THE EXPAT FILES

My Life in Journalism

Ken Becker

© 2017 Ken Becker
All rights reserved.

ISBN: 1978484844
ISBN 13 9781978484849

For Linda

*When I think back on all the crap I learned in high school,
It's a wonder I can think at all.
And though my lack of education hasn't hurt me none,
I can read the writing on the wall.*
    - Paul Simon

CONTENTS

Preface		ix
Chapter 1	The New York Times	1
Chapter 2	A murderous year	16
Chapter 3	The London-Zurich shuffle	36
Chapter 4	Adult education	45
Chapter 5	Dog day afternoon	59
Chapter 6	Is everybody happy?	77
Chapter 7	Rogue cop	87
Chapter 8	Crossing borders	99
Chapter 9	Kraut eats British nurse	110
Chapter 10	Tricky Dick and Trudeau	123
Chapter 11	Sleepy Toronto	147
Chapter 12	Congo out, Tanzania too	155
Chapter 13	Fighting the War of 1812	160
Chapter 14	New York stories	169
Chapter 15	The Gross Mile-a-Word Calculator	188
Chapter 16	Bar talk	197
Chapter 17	Bilateral relations	206
Chapter 18	Travels with Yaz	216

Chapter 19	Saved by Peter, Paul and Mary	235
Chapter 20	The celebrity interview	244
Chapter 21	Death in a small town	253
Chapter 22	Understand Newfoundland	261
Chapter 23	The Pope and the Queen	273
Chapter 24	Who's Jack Kennedy?	297
Chapter 25	Author! Author!	316
Chapter 26	Novel inspiration	327
Chapter 27	A novel retreat	346
Chapter 28	TV or not TV?	357
Chapter 29	Sound-up bagpipes	365
Chapter 30	'I hate those bastards'	376
Chapter 31	Up in the air	385
Chapter 32	School days	403
Chapter 33	Death far from home	417
Chapter 34	Last call	429
Epilogue		443
Acknowledgments		445

PREFACE

Journalists who write memoirs, at least the ones I've read, drop a lot of names. They tell us they were pals with a lot of big shots.

I've met a lot of famous people too. But I wasn't pals with any of them. They wanted something from me – publicity – and I wanted something from them – a good story.

Often, the personal experiences were more memorable than the pieces of journalism I wrote for newspapers and magazines. These are the stories I will share here. The ones I told in barrooms late at night.

Stories about the Nobel Peace laureate, the rudest person I ever interviewed; the prime minister of Canada who told me to fuck off; the cannibal bush pilot; the sad old king of the Jazz Age, who happened to be my uncle.

About too close encounters with Hollywood celebrities, a comatose Mafia don and a rogue cop charged with murder. About great writers who inspired me and trashy baseball players who disgusted me.

I'll return to the scenes of the crimes – a *Dog Day Afternoon* in New York, a massacre in Montreal, a family wiped out in a small town in California.

I'll return to the editor's chair, running a news desk when the bombs started falling on Baghdad, the planes hit the towers, soldiers died on battlefields, a queen and a pope came to visit. And to the college classroom, grooming a generation of young journalists.

Then, there are stories about *my* people – family, friends, colleagues – many gone, including my only son.

And *my* places. Big cities and small towns across North America and Europe. Places I lived or visited for adventure – a kidnap caper in Switzerland – and the pleasure of telling stories.

Work brought me to Canada. I stayed because this is where I met my wife, Linda.

I've now lived in Canada longer than I lived in the United States. But I remain an American and still think of myself as a New Yorker. Given a choice between being an immigrant in Canada or an expatriate, it's no contest. I'm an expat, an outsider, an observer.

It's a role I grew into, maybe from necessity, maybe by choice, maybe from a lifetime of clashes with bosses and other authority figures – cops, border guards – burning bridges along the way.

It's been a long and bumpy ride, from copyboy at the *New York Times* to international and national wire services, newspapers from coast to coast, and TV news. The life of the solitary writer also has its highs and lows.

Over the years, I've been asked the same questions: How did a guy who couldn't type and couldn't spell become a journalist? How did a college dropout become a college teacher? How did a no-bullshit nonconformist New Yorker wind up producing news shows at the most politically correct and anti-American TV network in Canada?

The answers are in the journey, every step and misstep. As it happened. No punches pulled. This is where it begins.

CHAPTER 1
THE NEW YORK TIMES

I come from a short line of short New Yorkers, a descendant of the great wave of Jews who fled the ghettos of Europe in the late nineteenth century. I was born in the Bronx in the 1940s and grew up in American ghettos – not exactly Minsk or Pinsk, but I didn't know many Christians – in Queens and Long Island.

My father, Hyman, Hy for short, was a salesman. My mother, Dorothy, was a homemaker. My sister, Janice, completed the family in 1950. That was around the time we moved to Clearview Gardens, a large labyrinth of two-story redbrick apartments, one family of post-war up-and-comers atop another, in Bayside, Queens.

The greatest academic and social achievements of my youth were earned in elementary school, at P.S. 184. In class, I gained a grasp of all I thought I would ever need to know – basic arithmetic, how to read and write, all the important dates in American history: 1492, July

4, 1776, December 7, 1941. I could find every state and most countries on a map.

My report cards were uniformly outstanding and, in sixth grade, I was elected school president and "king" of the school – my picture in the *Long Island Press*, alongside the queen, Roberta Kirsch, wearing our capes and crowns.

But then I went to junior high, skipped a grade, moved to Plainview, a sterile suburb for the aspiring *nouveau riche* on Long Island, and sleepwalked through high school.

The best times of my teenage years were the summers I was a counselor at Camp Williams in the Catskills. It was founded and supported by wealthy Jews as a haven for underprivileged kids from New York's poorer neighborhoods.

For me, from age fourteen to sixteen, it was an escape from the stifling mediocrity of Plainview. My fellow counselors were smarter, hipper – they read novels and listened to folk music – classier and more urbane than my high school classmates. They also were better looking.

For the campers, sunny days were filled with softball games and swimming, rainy days with arts and crafts, woodshop, and hootenannies – heavy on the Woody Guthrie and Pete Seeger.

I spent nights in the bushes or the backseat of a Buick Roadmaster with voluptuous Laura from Brooklyn, or Jeannie with the light brown hair from Park Avenue, or blonde and energetic Barbara, daughter of a district attorney. I was a boy and these were young women well-schooled in the book of love and the pages of literature.

In the fall of 1963, I went off to college at the University of Toledo, in Ohio. I never attended classes, woke up around noon, went to Franklin's, a nearby coffee shop. This is where I was having a breakfast BLT when a girl came in shrieking, "President Kennedy's been shot."

I passed most days either drinking beer bought with a counterfeit ID – I was only sixteen – or alone in my dorm room, listening to a tape of Carl Reiner interviewing Mel Brooks, the *2,000 Year Old Man*.

I did come to the attention of the university's administration a couple of times. Once, when I was placed on academic probation for scoring across-the-board incompletes the first term. And a second time when two FBI agents questioned me in the dean's office about a purloined calling-card number I used to phone my girlfriend, the voluptuous Laura, in Brooklyn. The G-men were not impressed with my you-can't-pin-that-rap-on-me-copper routine. I fessed up and paid the tab.

Anyway, I flunked out, or dropped out – How do you grade a student who never goes to class? – and went home to Plainview.

On my eighteenth birthday, November 19, 1964, I had my first legal drink – a vodka martini, shaken, not stirred – and got a draft notice. My student deferment gone, I was ordered to report immediately for induction into the army. There were already about twenty-thousand American soldiers in Vietnam. By the next year, LBJ and the boys in the Pentagon would meet their promise to increase troop levels in Southeast Asia to nearly two-hundred-thousand.

I wasn't worried – my doctor had told me I'd be rejected – when I arrived before dawn in the parking lot of my draft board in Great Neck, Long Island, in December. I had a briefcase stuffed with medical files as I boarded a bus with a few dozen other young men for the trip to the army induction center on Whitehall Street in Lower Manhattan.

Once inside, we stripped down to our underwear and paraded along an assembly line with hundreds of others for physicals, stopping to be checked out from head to toe. I clung to my briefcase. At each stop, I asked, "Can I show you my files?" The answer was uniformly "no, move along."

I started to become anxious until, after the last stop, I was steered into a small office where an army captain, a doctor, was sitting behind a desk.

He paged through my files. I added commentary, that I had had my spleen removed as a child, the remedy for a blood disorder called spherocytosis. He shook his head, came around the desk, and put his arm around my shoulders. "Sorry, son," he said, "but you'll never be in this man's army."

"Aw, shucks," I said.

I left his office, walked down the hall and watched my fellow draftees raise their right hands and be sworn into service. I hid my glee on the bus ride back to Great Neck. My relief wasn't only because I feared dying in Vietnam. I didn't want to spend two years taking senseless orders, eating bad food and sleeping in a barracks or a jungle.

Free of the threat of conscription, I went back to wasting my time at a series of mindless minimum-wage jobs. I also enrolled in a night course in English literature – I liked Shakespeare – at Nassau Community College but maintained my record of never reading a book from cover to cover.

My parents, concerned that I had not fulfilled their expectations and probably had no future, sent me to see my Uncle Jack, my dad's kid brother, who, according to family gossip, was hardly a raving success. I knew him as a failed actor and luckless gambler who changed his name from Becker to Banning.

At this time, Jack Banning was publisher of a leftwing tabloid called the *New York Free Press*. I met him in his grungy office on the Upper West Side of Manhattan.

"So," Uncle Jack asked, "what do you want to do when you grow up?"

"I have no idea," I said, laughing.

"Your parents say you might like working in the newspaper business."

"Yeah, I've thought about that," I lied.

"You want to work here?" he said

"I dunno," I said.

He lit a cigar, rose from behind his desk and snapped a question in my direction, "Who killed JFK?"

"Lee Harvey Oswald," I replied.

"Not the CIA? The FBI? LBJ?"

I shrugged.

Jack shook his head. "I think you're a little too straight for us," he said. "I know who you should talk to."

Jack made an appointment for me to see Wesley First. A former managing editor of the *New York World-Telegram*, First was the top PR man at Columbia University. I met him in his office on the campus in Washington Heights.

"So," he said, "your uncle tells me you're interested in being a newspaperman."

I nodded.

"Don't you think you should go back to school and get your degree first?"

"I'm not ready for that yet," I said. "I don't see any point in it now. I need to find out what I want to do first."

"That's not the way it's usually done," he said.

I didn't know what to say. But I knew I wasn't going back to school.

"Maybe I can help get you started," First said. He wrote down the names of his contacts at the *New York Times* and the *World-Telegram* and told me to send a letter to each of them.

I didn't read either paper. Or any paper. My dad would bring home a copy of the afternoon *Post* and I'd scan the sports pages.

I sent the letters, hoping for a shot at becoming a cub reporter, like Jimmy Olsen. I wondered who would be my Lois and Clark.

The *World-Telegram* replied first. In a letter dated December 9, 1965, assistant city editor Thomas A. Cornell wrote: *Unfortunately your qualifications fall short of the requirements for a beginning reporter. The only position available at the moment is a copyboy's position.*

I went for an interview with Cornell at the *World-Telegram's* downtown office on Barclay Street, near City Hall. It seemed to go okay and he said he'd get back to me.

In the meantime, I got a letter from assistant managing editor William A. Holcombe – did newspapermen all use their middle initials? – at the *Times*: *I'm not sure from your letter just what kind of employment you are seeking. If you are interested in copy boy work, while finishing college, please give me a call.*

I arranged to meet Holcombe, but wound up being interviewed by associate managing editor A.M. "Abe" Rosenthal, a very serious and somewhat scary man, who seemed to be sitting in a highchair and looked down at me through horn-rimmed glasses.

"Here at the *Times*," he said, "we view copyboy as an entry position. We expect our copyboys to show some initiative and rise through the ranks. Some of our best reporters started here at the *Times* as copyboys."

He paused and looked over my sketchy resume, which showed scant education and no career credentials. He frowned. "If we decide to give you a chance, it is with the understanding that you will go back to college," he said.

"Of course," I lied.

Within weeks, both the *World-Telegram* and the *Times* called to offer jobs. I was doubly lucky the *Times* phoned first, since it was my first choice and because the *World-Telegram* would fold a short time later.

In January 1966, when I walked into *the New York Times* for my first day on the job, I had no expectations and less chance of success.

I was nineteen years old. I thought I was smart, clever anyway, that I could excel if something interested me. But nothing had clicked yet.

My work experience included slicing lox in the deli section of Waldbaum's supermarket, selling toys during the Christmas rush at Korvettes department store, and disposing of body parts for the Mafia. I drove a delivery van for a butcher shop but occasionally the Italian gentleman who owned the establishment filled the trunk of his new Cadillac with sealed packages of mystery meat and had me unload it at the home of another Italian gentleman far outside our delivery area.

At the *Times*, I was assigned to the city desk, where one fellow copyboy was twice my age, had a PhD in literature, wanted to be a playwright and had no interest in journalism. So much for Rosenthal's assertion that all copyboys were on the slow track to becoming reporters.

The newsroom was mammoth, with scores of desks in rows, all facing the editors. It looked like a vast classroom of students facing the teacher.

A PA system was used to summon reporters. "Mr. Lindsay, report to the city desk," would echo off the walls and the high ceiling. Mr. Lindsay would amble to the city desk.

I was not permitted to amble. I ran – to refill paste pots, sharpen pencils and deliver copy from reporters to editors, or from editors to the composing room, via a system of pneumatic tubes.

Within weeks, however, I moved to the Financial-Business department, in a separate space about the size of a football field end zone. There, I was the only copyboy.

It was the same hierarchical arrangement of desks. At the front was the business editor, Thomas E. Mullaney, a stiff and formal middle-aged lifer at the *Times*. I shared a desk with the department's secretary and clerk, answering phones and opening mail when I wasn't being summoned to run errands. One of the two women reporters, Clare Reckert, shouted "Boy!" whenever she had a chore for me.

Often working into the evening, my rounds would take me across Forty-third Street to Gough's bar, to get alcoholic inspiration for the editors on the copy desk. The Dixie Hotel was also on the south side of Forty-third Street, which was convenient for the men spending their lunch hours with the young and attractive secretaries and clerks who populated the New York Times Building.

I wasn't long at the *Times* when I learned the line: "Drink is the curse of the *Herald Tribune*, sex is the curse of the *Times*." From what I could tell, many *Timesmen* were twice cursed.

Occasionally, I delivered sealed envelopes – eyes-only memos – from Mullaney to the private offices of executive editor Turner Catledge, a courtly Mississippian, or managing editor Clifton Daniel, the silver-haired dandy married to Margaret Truman, daughter of a president. Instructed early in the *Times*' Dickensian hierarchy, I would always enter an office by saying "good morning, Mr. Daniel," or "good afternoon, Mr. Catledge."

Daniel would usually reply with a nod. Catledge never looked up from his desk. These were very intimidating – or rude – men.

So was Gay Talese – not the rude part – who I often encountered on my many trips to the morgue. Everyone in the building knew the former *Timesman* was researching a book on the paper.

While I would be picking up files on General Electric's earnings or pork-belly futures for the business reporters, Talese, in his finely tailored suit, silk tie and matching handkerchief, would be sitting at a small circular table, shuffling through clippings.

So, Gay, you gonna blow the lid off this joint? I wanted to ask.

The gossip was that the big boys at the *Times* were very nervous about what Talese would write. But the *Times* gave him full access to the building, including the executive offices.

(*The Kingdom and the Power*, published in 1969, would paint a less than flattering portrait, focusing on the often petty politics and power plays within the *Times*.)

The people I met at the *Times* had a sophistication and self-assurance unlike anyone I had known growing up – one smoked *Gauloises!* They knew they were the personification of the power of the press. Their professional lives put them in close proximity to presidents, kings, dictators and movie stars.

I visualized their Manhattan apartments or homes in Westchester, filled with antiques and floor-to-ceiling bookshelves. I assumed they spent their nights at the opera or front-row-center at the hottest Broadway play, dined at the Four Seasons, drank cognac from snifters into the wee hours listening to jazz in the Village. And that they traveled the world with the same ease they ruled Manhattan.

Hy Maidenberg, one of the business reporters, who had worked in Latin America, often expounded on his idea of taking over a small Caribbean country. "I could probably steal the treasury in a day or two and be proclaimed dictator within a week," he concluded.

Another reporter, Bob Walker, told me he was from Canada. The only others I knew from Canada were Sergeant Preston of the Yukon and Nanook of the North.

Walker always wore suspenders over a crisp white shirt and dark suits rather than Preston's red serge or Nanook's caribou skins, so he must have been from a different part of Canada.

I didn't learn much about journalism at the *Times*. No one talked to me about reporting or writing. I didn't ask either. But I paid attention.

The *Times* was insufferably full of itself and its perceived place in the world. It took a conservative, puritanical, approach to news.

I witnessed the internal debate, the angst and the naval gazing, when the *Times* featured on the front page Richard Speck's slaughter of eight student-nurses in Chicago in July 1966. The reaction was intense. Some cried, *Heavens to Betsy, the Times has stooped to sensationalizing a scummy crime story. What's next? Sports on the front page?* Others declared it was about time the paper recognized what readers were interested in and talking about.

I also found it pretty uncool that the *Times* still referred to blacks as "Negroes" in 1967, when black rage erupted in riots in nearby Newark and in Detroit. As a copyboy and the youngest person in the newsroom, it was hardly my place to raise such issues.

Besides, I was too busy soaking up the stories the reporters and editors told me, giving me a taste for the life, if not the craft. I'd hang around the desks of guys like Gene Smith, a burly business reporter whose wife was a show biz press agent.

"Guess who was passed out in Peggy Lee's dressing room at the Copa Saturday night?" he said one Monday morning, not waiting for an answer. "Joe Namath. Dead drunk. Then, yesterday, he goes out and throws four touchdown passes."

This was serious coin for a kid making sixty-six bucks a week. While anyone with a dime could read Harrison Salisbury's 1966-67 dispatches from North Vietnam in the *Times*, I knew that Broadway Joe was comatose at the Copacabana the night before the big game.

There were other perks too. I quickly learned a lesson in the trickle-down economics of the newsroom, that even lowly copyboys could score free tickets to a Broadway show or box seats at Yankee Stadium. I could also tag along when a press agent picked up the tab at Sardi's, or to an after-hours party in a complimentary hotel suite stocked with a full bar and pretty girls from a friendly PR firm. I was a wallflower on such occasions, the kid in the corner, a mascot, not one of the crowd.

At Christmastime, I delivered gifts to the reporters from the companies they wrote about – cases of premium booze, color TVs, cashmere scarves and silk neckties. I never considered whether such swag influenced the coverage of their beats.

Late in 1966, I wrote to Wesley First at Columbia, thanking him again for his help getting me a job. I said I was enjoying the *Times* and lied again about plans to go back to college. He replied:

I am delighted about the job, and even more delighted about your decision to pick up your educational responsibilities again.

What I wanted was to be a real newsman, with an apartment in Manhattan. But I wasn't qualified for one, and couldn't afford the other.

Living with my parents in Plainview was stunting my growth as a person, as well as my sex life. The back seat of my 1959 Buick Electra convertible – black, with red interior, and big fins in the back – was roomy but hardly an alluring love nest. When a girl insisted on a proper bed, the only option was mine. We had sex behind my bedroom door, with my mother and father, hopefully sleeping, across the narrow hallway. I spent more energy shushing than *shtupping*.

Traveling to the *Times* from Plainview was also a drag. Sometimes I'd catch the Long Island Railroad in Hicksville, the name of the town a reminder of my predicament.

Oftentimes, I hitched a ride with my dad's carpool. At an ungodly hour of the morning, the carpoolers seemed nauseatingly chipper, constantly kibitzing. Arriving at the subway in Jamaica, Queens, the men would pile out and take the train into the city – that's what everybody in the boroughs and the suburbs called Manhattan, The City.

When I worked late at the *Times*, I occasionally stayed with my Aunt Fay in the Bronx. I took the D Train from Midtown to Jerome Avenue and 161st Street, the Yankee Stadium station. She lived in a tall apartment building with a rooftop view of the ballpark.

Fay was my mother's older sister. She was single, the independent working girl in the family, an executive in a company in Manhattan that made patterns for dresses. When I was a kid, she had a snazzy, turquoise Studebaker convertible and took trips to exotic foreign locales.

When I arrived at her apartment late on a workday, she would grill me a tenderloin steak under the broiler and heat up a can of corn niblets as the trains on the elevated tracks regularly rumbled past her kitchen window.

She'd serve me dinner on a tray in front of the TV. We'd watch the eleven o'clock news on WCBS. When it was over, there was a *Times* commercial that said something like, *If you want to learn something more about these stories, pick up a copy of the New York Times in the morning.*

Toward the end of 1967, I was tired of running every time Clare Reckert shouted "boy." I asked Tom Mullaney if I could get a crack at writing something – anything, even reworking a press release – but he said the same thing Rosenthal had told me. "You have to first go back to college."

But I wanted to be a reporter. I didn't have any skills but I wanted the life. I'd bought a trench coat, a London Fog. I'd had lunch at The Algonquin. I understood some of the cartoons in *The New Yorker.* I'd read a book, *Catch-22,* from cover to cover.

I chain-smoked cigarettes and drank scotch. I could stay out all night and show up at work with a hangover. I was ready.

I wrote Tom Mullaney a letter of resignation, thanking him for his kindness. His reply concluded: *I am quite confident you will do well in whatever task you turn your talents to, whether it be journalism or something else.*

One of his assistant editors, Lee Kanner, mumbled through his ratty moustache an equally encouraging farewell. "The rate you're going, you probably won't live past twenty-five."

With those votes of confidence, right after New Year's Day 1968, I packed my new Mustang – a white hardtop with red interior, three-speed on the floor – and headed west, for California. The only thing I took from the *Times* was a taste for the high life and the belief that a really pretentious byline that included a middle initial – one of the finance reporters I ran errands for was Vartanig G. Vartan – was a prerequisite to a career in big-time journalism.

I was now Kenneth M. Becker. And I had a resume that said I'd worked the past two years at **THE NEW YORK TIMES**.

CHAPTER 2
A MURDEROUS YEAR

As a twenty-one-year-old who had traveled little, I loved being alone on the road, crossing the country, cruising along Route 66 through Amarillo, Albuquerque, Flagstaff, crossing the Mojave from Needles to Barstow.

I made it to Los Angeles in less than a week and checked into a cheap motel in Glendale. The only thing I knew about Glendale was that Casey Stengel was from there. I didn't have Casey's number.

But I had a list of California newspaper and PR contacts, thanks to some of the business reporters at the *Times*. I called everyone on the list in L.A. and played solitaire in my room for a couple of days, waiting for the phone to ring. It didn't.

I went farther afield, phoning people on the list in San Francisco. One called back, a PR guy for Sylvania Electric, named Ralph Waldo Emerson.

He said that if I would come to San Francisco, he would help get me settled and give me some ideas on how to find work. I packed up the Mustang again and headed north.

The drive along the Pacific coast was glorious. But I was preoccupied, scared shitless, three-thousand miles from home without much money and no real prospects. What would I do if I couldn't get a job?

As I approached San Francisco on Highway 101, I stopped near the airport to meet Ralph for lunch at the Hyatt hotel. The restaurant was dark, with spacious faux-leather booths. In one of them I found Ralph, a tall, thin, ruddy-cheeked fellow in his thirties.

"Is your name really Ralph Waldo Emerson?" I asked, knowing it was a famous name but not knowing anything about his namesake.

"Yes, it is," he said.

"Are you related?" I asked.

"Distantly," he said.

I was relieved he dropped the subject, since I was not prepared for an Emerson quiz.

Ralph bought me a steak and a scotch – or three – and suggested I check into a place called the Post Residence, on Post Street, in the heart of San Francisco.

The Post was basically a boarding house for young people. These were not the hippies who had flocked to San Francisco the previous year, the "Summer of Love." Most of the people at the Post had followed the usual migration routes to the big city, looking for a better life. There was Jim from Utah, Fred from Texas and Frank from Oklahoma, who taught me how to use a plastic card to break-and-enter when I got locked out of my room one night.

I had a private room – a bed, dresser, sink and toilet. The only window offered a view of an alley that was the driveway for Trader Vic's restaurant. The shower was down the hall.

There was a common room with a TV, where we all gathered during my first week in town to watch the network premiere of *The Great Escape*, cheering Steve McQueen, who I would soon encounter at San Francisco airport.

But on this night, I only had eyes for the sultry German girl who was flirting shamelessly with me. After the movie, Doschia invited me to her room for a glass of wine. I knew little about life and less about how to become a newspaperman. But, I thought I knew something about girls.

I went to Doschia's room with hope and a hard-on, only to watch her Swiss roommate tag along. We drank cheap Chianti, poured from a jug in a straw basket. Doschia kept flirting with me while I talked to her roommate, Anita.

She was interested that I was a journalist – I wasn't, of course – and said she had a passion for good writing. Since I had not written anything, nor read much either, I lied.

"What do you think of Hemingway?" she asked.

"Well, my friend Gene Smith – at **THE NEW YORK TIMES** – knew Hemingway," I said. I wasn't sure about this. Maybe it was true. Maybe it wasn't. It sounded good, though.

The only thing I knew about Hemingway was that he was dead – took himself out of the game with a shotgun. I did follow the news, even if I didn't know how to report it or write it.

"What's your favorite Hemingway book?" Anita asked.
"The one with Jake Barnes," I said.
"*The Sun Also Rises.*"
"Yeah," I guessed. I hadn't read it. "Did you hear what happened at **THE NEW YORK TIMES**?"
"No."
"Well, when I was working at **THE NEW YORK TIMES**, one of the college correspondents sneaked an announcement into the paper. It was for the 'Brett award: to the student who has worked hardest under a great handicap – Jake Barnes.' The guy got fired. It was the talk of the newsroom for weeks. Only at **THE NEW YORK TIMES** would there be a prank with a literary connection."

Anita and I talked into the night. I asked if she had seen *The Graduate*. She hadn't. I had stood in line on Third Avenue to catch the movie just before I left New York. I felt now like I was living it.

I'd driven Benjamin's route to San Francisco. I too was uncertain about my future. His solution had been to break the boredom by falling in love and rushing into marriage. Mine would be too.

Anita and I went to see *The Graduate* together. We sealed the night with a kiss. Even though she was more than six years older than me, I saw her as Elaine. Would she turn out to be Mrs. Robinson?

During my first weeks in San Francisco, I made the rounds of the San Francisco papers. *The Chronicle* told me to go back to college. *The Examiner* held out some hope but I never heard from the editor again.

I spent my days driving around the city – at least I had a cool car – or over the Golden Gate to Sausalito, sitting on the dock of the bay, eating fish and chips, drinking beer at the No Name bar, heading back across the bridge in the evening, picking up the best looking hippie chicks hitching on the entrance ramp, smoking some dope and hoping to get lucky.

At night, I'd ride the cable cars with my Texan friend, Fred, who confessed he was an army deserter, AWOL from Vietnam. I'm not sure I believed him but it was a good story.

We all had our stories. I told him my true one, that I avoided the army – and Vietnam – because I had a non-essential organ removed as a child, which classified me 4-F. "It's a family tradition," I said. "My dad had a bleeding ulcer that kept him out of World War Two."

Fred and I would jump on and off the Powell/Mason car, never bothering to pay. The conductors didn't seem to mind. Whether we got off in North Beach, or went the distance to Ghirardelli Square or Fisherman's Wharf, the streets were filled with music – Beatles, Stones, Doors, Airplane – and hippies ready to share a joint, a bottle of wine or a whiff of sex.

Fred and I weren't committed to the whole hippie scene. We dabbled in sex, drugs and rock 'n roll. We also checked out the strip joints at Broadway and Columbus, Carol Doda's famous 44s for all to see at The Condor. Fred kept promising we'd get together with some strippers he knew, who would show all without a cover charge. It never happened.

We did get together with Janis Joplin – he said he knew her from Texas – one night at the Fillmore, not inside the club but drinking Southern Comfort outside. Or did we? With all the grass and beer we'd consumed earlier that night, for all I know we were sitting on the curb, passing a pint of hooch, with a scraggly-haired, hard-bitten hooker from Fresno. But, a couple of years later, when I heard her cackle at the end of *Mercedes Benz*, it sure sounded familiar.

Getting stoned proved to be a good excuse for not looking for a job. But I still got together regularly with Ralph Waldo Emerson, whose office was down the peninsula, near the airport. I'd meet him at the Hyatt, where he'd buy me lunch and give me pep talks.

"How about PR?" he asked one afternoon, between bites of steak and gulps of scotch.

"No," I replied, "I want newspapers."

"You need a job," he said.

"I know."

Leaving the Hyatt in mid-afternoon was strange enough. Going from the dark restaurant into the sunshine was always a shock. But more unsettling was the fear that I'd never get a crack at being a reporter. I knew I didn't have credentials or experience. Yet I believed that if I got inside the door somewhere I could do the job. I thought I could write. And I wanted the life.

Rejected by the *Chronicle* and the *Examiner*, I hit the road, each day going farther from the city. I drove south, stopping at every paper between San Francisco and San Jose; went north through Marin County; east from Oakland. No one was hiring. At least they weren't hiring me.

Anita and I, both being new to the Bay Area, didn't know a lot of people. But one of my closest childhood friends, Barry Ginsberg, was somewhere in Marin. We managed to get in touch and arranged to meet.

Barry and I lived in the same Clearview Gardens development in Queens. But we went to different elementary schools and didn't meet until we were placed on the same little league baseball team in the summer of 1954, when we were seven years old. I was the pitcher. He was the catcher.

My dad managed our team. Barry's mom, Flossie, was the team mother. That was an actual title – team mother. She was in charge of the drinks and snacks.

One year, I won the league batting title. More than half my hits were bunts. Barry called me a "sissy bunter" and tried to swipe my trophy.

Still, Barry and I became best friends. Our families became close, went on vacations together. But then, Barry and I went to different high schools and colleges, had separate sets of friends, and drifted apart when he became a dedicated hippie and I stayed straight.

Anita and I met up with Barry and his girlfriend on the Marin side of the Golden Gate. He suggested a drive to the top of Mount Tamalpais to watch the sunset. Much alcohol and cannabis was consumed.

Walking back to the lot where I'd parked my Mustang, we spotted a Hells Angel making off with the hubcaps. "Let's get him," Barry said. I tossed him the keys. "You drive."

It wasn't until we got to the bottom of the mountain, no sign of the biker, that I smelled something burning and realized Barry had neglected to release the emergency brake. We spent the rest of the night in a gas station garage.

By March, Anita and I had moved in together, into a one-room apartment at the corner of California and Laguna in Pacific Heights.

Having sampled English cuisine during a brief period as an au pair, she introduced me to the frugal practice of serving meals on toast. Sometimes we ate baked beans on toast. Other times, scrambled eggs on toast. Being my father's son, I never considered cooking.

We didn't have a television, but I'd brought a record player from New York. I played my Simon and Garfunkel albums over and over again. *Wednesday Morning 3AM, Sounds of Silence, Parsley, Sage, Rosemary and Thyme.* When *Bookends* was released, I went to Tower Records in North Beach and shelled out a couple of bucks I couldn't afford to spend. We went to Tower Records together, and got in line, the first day the White Album went on sale. Anita loved my Beatles' records: *Rubber Soul, Revolver, Sgt. Pepper,* and *Magical Mystery Tour.*

She worked nights at the Hertz counter at San Francisco airport. I drove her and picked her up when her shift ended at eleven.

McQueen was filming *Bullitt* in the city that spring, shooting scenes at the airport. While I was waiting for Anita to come off shift one night, McQueen sat down next to me in a row of chairs near the Hertz counter. He nodded. I nodded. He sat. I sat. He got up and walked away. I thought later that if I had been a journalist, I would have had a notebook and a pen and tried to interview him.

On the night of April 4, 1968, after picking up Anita, the radio blared news of riots in cities across the country, after Martin Luther King was assassinated in Memphis.

"What's going to happen?" she asked.

"It's going to be bad," I said.

From our fourth-floor apartment high in Pacific Heights, after midnight, we looked west toward the Fillmore District, the city's black neighborhood. There were no signs of trouble, no fires burning as they were in Washington and Chicago and elsewhere.

After the King assassination, I went downtown to Robert Kennedy's campaign office. Since I was over twenty-one, this would be the first year I could vote.

My earliest political memory was the 1960 Democratic convention on the radio. It went late into the night and, tucked into bed, I listened to the nomination of JFK on my little transistor radio. I was a Kennedy man, or a Kennedy boy, since I was only thirteen.

I'd watched Walter Cronkite give the news of JFK's death on the TV in a rec room of my dorm in Toledo. A football player, a kid from western Pennsylvania named John, laughed and said, "Good." I retired to my room, stayed up all night staring into the dark, and caught the first DC-3 home to New York in the morning. In my parents' house in Plainview, I watched Oswald shot dead on TV.

In the rowdy political season of 1968, I was again a Kennedy man. Bobby looked like a winner. And, since I wasn't doing anything, I volunteered to help.

I walked into the busy campaign office on Market Street, introduced myself as a former newsman with **THE NEW YORK TIMES**, and was directed to the office of Phil Burton, the California congressman running the Kennedy campaign in San Francisco.

"Have you ever written a press release?" Burton asked.

"No."

"How about speeches?"

"You want me to write speeches for Bobby?"

Burton laughed. "No, but we all give speeches on his behalf."

"I could try," I said.

"Well, let's start with a press release. There's an event coming up and we need to send out a release. See the girl out there" – he pointed – "and she'll give you all the information."

I saw the girl. Got the information. Took it home. And never went back. I had other things on my mind.

Anita was pregnant. I was determined to do the right thing, or maybe I was just lonely and wanted a mommy. The proposal was less than traditional.

We often took walks in the foggy streets of Pacific Heights after midnight, after Anita finished work. Sometimes, we'd just go up the hill to Lafayette Park, stroll along the paths, amid the tall palms.

On one occasion, after we smoked some shockingly potent dope, Anita was mesmerized by the sight of oncoming headlights and stood frozen the middle of California Street until I tugged her to the curb.

In early May, we walked down California, across Van Ness, heading for a twenty-four-hour supermarket. Anita stopped to look in a shop window.

"You like that dress?" I asked. It was a simple white, cotton number that suited her style – Swiss bohemian.

"I do," she said.

"It would make a nice wedding dress." That was it – the proposal.

The next day, we went back to the store and bought the dress. Anita booked a few days off work.

We drove to Reno – Nevada, unlike California, did not require blood tests or any such marital prerequisites – late at night and went to city hall the next morning. We waited our turn in the office of the justice of the peace.

"Yours knocked up too?" asked a cowboy and his very pregnant bride.

I laughed. Not exactly an answer.

I was wearing my only suit, navy blue, with a white shirt and tie. Anita was wearing the white dress.

After the vows, we took a couple of snaps of each other on the steps of city hall and headed west, for a brief honeymoon in Lake Tahoe. I stopped for gas on the way out of town. The pump jockey asked me, "Here for a quickie divorce?"

"Just got married," I said.

"You'll be back."

By the time we reached the freeway exit for Tahoe, the snow had been coming down for a while. We'd packed for May in California, not January in Colorado.

I made my first executive decision as a husband, and drove five more hours to Carmel. We checked into a small inn, surrounded by flowers and bathed in sunshine.

Money was always an issue – one of us wasn't earning any – but we decided to splurge and feed our extracurricular passions during our one full day in Carmel. Anita would go horseback riding, and I would play golf at Pebble Beach.

But, when I got to the clubhouse, and found out the green fee was eighteen dollars, I balked. "This is outrageous," I said to the guy in the pro shop. "Back home, I play Bethpage Black for four bucks."

I came back at dusk, parked my Mustang on the shoulder off 17-Mile Drive, got my clubs out of the trunk, walked onto the course and played a couple of holes. Anita sat in the car. Presumably embarrassed.

By the time Bobby was shot in Los Angeles in June, Anita and I had moved into a one-bedroom apartment, the second floor of a two-story house, in the Avenues. We were close to the ocean, the beach, and Golden Gate Park, but the clock was ticking on her pregnancy. It was getting tougher for her to squeeze into her yellow Hertz uniform, and I still didn't have a job.

I spent the summer driving farther and farther from San Francisco, stopping at every newspaper office, dropping off resumes, filling out applications and sitting for interviews.

In August, the city editor of the *Livermore Herald & News*, Barry Schrader, called and offered me a $110 a week reporter's job. "I'll give you a try," he said.

Anita quit her job. I packed up the Mustang. We drove over the Bay Bridge, forty miles east on the freeway, and moved into a little one-bedroom apartment with a patio.

Livermore was a sleepy town in a valley of ranchland and vineyards – the Wente family started their winery in 1883.

The town's major employer was the Lawrence Radiation Laboratory – it was later renamed the Lawrence Livermore National Laboratory to remove the scary R-word – where, behind a security fence, Cold Warriors designed bigger and better nukes.

The physicists and their wives drove around in Karmann Ghias and Volvos. The ranchers sometimes came to town on horseback. It was an interesting clash of cultures, which made for lively discussions at city council and school board meetings. The town's elders had to satisfy the competing interests of those who wanted better schools and libraries for their kids and those who wanted to roll back the clock, especially on the weekend of the annual rodeo.

I was one of the two reporters on the city desk. The other, Ron Iscoff, a few years older, read my first clumsy attempts at newspaper writing and tried to wise me up to the inverted pyramid and AP style.

But I had my own style – I started most stories with a quote, which I believed was a literary approach – and an agenda, to be the voice for alienated youth and others on the fringe.

I began a story on teenage runaways with Lennon/McCartney lyrics from *She's Leaving Home*. Poignant stuff. Heavy message.

My role as the paper's resident young radical was tolerated, partly because I seemed like an average young man with a wife and baby on the way, got haircuts occasionally, and wore a shirt and tie to work.

I thought I was being subversive when I wrote about hippies and blacks. But the editors had the big knife, changing the word black to Negro and writing headlines that conformed to the paper's conservative Republican editorials.

After covering a speech to the local GOP club and writing a solid story, I imagined the headline to be: *Racist Uncle Tom a Republican toady*. The front-page headline read: *Negro GOP Leader Raps Welfare*.

Still, I hadn't been fired or judged a fraud, and even got a compliment or two from the bosses. The city editor liked when I used "the eleventh hour" cliché in a lead.

Iscoff seemed to be the only one who knew I was faking it and kept trying to get me to turn out leads worthy of the AP wire. But, when I tried to write straight, it just came out lame: *After a 30-year reign as king of Livermore's morticians, Leo Callahan has turned in his embalming fluid for a two iron*. This was the lead of my story on the town's undertaker, who was retiring and planned to play more golf. I took a picture of him – reporters took their own pictures with one of the paper's twin-lens Argus box cameras – wearing his Perry Como cardigan and posing with his two iron.

My education as a journalist seemed stalled until November 13, 1968. It was a week after Richard Nixon was elected president – I cast my first ever ballot for Eldridge Cleaver of the Black Panthers, who was the candidate of the Peace and Freedom Party.

On a Wednesday evening the next week, I was the only reporter in the office when a call on the police radio announced, "One-eighty-seven at 353 North I Street."

I had learned the California police codes. I knew 187 was a homicide. I jumped in my Mustang and sped to North I Street. There was an empty cop car with lights flashing. I spotted a door wide open to a second-story apartment.

I walked in. The first thing I noticed was the place smelled like stale vomit. The second thing was that the television was on and, lying in front of it, on his stomach, was a young boy. He was wearing pajamas. He wasn't moving.

I walked closer. The hair on the back of the boy's head was matted with dried blood. I heard voices and followed the sound farther into the apartment. I passed the small kitchen. Breakfast for four – untouched bowls of cereal, a quart of milk – was on the table. Entering a back bedroom, I saw three cops standing over a man's body.

"What the hell are you doing here," shouted one of them, the chief of police, John Michelis.

"The door was open," I said, straining to look beyond them, into a closet, where two more bodies – a woman and little girl – were slumped in a corner.

"Well, get the hell out," ordered the chief.

I stood outside and scribbled in my notebook, every detail I could remember. I noted the uneaten breakfast as evidence of when the murders might have been committed. I drew a diagram of the apartment and where the bodies lay. I should have been repulsed by what I'd seen. But I was excited.

Iscoff showed up. We decided – he decided – that I would stay at the scene and talk to the cops and neighbors, and he'd go back to the office and work the phones.

We had the name of the family and a strong hint from the cops that Paul Cranfill, 27, had shot his wife, Lynn, 25, and their two children – five-year-old Bobby and two-year-old Cathy – before turning his pistol on himself.

We collaborated on a pretty good story that night – me writing and Iscoff rewriting – including most of those Ws: who, what, when, where. The next day we would try to figure out why.

We filled the front-page with an impressive amount of information gathered over only a few hours. The cops had told me that Cranfill's brother, Carl, had come home at about 4 p.m., walked into the dark apartment – the lights were off and the drapes were drawn – and taken a two-hour nap on the living room couch, within a few feet of his nephew's body. He called the police when he saw the boy, apparently hoping he could be resuscitated – a word that sent me to the dictionary, since I was the world's worst speller.

My uninvited walk through the crime scene gave us a good description of where the bodies were found. The cops told me it looked like a triple-murder-suicide and that all had been shot in the head. When I asked the chief if the breakfast dishes suggested the time of the crime, he confirmed it probably occurred that morning.

We got some good quotes from the owner of the small apartment complex – "they were a real happy family" and "excellent tenants" – and from Cranfill's employer at an electronics factory, who called him "a good worker."

We also learned that police had found a newspaper clipping on gun control. A neighbor who took target practice with Cranfill said he was "a good marksman."

A search of the *Herald* morgue unearthed an article from the previous summer, when Lynn Cranfill had been featured as "Homemaker of the Week." She had described her husband as "a kind person." All this went into the story.

On the front page, the paper reprinted a photo that had accompanied the homemaker article, of Lynn Cranfill in the apartment with little Cathy and Bobby sitting beside her.

When the paper was put to bed that night, Iscoff and I had a celebratory drink and plotted the next day's follow-ups.

For several more days, we shared a byline, alphabetically, me on top, and tried to get at what was in the killer's head before he put a nine-millimeter slug in it.

We found out that Cranfill was a gun nut, that besides the murder weapon – a P.38 automatic – he also owned a .357 Magnum, a .22-caliber pistol and a .30-caliber carbine. He was also apparently nuts. A doctor told us Cranfill had a "paranoid-schizoid personality," that he had been taking Thorazine, an antipsychotic tranquilizer, and that his family had been advised to put him in a mental hospital. His wife refused.

We learned that Cranfill was "up to his neck" in debt. "He must have owed well over $6,000" and had been planning to file for personal bankruptcy, a relative told us.

Iscoff and I had a good run with the story. The Cranfill tragedy wasn't exactly the crime of the century but, for me, the rush was extraordinary, everything I'd hoped for when I stumbled into the newspaper racket. When it was over, I went back to covering meetings and checking the police blotter.

Chief Michelis, to punish me for invading his crime scene, called me into his office, sat me down for a good scolding, and showed me his photo collection of gunshot victims, mainly of men who had blown away their faces with shotguns. As Hemingway had, I thought. Instead of puking my guts out, as Michelis had presumably expected, I asked questions about the story behind each picture.

Since there weren't triple-murder-suicides every day in Livermore, I was getting restless. The routine town meetings and petty crime – I did a story on kids stealing piggy banks – didn't pump adrenaline, my new favorite drug.

I especially hated the chore of "pickups," going to the home of someone who had died to pick up a photo, mostly of kids my age and younger killed in Vietnam.

I thought I was ready to move out and move up. But, having been at the *Herald & News* only a few months, I didn't think a big city paper would take me on. I grudgingly accepted the fact I'd have to pay my dues, as much as several more months, anyway.

Looking for some spice, I talked my editor Barry into allowing me to write reviews of every film that opened at the town's only movie house, the Vine Theater. I titled the weekly column *Current Cinema*. I figured no one in Livermore read *The New Yorker*.

I had my byline printed in lower case: kenneth becker – very e.e. cummings. The *Herald* had a policy against middle initials, so Kenneth M. would have to wait.

The Vine provided passes – finally, a perk – giving Anita and me a free night out once a week.

She was very pregnant when she joined me backstage the last weekend in October for the San Francisco Pop Festival, at the fairgrounds in the neighboring town of Pleasanton.

I was there providing the coverage, of course, as the resident cool kid on the *Herald*, able to translate into English the musical menu that included Iron Butterfly's *In-A-Gadda-Da-Vida*; Procol Harum's *A Whiter Shade of Pale*, The Animals' *House of the Rising Sun*.

While Anita and I went home Saturday night, a couple of thousand people camped on the grounds for the next day's show, which featured a new group that called itself Creedence Clearwater Revival.

When I got back to the office late Sunday to write my story, my editor asked about the riot.

"What riot?"

"The police say five-hundred people crashed the gates, the cops had to call for reinforcements."

"I didn't see anything, or hear anything about that." I wrote my story. Opening with a quote, of course.

PLEASANTON – "You and your damn music. I have to exercise my horse and the track is swarming with dirty hippies," an elderly cowboy said walking his horse up and down the sidelines.
Thus, another nail was hammered into the generation-gap casket as a result of the San Francisco International Pop Festival, held at the Alameda County Fairgrounds in Pleasanton this weekend.

I inserted info from the cops. It ran under the headline: *Pop Festival Success Despite Youth Melee.*

In the United States, 1968 was a banner year for youth melees, race riots, police riots – at the Democratic convention in Chicago – assassinations and, for me, fatherhood.

On the night of December 4th, after an hour and a half of staring at Jane Fonda's pointy tits in *Barbarella*, as the credits were rolling, Anita nudged me and said, "I think we better go to the hospital. My water broke about an hour ago."

"Why didn't you tell me?" I asked.

"You have to review the movie, don't you?"

We rushed home, grabbed the suitcase that had been packed for a week, called the doctor and, after midnight, hit the freeway. Since Anita had started her pregnancy with an obstetrician in San Francisco, that was where we were headed. I pointed my Mustang west, toward the Bay Bridge and Children's Hospital in the city, about forty miles away.

Katherine Lisa Becker arrived at about 4 a.m. on December 5, 1968. We would call her Kate. She was supposed to be Katharine, like Katharine Hepburn, but I couldn't spell.

I had wanted to name her Jennifer and call her Jenny but Anita didn't like it. We named the cat Jenny instead.

I didn't much care for the cat and was getting tired of living in the sticks. I played the nepotism card into a job offer back in Gotham.

In April 1969, I quit the Herald, gave away the cat, sold my '67 Mustang for $800 and flew to New York. I didn't know we'd soon be going farther east, across the Atlantic.

CHAPTER 3
THE LONDON-ZURICH SHUFFLE

Arriving in New York with my wife and baby, I considered my start in newspapers a success. Writing seemed to come naturally. I enjoyed the pressure of deadlines and craved more action inside the crime-scene tape.

I couldn't type very well – hunting and pecking with two index fingers, more often than not striking the wrong key – and spelling remained a challenge. But, I figured I was on my way.

My Uncle Jack, the same one who sent me to Wesley First at Columbia more than three years earlier, had offered me a job as associate editor of a magazine he was starting. It was to be called *Changes*.

"It'll be the East Coast answer to Rolling Stone," Jack said. My salary would be $150 a week. Pretty good money, I thought. And we'd bank most of it by initially staying with my parents, who'd moved back to Queens from Long Island.

Each day, I took the subway from Rego Park to the magazine's shabby office on Fifth Avenue, at 14th Street, in Manhattan. From the first day, I knew I was in trouble.

I was just starting to build some confidence as a writer and now I was expected to be an editor, whatever that was. The magazine had a small staff: Jack as editor, his co-publisher Sue Ungaro as advertising manager. Terese Coe and I were associate editors. The writers, if you could call them that, were all freelancers plucked from the counter culture Rolodex.

Terese seemed to know what she was doing, and showed me the respect I deserved – none. She made it clear that my only qualification for the job was being Jack's nephew. I never really figured out what I was supposed to do, or what anyone else was doing.

I hung around the office and tried to help out, which meant mainly running errands, which made me a copyboy with a title. My big editorial decision was making Iscoff, from his listening post in Livermore, the West Coast correspondent. It looked good on the masthead but didn't mean he had to write anything.

My one assignment for the first issue was to meet with Richie Havens and edit a short essay he wrote for us. I was jazzed about meeting the soulful singer.

His first album, *Mixed Bag*, was a favorite. During my time on the West Coast, I wore out the tracks of *San Francisco Bay Blues* and his version of *Just Like a Woman*.

I met Havens in the magazine's dingy back office. He asked me for guidance. I didn't have any. But he was gracious and I was puffed up by meeting a celebrity who seemed to enjoy my company. I'd see him again – twice – in Paris and Toronto.

He handed me his story, which he titled *Everything is Music*. It began: *How many times have you lay awake at night and listened to the city? A conglomeration of sounds that almost sub-passes your listening, when you are of course moving within it.*

I, of course, had no idea what he was talking about. But I read on, all the way to: *So like the sound of one hand clapping, so like the sounds of the entire universe (heard from the moon).*

"Far out, man," I said, about all the editorial judgment I could muster.

We sat and talked for a while, shared a joint, and talked some more. Other people came in, more drugs came out. When we ran out of refreshments, Sue Ungaro and her boyfriend, the jazz bassist Charles Mingus, took me for a ride in his Cadillac to get more.

One of my jobs at *Changes* seemed to be keeping Mingus company when he drove Sue to sales calls. He and I would sit in his Caddy while Sue went about her business. We didn't say much, since I knew nothing about jazz or other cool Greenwich Village stuff and he knew nothing about growing up in the suburbs and living with your parents in Queens. The one subject that interested both of us was how he had taught his cat to shit in the toilet.

"It took me only a couple of weeks to toilet-train Nightlife," Charlie said with great pride. "He's even learned to flush."

The debut issue of *Changes* came out in May and was dated June 1, 1969. It was large tabloid size, on rough newsprint, sold for fifty cents, and had a psychedelic drawing of Dylan on the cover.

Terese wrote the cover story, defending Dylan's *Nashville Skyline* album against criticism of its country bent. At least that's what I think it was about, since I found it as incomprehensible – with references to Camus, Beckett, Genet and Antonioni – as the rest of the stories in the magazine. All seemed to be written on speed, in a language with which I was not familiar.

I had expected *Changes* to be more like a real magazine, concentrating on music, the youth culture and the antiwar movement. What I read in the first issue was indecipherable. I assumed I was too uneducated and too unsophisticated to understand the articles, not hip enough or professional enough to cut it in New York. I was miserable.

It didn't help that no money was coming into the magazine and the staff was forced to sacrifice a couple of paychecks for the cause, which meant Anita and I couldn't afford an apartment of our own. The tension in my parents' place was on the rise.

Anita's solution was to move again, this time to *her* home. She had been writing to her sister, Pia, who was trying to find me a job in Switzerland.

Pia had been in contact with the bureau chief for United Press International in Switzerland, an Austrian named Franz Cyrus. I would learn that he wanted to sleep with Pia, not hire me.

On May 24, 1969, I received a telegram:

PLEASE CONTACT MR. JACK FALLON UPI NEW YORK 220 EAST 42ND STREET
TELEPHONE MURRAYHILL 2-0400
FOR INTERVIEW
REGARDS
FRANZ CYRUS/UPI/ZURICH

I met Fallon, UPI's foreign editor, in the reception area outside the news agency's headquarters in the Daily News Building, on the south side of 42nd Street, between Second and Third Avenues. He didn't shake my hand and said only, "let me see your clips."

Anita had pasted my *Livermore Herald & News* stories onto three-hole loose-leaf paper and collected them in a black binder. Fallon took it, walked back through the doors into the newsroom, and left me sitting alone on a sofa near the reception desk.

He returned about ten minutes later, handed me back my life's work, sat down next to me and said, "Why do you start all your stories with a quote?"

"It seems to work for me," I replied.

"Well, it doesn't work all that often."

He stood up, said he'd be contacting Cyrus in Switzerland. "Maybe you'll hear from him," Fallon said. I was dismissed.

Cyrus did call, sometime in June. He told me to come to Switzerland, stopping first in London to meet with the UPI's European news manager, Danny Gilmore, and spend some time training there.

On July 1, Anita and I and baby Kate, now nearly seven months old, took off from Kennedy Airport – and came down for refueling in Bangor, Maine, in a thunderstorm. As the plane wobbled and bounced through the clouds, I screamed and puked. Once on the ground, I told Anita we were getting off.

"We can't get off here," she said.

"Why not? We'll take a boat or something. There's no way I'm going up again in this plane."

"I didn't know you were afraid to fly," she said.

"I wasn't – until about twenty minutes ago."

She went off to talk to a stewardess. I stayed with Kate and began gathering our carry-on.

Anita returned with a cup filled with scotch. "Drink this," she said. "You'll calm down."

I gulped some scotch and looked around the cabin. A few passengers were staring at me. Some had been screaming and puking too, as the plane rocked and rolled. But they didn't seem ready to get off. I felt embarrassed enough to settle back into my seat with my family and my scotch.

We landed at Gatwick airport just before midnight. The tourist bureau in the terminal sent us to the nearby Russ Hill Hotel, in Surrey. The night clerk opened the bar for us, illegally poured us a couple of beers – I never did figure out England's drinking hours – and fixed some thick-cut ham sandwiches on pumpernickel. I was starving after having my appetite arrested by fear.

The next morning, we took a taxi to Heathrow where Anita and Kate caught a flight to Zurich. Her father would pick them up and drive them to her parents' home in Bern.

I went into London, after the tourism bureau at the airport got me a reservation at the Cadogan Hotel, near Sloane Square. I checked in, left my bag with the porter, had the doorman hail a cab and rode to Bouverie Street, off Fleet.

I took a rickety lift to the UPI office and asked for Mr. Gilmore. He invited me to his office and asked, "Who are you again?"

"Ken Becker. From New York. Franz Cyrus told me to see you on my way to Zurich. He offered me a job there."

"I know nothing about this," Gilmore said.

He asked me to wait in the newsroom while he phoned Cyrus. I stood alone, amid the clatter of the teletype machines. Men in white shirts and ties, their sleeves rolled up, pounded on typewriters, cigarettes dangling from their lips. A London fog of smoke rose and settled near the high ceiling. I loved it. I couldn't wait to start working here, to be back in the news biz.

Gilmore came out and led me into his office. "I'm afraid there is some misunderstanding. There is no job for you with UPI in Zurich. All we have in Zurich is an inner-Swiss service – in German, for Swiss papers. There is no UPI correspondent there. And there can't be one there unless I hire one." He paused. "And, if I wanted a correspondent in Zurich – which I don't – I wouldn't hire you because such a plum position – if there was one – would be for a seasoned reporter transferred from another bureau."

"But," I pleaded, "Mr. Cyrus told me to stop and see you, that I would get some training here and then start working in Zurich."

"That's not what he says. He says he has been in touch with you but never offered you a job."

"But I packed up my wife and baby in New York and we came here – she's on her way to Switzerland now. What do you suggest I do?"

"I'm sorry," he said.

I found a cab on Fleet Street and told the driver to take me back to the Cadogan. I went straight to the bar, which wasn't open, went for a walk instead, sprained my ankle jumping over a stone wall in the middle of a roundabout near Piccadilly Circus, and limped back to the Cadogan.

The doorman suggested I go to the hospital. "I'll fetch you a taxi," he said, "as soon as I take care of these folks." A couple in their thirties, dressed more appropriately for a Vegas nightclub than afternoon tea in a hotel in Chelsea, was waiting with their bags. He was steamed. He turned to me. "Back in Toronto, at least we know when the bars are open," he told me. "We're off to Paris," he added, taking the arm of the floozy at his side. "We've had it with this country."

When a taxi pulled up, they were off. The doorman hailed another one for me. At the hospital, I had my ankle taped – free of charge, my first experience with socialized medicine.

Back at the Cadogan, I made a reservation for a flight to Zurich the next day, went to the bar – it wasn't open at this hour either – went to my room, went back to the bar when it opened, had a scotch, had another scotch, had a double-scotch, went to my room and thought about Oscar Wilde, Lillie Langtry and King Edward VII.

The barman had told me some of the racy history of the Cadogan. He said that Wilde – I'd heard of him but otherwise knew nothing about him – had been arrested in Room 118 and taken to prison for a sexual escapade with a much younger man, and that the king and Langtry – I knew nothing about the son of Queen Victoria and had never heard of the apparently famous and beautiful actress – had had their trysts in Room 109.

I would learn more about Wilde and a lot of other things in the coming months, after arriving in Switzerland with no job and no prospects.

CHAPTER 4

ADULT EDUCATION

"Do you have any books by Hemingway?" I asked the older woman who was smoking and reading in the basement English-language section of a bookshop on Neuengasse in Bern.

"Of course," she said with a Swiss-German accent, rising and escorting me to a bookcase labeled fiction. "Any particular title you're looking for?"

"*The Sun Also Rises*," I said, recalling the book I'd discussed with Anita the night we met in San Francisco.

"Ah," said the older woman, "Robert Cohn was once middleweight boxing champion of Princeton."

I knew lots of Cohens – Dotty and Eddie Cohen, and their kids, Alan and Kathy, lived upstairs from us in Clearview – but none of them went to Princeton. I didn't know anybody who went to Princeton, or Harvard, or Yale, or any of those other ivy-covered colleges. I didn't know what the lady in the bookshop was talking about, either.

She pointed to a shelf lined with Scribner paperbacks. Some of the titles were familiar: *For Whom the Bell Tolls* (Gary Cooper and Ingrid Bergman), *The Old Man and the Sea* (Spencer Tracy). Why would anybody read a book when they could go see the movie?

I turned the first page and began reading ... *Robert Cohn was once middleweight boxing champion of Princeton.*

My god! So that's what this Swiss lady was doing. Showing off. Did she know the first line of every book in the store? Was it a trick to fleece francs from unsophisticated Americans? Didn't care. I was damned impressed.

Her small world, surrounded by British and American books, would become an oasis for me during the year I would spend in exile in Switzerland. She would become my professor of literature. Anita and others would tutor me in other aspects of my education.

I arrived in Bern with the same sense of uncertainty that I felt during all those months of unemployment in California. I was back to square zero, only now I had a wife and baby.

We moved into the upper floor of Anita's parents' house on *Altenbergstrasse*, on a bank of the fast-flowing River Aare.

Arriving that first week in July, on a hot, sunny day, I was first introduced to my sister-in-law, Pia. "I could really use a nice cold douche," were the first words she said to me.

I looked at Pia quizzically. Anita laughed. "In German," my wife explained, "*dusche* means shower." I laughed. Anita told Pia what she said. She blushed, then laughed.

My German vocabulary would grow to *guten morgen, gute nacht, auf wiedersehen, einen kaffee, bitte* and *zwei biere, bitte*. For the rest, I had Anita as my spokesperson and interpreter. Why doesn't everyone speak English?

The fact that I couldn't communicate with my in-laws was probably a blessing, since they didn't seem to like me very much. I couldn't blame them. I'd married their daughter and knocked her up – not in that order – moved into their house and didn't have a job.

Anita went back to work at Hertz in Bern – she'd gone to San Francisco on an exchange program. To keep me busy and broaden my horizons – or maybe just get me out of the way – she arranged for me to "deadhead" cars for Hertz.

The way this worked was that when a customer dropped off a car that belonged to a Hertz agency in another city, it had to be returned. I'd do that, and take the train home to Bern; or I'd take the train to another city and bring a car back. If it involved travel to another country – you don't have to go far to cross the border from Switzerland – Hertz would also pay for a night in a hotel.

I got to see a lot of Europe. I went to Amsterdam, where I briefly checked out the hookers in the windows in the *Rossebuurt* and the Rembrandts in The Hague, before returning to my little hotel room to read Norman's Mailer's *The Armies of the Night*.

I was chewing through books every waking hour, starting with the classics of 20th century literature – Steinbeck, Hemingway, Fitzgerald, Faulkner, Somerset Maugham, Evelyn Waugh. I tasted Thomas Wolfe and spit it out before finishing. I read some of Oscar Wilde's poetry and plays

– not as exciting as his naughty business at the Cadogan – and stories by Ring Lardner Jr. and Damon Runyon.

I caught up with more contemporary writers: Capote's *In Cold Blood*, Jimmy Breslin's *The Gang That Couldn't Shoot Straight*, Tom Wolfe's *The Electric Kool-Aid Acid Test*, which reminded me of the stuff we'd printed in *Changes*.

I read Jack Kerouac's *On the Road* for the first time – didn't much like it, but would take another crack a few years later, after I came under the tutelage of his buddy, Lucien Carr – and a book Anita had given me while we were in San Francisco, *The Hells Angels*, by Hunter S. Thompson.

I was starting to realize that these guys – yeah, they were all guys – were giving me lessons that could be applied to writing journalism. Some of them – Mailer, Capote, Thompson – were in fact writing journalism.

It wasn't the newswriting I practiced in Livermore, or the AP style Iscoff tried to steer me to, or the gibberish I saw in *Changes*, but a type of storytelling that took a reader on a more satisfying ride.

Far from home, but still feeling a hangover of the previous year – the riots and assassinations, the Democratic debacle in Chicago, Nixon's victory in November, the war without end – I retraced the events with Theodore White's *The Making of the President 1968*, as well as a book by three British journalists called *An American Melodrama: The Presidential Campaign of 1968*. I gobbled up David Halberstam's and Jack Newfield's books on Bobby Kennedy as soon as they came out.

In Bern, most of my days began with a walk across the river to the medieval Old Town, to the newspaper kiosk near the city's famous clock tower, the *Zytglogge*. I'd pick up the *International Herald Tribune,* settle into a café – *einen kaffee, bitte* – at the *Barenplatz* and read from front page to back, saving the best for last on the days there was an *Observer* column by Russell Baker. I had a weakness for Art Buchwald too.

Keeping up with the news from home wasn't too difficult. Though we didn't have a TV, I did watch the moon landing on July 21, 1969 in my in-laws' living room.

That same summer, I found enough words – in the *Trib, Newsweek* and *Time* – to get a picture of Woodstock, Teddy Kennedy's fall off a bridge on Chappaquiddick Island, and the slaughter of actress Sharon Tate and her Hollywood friends, which was front page for days and a great mystery.

Fortunately, I got the straight dope from a couple of stoners about my age who said they were from L.A. and hitchhiking around Europe that summer. We met one evening in a café in Bern.

"Jimmy Coburn did it," one told me.

"James Coburn?" I asked. "The actor?"

"Yeah," the other said, "crazy fucker, that Jimmy. Still got the knife from *The Magnificent Seven.*"

"Are you saying that James Coburn, the actor, used a movie prop to carve up those people?" I eyeballed both of them.

They responded with shit-eating grins, rose from the table and tripped off into the night.

Ugly Americans, I thought. Too much money, too much free time to get high and goof on people. I desperately wanted to move into responsible adulthood, not regress into adolescence.

By this time, the autumn of 1969, Anita, Kate and I had moved out of my in-laws house and into a one-room apartment across the river. On the edge of the Old Town, the building was called *Mohnhaus* – poppy house – appropriately named, since most of the residents were junkies and hookers. They fawned over Kate, who was starting to walk and talk and exude a magnetic charm she would never lose.

I was still driving cars for Hertz. On one trip, behind the wheel of a snazzy Mercedes convertible, I arrived in Geneva to a flirty call of "ooh la la" from a couple of fashionable ladies.

I was meeting that afternoon with John Callcott, the UPI correspondent in Geneva, at his office in the large United Nations complex. He dashed off some work and we retired to the bar at the Intercontinental hotel.

I'd called Callcott from Bern and he was eager to hear the story of how Franz Cyrus conned me into coming to Europe, about my suspicion the Swiss bureau chief was only interested in bedding my sister-in-law Pia.

"Sounds like Cyrus, anything to get laid," Callcott said.

"So what do I do?" I asked.

"Well, there will never be a job for you here in Switzerland, or anywhere in Europe for that matter. UPI just doesn't hire people on the spot overseas. I got on in Germany in the '50s, but they just don't do that anymore. Your best bet is to go back to New York, try to get on with UPI there, and, after a couple of years, if you still want to work in Europe, try to get transferred over here."

I didn't think I had the patience to follow Callcott's advice. Yet he was an inspiration – handsome and well dressed, smart and sophisticated, spoke French, German and Italian. An American who had made a life in Europe, as Hemingway had. About ten years older than me, he had some great war stories: about covering the building of the Berlin wall in the early '60s, and standing near JFK a couple of years later when the young president declared *"Ich bin ein Berliner."*

Callcott invited me to his home nearby – he was between marriages – a tasteful townhouse that reminded me of the brownstones on the East Side of Manhattan, except the stones were gray. Settling into a chair at the dining room table, John poured me a scotch, which I sipped while he roasted a fillet of beef and sautéed fresh vegetables.

"It's a good life," he said as he poured glasses of Bordeaux for dinner, "but you really can't survive on a UPI salary over here. I have to write on the side – under about ten different names – to get by, while the UPI bureau manager in Des Moines is living like an emperor."

"You want to live in Des Moines?"

He smiled. "Guess not."

I crashed at Callcott's place that night and found my way to the station the next morning. Waiting for the train, I read in the *Trib* that the Mets – the lovable losers of Breslin's *Can't Anybody Here Play This Game* – had won the World Series.

On the ride back to Bern, sitting in a second-class compartment, I was more determined than ever to become a real journalist, preferably a dashing foreign correspondent like my new friend, John Callcott.

I wanted the lifestyle, the adventure and glamour. But I also wanted to be good at it, a reporter with guts and instinct, a writer with flair, above the ordinary. I knew I was learning by reading and traveling. Alone, on the road, I would build stories in my mind, from the things I saw and the people I encountered.

On another trip for Hertz, from Bern to Munich, I passed a campground in Bavaria that was hosting a rally for the National Party of Germany. A large field was filled with neo-Nazis, young and old men yearning for the good old days.

I wondered what would happen if I stopped and joined them, introduced myself as a Jew from New York, started asking questions and taking notes, taking charge. *Okay, boys, drop your drawers – want to check if any you Nazis are Jewish.*

I was thinking of a legendary *Times* story, how reporter McCandlish Phillips had learned that the head of the Ku Klux Klan in New York, a former second-in-command of the American Nazi party, was Jewish.

In Munich, I stayed with Anita's friend Gaby, whose highrise apartment overlooked the construction site for the 1972 Olympics. I imagined what it would be like to be here as a reporter three years later, obviously not knowing the big story of the Games would be Black September terrorists murdering Israelis, or that in a few months I'd be covering the trial of three Arab terrorists in Zurich.

Through the summer, I'd kept in touch with Franz Cyrus, periodically reminding him of what I called his "promise" and he called my "misunderstanding."

The last I'd heard from Danny Gilmore, UPI's European news manager in London, was a note that began *I share your disappointment that UPI hasn't been able to place you immediately* and ended with: *All I can suggest is to keep in touch with Cyrus to see if the situation changes there.*

It didn't. But there was a temporary opening as the winter of 1969 approached. I jumped at it.

Earlier in the year, before I arrived in Europe, there had been an attack on an Israeli El Al jetliner at Zurich's Kloten Airport. Three men and a woman, disciples of the Popular Front for the Liberation of Palestine, managed to drive onto the tarmac, where the Boeing 720 was starting to taxi for takeoff to Tel Aviv.

From the ground, they opened fire on the cockpit with AK-47s, killing the pilot and wounding the co-pilot. They also had grenades, presumably to blow up the plane and kill everyone aboard.

But, before they could complete their mission, an Israeli air marshal, armed with a handgun, returned fire, killing one of the PFLP men and keeping the others occupied until they could be arrested by police. The Swiss charged the three surviving terrorists – and the Israeli – with various crimes.

Cyrus hired me as a stringer to cover the trial for UPI's main, New York-based, English-language wire.

So, in late November, I took the train from Bern to Zurich. I walked to my hotel on Weinbergstrasse, down the street from the UPI bureau. It was cold. The streets were filled with slush.

I was on my own again in an unfamiliar place. I was getting used to that, the tingle of anxiety and exhilaration.

Cyrus invited me to dinner my first night. He picked me up at about eight o'clock in his big Mercedes. "We're going to my favorite restaurant," he said.

Middle-aged and stocky, he appeared extremely pretentious, with his Mercedes and rumpled but expensive suit, wool topcoat and alpine hat from the wardrobe department of *The Sound of Music.*

The maître d' at Restaurant Kronenhalle greeted Cyrus by name – *Herr Cyrus* – and seated us at a small table under an original Miro. Anita had been teaching me about art, and she was especially fond of Miro.

"That's a Picasso over there," Cyrus said, pointing, "and that's a Matisse. The owner here collected all these paintings."

If he was trying to impress me he was succeeding, as he did when he suggested I order the rack of lamb and selected a bottle of Chateauneuf-du-Pape.

I really wanted to ream this guy out for luring me across the ocean and stringing me along. But I didn't want to jeopardize my chance at finally getting a crack at a job with UPI.

Cyrus was just as I imagined him, a bit pompous, smarmy, and thoroughly untrustworthy. We spoke English – I didn't have a choice – and I quickly realized that when he started talking faster he was probably lying. He was more of a salesman than a journalist, which was what UPI wanted in its bureau managers, since their main job was signing up clients.

"Your sister Pia is very charming," he said over dinner.

"Sister-in-law," I corrected, wanting to add, *Too bad you'll never get to fuck her.*

"How good is your German?" he asked.

"I can order a beer," I said.

"You don't like the wine?"

"No – I mean, yes, I like the wine. What I'm saying is, that is the extent of my German – being able to order a beer."

"That could be a problem," he said.

"You knew that before I left New York," I said.

"Yes, but I thought you'd have learned German in the time you've been here."

Slick move, Franz, pretending this was your plan all along.

"You said there is a problem," I said.

"Well, the trial will be in German. But I suppose I could have my reporter file in German and have my editor, Paul Stierli, translate for you."

The next day, I took a taxi to the courthouse in the town of Winterthur, near the airport, for my only look at the courtroom for the trial I would be "covering" for UPI's clients in the United States and other papers around the world.

Reporting for work at the bureau that day, I was given a small office off the newsroom, where half a dozen men churned out UPI's German-language service for Swiss papers.

We quickly settled into a routine. The reporter at the courthouse would dictate his story to the desk by 4 p.m. – 10 a.m. in New York. Stierli would write a translation for me, and I would do my best to turn it into about four-hundred words to be teletyped to the rewrite desk in New York in time for the early deadlines for the next day's East Coast morning newspapers.

I got off to an inauspicious start, when I spelled Israel "Isreal" – and received an appropriately snotty note from an editor in New York – but it seemed to go well after that. Stierli, who was a good editor in both English and German, was a great help, smoothing out the rough spots and drilling me in the finer points of UPI style. We were about the same age, but he had prepared for his career by going to university and working his way through the ranks, not driving around North America and Europe.

The trial – and my paid gig – lasted about a month. When it ended, a couple of days before Christmas, I was able to pound out a decent wire-service lead:

By Kenneth M. Becker
ZURICH (UPI) – Three members of the Popular Front for the Liberation of Palestine were convicted and an Israeli security guard was acquitted Tuesday for their roles in a deadly shootout at Zurich's Kloten Airport last February.

I was now – finally – Kenneth M. Becker. I didn't have a job in Switzerland, but I did have an offer from UPI in New York, starting in the new year.

Anita and I decided I would go ahead, and she and Kate would follow after I found a place to live. Meanwhile, we spent Christmas together in the *Mohnhaus* apartment, with a tiny fresh-cut tree and Anita introducing me to the Swiss tradition of decorating it with real lighted candles.

The season's *piece de resistance*, the culmination of my European education, was a trip to Paris. Anita and I took the night train from Bern, which put us into the darkened City of Light just before dawn. We went up to Sacre-Coeur to watch the sunrise, then checked into a small hotel on the Left Bank.

It was helpful having an older wife who was a more experienced traveler and spoke the local lingo across borders. She knew the ins-and-outs of dealing with hotel clerks, and managed to get us into our room early, arranging for a tray of *café au lait* and croissants to be delivered.

"Ahhhh, Paris," I said.

For two days, we walked the city. I'd read Hemingway's *A Moveable Feast* on the train from Bern. I felt like I was following his footsteps, from Cafe Select on Boulevard Montparnasse, where he drank with Henry Miller, to the Louvre, where he took Scott Fitzgerald to show him the nude statues, to assure Scott his penis was a normal size.

We walked through the Tuileries in a cold rain to the Jeu de Paume, where Anita continued my education in the Impressionists.

We spent our final evening in a small bistro, dining on steak frites and drinking cheap red wine.

"Ahhhh, Paris," I said.

Near the station to catch the night train to Bern, we stopped at a café for a late night drink. Anita ordered while I went to the men's room. I was back at our table a minute later.

"I have to show you what's in the bathroom," I said to Anita.

"I'm not going in the men's room," she said.

"It doesn't seem to matter here."

It took some persuading but we entered the men's room together. "Look," I said, pointing to a wall smeared with semen, a used condom, stretched to its limit, stuck to it.

Anita turned and left without a word. I used the john and returned to the table.

"Ahhhh, Paris."

I was twenty-three years old, a world traveler, and a married father of a year-old daughter. I was going home, to get my first crack at big-time journalism.

CHAPTER 5
DOG DAY AFTERNOON

I was panic-stricken as soon as I walked in the door of UPI's New York headquarters, on the twelfth-floor of the Daily News Building, for my first day on the job early in 1970.

The cavernous newsroom reminded me of the *Times*, though the energy level was much higher. The clatter of dozens of teletype machines – and people shouting over the din – punctuated the point that some serious shit was happening here.

"What's all the commotion?" I asked Eugene Haggerty, the New York bureau chief, who had met me in the reception area and escorted me to his desk in the newsroom. "It's only nine o'clock in the morning."

"Yes," said Haggerty, nodding, his red nose shining in the fluorescent light, "but it's tea time in London, the cocktail hour in Moscow and tomorrow in Australia."

I didn't know if he was right and didn't care. I was too concerned with how I was going to fit in with people who always knew what time it was in Moscow. I looked around the newsroom. Men in white shirts, looking like extras from Citizen Kane, hammered away at typewriters.

"There's a deadline every minute in this business," Haggerty added, introducing me to a line I would hear repeated many times at UPI – and would one day pass on to another generation of wire-service journalists.

Haggerty told me I'd be assigned to the Local Desk, which covered news from the city and its outskirts but also do some editing stints on the General Desk, which handled stories from across the country, and the Cables (foreign) Desk

"You're on three months probation," he said. "If you can do the job, you're in. If you can't, you're out."

I was leaning toward "can't" and "out" as soon as I met my new boss. Tommy Zumbo was a tough-looking fireplug who spit out his words with an Archie Bunker accent and attitude.

"It wasn't my idea to hire you," were his first words to me. "But Danny Gilmore seems to think we owe you a break."

"Yeah," I said, "I went all the way to London to meet with Gilmore, thinking I had a job in Switzerland, but he told me there was no job and I sat there for months with my wife and kid, driving cars for Hertz, before this job opened up to cover a trial in Zurich ..."

Zumbo cut me off. "I don't give a shit about any of that. You're here now and you're working for me. I'll get you started with some rewrites, taking dictation over the phone from reporters, working the night desk. We'll see."

He pointed to a cluster of four desks, each with a typewriter, and told me to take a seat. "Can you type?" he asked.

"Sure, with two fingers, but I'm pretty fast."

"We'll see," he said before turning his back and walking off.

I hoped this was the way Zumbo treated all the new guys. If it wasn't, I was in trouble. There was no way I was going to bullshit my way through three months in this place. It wasn't Livermore. Or some half-assed hippie magazine. Or a couple of weeks conning the Swiss-Germans in Zurich.

I was now working for one of the two international wire services in the United States. Every paper in the country, in the world, was filled with columns from UPI and AP. They churned out millions of words from all over the world. These people were pros. And I wasn't.

Zumbo kept me on the desk rewriting piddling press releases or taking dictation from real reporters. He expressed his opinion of my work in less than subtle ways.

"This is shit, do it over," he'd say, crumpling my copy into a ball and throwing it at me. "And, for Christ's sake, learn how to type."

My copy was shit and I couldn't type, which was obvious by all the words Xed out and all the typos corrected in pencil. But I kept plugging away.

Pretty soon, more often than not, I got the lead right and wrote clean if uninspired sentences. I was gaining confidence and the acceptance of some of my colleagues.

We drank together after work, often starting at a hole-in-the-wall bar around the corner on Second Avenue called the Edison, then moving downtown to the Lion's Head on Sheridan Square in the Village, a popular haunt of newspapermen and more literary types.

Most of my fellow bar-hoppers were single, not stepping out on a wife and kid in Queens. I'd found an apartment in Rego Park, a few blocks from my parents.

But I wasn't about to sacrifice what I considered an essential aspect of the journalist's life – drinking and smoking too much, talking shop and telling tales. I soaked up all the slurred stories and told some of my own – about my summer after the Summer of Love with Janis Joplin in San Francisco; about hanging out with Charlie Mingus and Richie Havens; about the cafes of Paris and the hookers in the windows in Amsterdam.

I got better at showing up for work with a hangover and making it through the day on coffee and cigarettes. I managed to pass my probation period without being fired.

"You still got a long way to go," Zumbo said.

Nonetheless, I was officially a Unipresser, which is what UPI people called themselves. We also called ourselves Downholders, which came from the admonition "down hold expenses" when traveling on assignment.

Unlike the Associated Press, which was a cooperative owned by daily newspapers across the country, UPI was a free-enterprise operation, founded in 1907 by E.W. Scripps, who believed that some competition for AP would be good for the industry and, perhaps, the country.

I soon learned that working for UPI, with fewer staff and a lot less money, you had to work harder, write better – and faster – than the enemy. Beating the AP by a few minutes with a bulletin was considered a major victory, as was getting your story published in more newspapers than the AP. Daily logs were compiled to keep score, with the results sent to all bureaus on an internal message wire.

Each bureau had a two-letter code. New York was NX. Such codes were designed, in part, to save money, since every character transmitted by teletype carried a cost. This necessitated a shorthand when sending messages – cheaper than long-distance telephone rates – between bureaus.

By the same token, every staffer sent messages using his or her wire service initials. Mine were kmb, always lowercase, in the e.e. cummings tradition established in Livermore.

This shorthand – decades before it was called text messaging – also proved valuable for me when taking notes. Along with improvements in my typing and spelling – I memorized the correct spelling of every word I ever spelled wrong, starting with Israel – I sharpened my skills at scribbling notes.

By 1972, standing in the balcony of a New York hotel ballroom, covering a twenty-minute speech by presidential candidate George McGovern, I got every word down.

During the three years I was at UPI-New York, the social order in the city and the country was shattering. There was the war in Vietnam and wars at home – between young and old, black and white, rival Mafia gangs.

Long-haired kids marching for peace were routinely savaged by cops and their blue-collar allies – or shot dead by the National Guard on the campus at Kent State, where one of the casualties was from Plainview, the kid brother of a high school classmate.

Black Panthers on rooftops in Harlem were shooting at police; mainly black prisoners battled mainly white guards at Attica to a deadly standoff; the Gallo and Colombo crime families gunned each other down in the streets of New York.

Zumbo kept me chained to the desk for most of 1970 and '71, doing rewrites or working the phones on minor stories. One of the many teletype machines at the local desk received cryptic messages from police headquarters – just the crime and an address, such as: *homicide: 125 E. 105th St.* I learned quickly that we only chased stories on crimes in white neighborhoods.

I did get out of the office occasionally to do some reporting, mainly on weekends or to help a more experienced hand on a big story, which is how I wound up at the hospital bedside of Joe Colombo in June 1971.

Colombo was a Mafia don with chutzpah. Fed up with being shadowed by the FBI and angry at the portrayal of the family business in Mario Puzo's book, *The Godfather*, Colombo went public, saying he and his *paisans* were discriminated against not because they were gangsters and killers, but because they were Italian. He founded the Italian-American Civil Rights League, the Mafia's answer to the Anti-Defamation League of B'nai B'rith and the NAACP.

On June 29, 1970, the league, with Colombo its star attraction, held its first Italian-American Unity Day rally, drawing fifty-thousand people to Columbus Circle in Manhattan. Many ordinary Italian-Americans bought

Colombo's con, as did politicians courting the large Italian-American vote.

Nelson Rockefeller, then New York's governor, was an honorary member. In November 1970, Frank Sinatra headlined a benefit concert for the league at Madison Square Garden.

I was working the desk, as usual, when all hell broke loose at the second unity day rally, on June 28, 1971. When word came that Colombo had been shot and taken to Roosevelt Hospital, a few blocks from Columbus Circle, Zumbo sent me there.

It wasn't hard to find Colombo – I just followed the herd right into his room. My UPI colleague Cass Vanzi was already there, as were about a dozen other reporters and Colombo's wife and sons.

While the wife cried, and the sons talked about revenge – though Jerome Johnson, a black man posing as a news photographer shot Colombo, and was himself shot dead at the scene, everybody suspected the rival Gallo brothers had set up the hit – the reporters were shouting questions at the man lying unconscious in the bed, some sticking microphones within inches of his mouth, which was hooked up to a ventilator.

"What happened, Joe?"

"How do you feel, Joe?"

"Who did it, Joe?

"You going after the Gallos, Joe?"

It would be Joe Colombo's last news conference. He never said a word. The fact that the sons allowed the press inside the hospital room seemed to reflect some weird kind of respect for their father's campaign to court attention.

Cass and I stepped out of the room to discuss how long we should stay. She was only about a year older than me, but already a respected reporter with talent and street sense. There was no question who was the senior staffer on the story.

Cass told me to talk to the sons and phone in some quotes to the desk, which I did, and go back to the office. She remained, in case Colombo woke up. He never did – was "vegetabled," as Joey Gallo put it – but hung on for another seven years.

Jimmy Breslin's novel, *The Gang That Couldn't Shoot Straight*, which I had read in Switzerland, was a comic take on Crazy Joey's Brooklyn crew. They kept a lion in their basement, and unleashed it when they needed help persuading deadbeats to pay up.

The Colombo-Gallo war was effectively over less than a year after Joe went into a coma, when Crazy Joey was gunned down in Umberto's Clam House in Little Italy.

Reporters working for UPI on breaking news often phoned in just notes and quotes, with the story being crafted by the top rewrite artists in the business. But we were also expected to be able to dictate a story word for word, including punctuation, from the scene – and beat AP in the bargain. That meant always having a large supply of dimes for payphones. And, if there was only one phone in the vicinity, I was instructed to unscrew the mouthpiece and pocket the speaker for exclusive use.

My weekend assignments were often antiwar marches – there seemed to be one every Saturday in New York in the early 1970s. Police would cordon off the parade route and I would walk along, inside the barricades but outside the line of protesters, taking notes.

I'd look for signs of trouble – hoped for it, really, since these events took on a sameness – check the cops for the official crowd count, and call in my story.

Though I sympathized with the marchers, I played these stories straight. Still, by showing up regularly, I formed a relationship with the leaders of the antiwar movement, including Cora Weiss and Dave Dellinger – one of the defendants in the infamous Chicago Seven trial – of the Mobilization Committee to End the War in Vietnam.

One of them would phone me when they were planning a press conference or demonstration. One call from Dellinger in 1972 was exceptional. He confided that he and Weiss were planning a trip to Hanoi, to bring back some American prisoners of war.

"Would you like to come along?" he asked.

"I'd love to," I said, trying to keep the shock and excitement out of my voice. "I'll have to check with my bosses, though."

"Well," he said, "let me know."

"Can we report that you're going?"

"No," he said, "that's off the record for now."

"Are any other reporters going?"

"Not that I know of."

I called Zumbo. He didn't share my enthusiasm. "We'll talk about it tomorrow."

There was a lot of talk. Zumbo talked to me. Zumbo talked to the editor-in-chief, H.L. "Steve" Stevenson. I talked to Stevenson. I quickly got the message: They wanted the story, but didn't think I was up to the job.

"Can we pick who goes?" Stevenson asked.

"That's not up to me," I replied.

"How much will it cost?"

"I have no idea."

"I'll let you know," Stevenson said.

I called Dellinger. I didn't ask him whether UPI could send someone else.

"When are you leaving?"

"Soon," he said.

"Please let me know when you know."

A couple of days later, Dellinger called me at my office. It was early in the morning. I'd just taken off my jacket, rolled up my sleeves and was on a first cup of office coffee. "We're leaving tonight. From JFK. I made a reservation in your name." He gave me the airline and flight number.

I told Zumbo. He went into a meeting. When he came out, he said, "Go home. Get your passport and pack a bag. But don't leave for the airport before you call me to get the go-ahead."

I rolled down my sleeves, put on my jacket and stubbed out a cigarette.

"How much is this going to cost?" Zumbo asked.

"I have no idea," I said.

"Gimme the flight number and we'll call to find out. Don't forget to call before you go to the airport."

I jumped on the subway and rode home to Queens. Living in Rego Park, near my parents, was convenient, since my mother looked after Kate while Anita worked as a temp. Our apartment building, a six-story pile of red brick like thousands of others throughout the boroughs, was just blocks from the Long Island Expressway, not far from JFK or LaGuardia.

Anita came home before it was time for me to go to the airport. I told her what was happening and asked that she drive me to the airport. I phoned Zumbo.

"It's no go," he said.

"Why?" I asked, though I really wasn't surprised.

"Too expensive." He was kind enough not to say I wasn't up to handling the story. I unpacked, put my passport back in my sock drawer and poured a scotch.

Two days later, Peter Arnett of the Associated Press, who had already won a Pulitzer Prize for the AP for his reporting from Vietnam – and would become famous as CNN's man in Baghdad when the bombs started falling in 1991 – sent his first dispatch from Hanoi, where he was the only journalist traveling with Weiss and Dellinger and the rest of the American delegation. Needless to say, UPI was shut out on this story.

For me, it was tough to take. I told colleagues that UPI had screwed up in not allowing me to go to North Vietnam. But I knew my bosses were probably right. Even if they had known AP was on the trip to Hanoi and let me go, I feared I couldn't compete head-to-head with a pro like Arnett.

I was still learning the craft. And it was hard. I felt competent to cover a two-alarm fire in the Bronx – Zumbo liked to say, "Don't expect any big assignments before you can cover a two-alarm fire in the Bronx" – but every new challenge was accompanied by a fresh case of insecurity.

I knew I couldn't write as well as Cass Vanzi or another star reporter on our desk, Peter Freiberg, that I wasn't fast enough to beat most AP reporters on a competitive story, that I'd miss the lead or screw up something else.

Peter had taught me the trick to organizing my notes and dictating a story on the phone – find the key quote, make it the second paragraph and scribble a lead that flows into it. "Then, add info as you go," he explained, "dropping in more quotes. Before you know it, you have a three-hundred-word story."

He was right. It worked. But I felt far from prepared to cut it alongside reporters who'd covered wars and presidential campaigns. Still, I was getting some good assignments. One of them scared the shit out of me.

New York could be a dangerous place in the early 1970s. Even walking the streets of Midtown could be risky. Wandering into the wrong neighborhood could be fatal.

But reporters were expected to go where the news was. On April 14, 1972, the news was at a Black Muslim mosque on 116th Street at Lennox Avenue in Harlem.

All I knew when I got in the cab outside the Daily News Building – and bribed the cabbie to drive me up to Harlem – was that a cop had been shot. I didn't yet know he was dead. I didn't know that the Nation of Islam – not renowned for putting out the welcome mat for whitey – was involved.

I arrived to find a huge crowd of angry black people gathered outside the mosque, surrounded by dozens of jittery cops. There were also a lot of TV cameras for the mob to play to. And that's what it seemed like at first, a theatrical production, with all of us playing our parts: the menacing Muslims on the steps, guarding the mosque; the grim-faced cops trying to shield their rage after one of their own took a bullet; the gathering storm of mainly young blacks filling the street; the petrified press, hoping to get the story and get the hell out of there.

The main character in the drama, Officer Phillip Cardillo, was already gone, having been shot inside the mosque and whisked away. He and three other officers had rushed into the building, responding to a 911 call – it turned out to be phony – that a fellow cop was in trouble. What they found was a large group of men who took offense at having their religious house invaded by the enemy, responding with fists and the bullet that killed Cardillo.

By the time I got there, cops were inside the building questioning suspects and the crowd in the street was shouting for the police to leave the Muslims alone and go away.

I stood on the sidewalk, between the Muslims on the steps and the commotion in the street. It was early afternoon, a beautiful spring day, unseasonably warm and sunny. I wondered why all the kids in the crowd weren't in school. Then I heard a gunshot and watched the crowd compress, not running away but toward the sound of the shot.

It turned out a lone cop had been pinned in the mass, fell to one knee, raised his revolver, and accidentally fired into the air. But the crowd was in a frenzy. So were the cops, running around, trying to restore order. Next thing I knew, the men in blue were pulling out and a little kid who couldn't have been more than twelve walked up to me, smiled, hoisted his T-shirt, showed me a big gun stuck in his belt, nodded toward the cops and said, "When they're gone, you better be gone too."

He melted back into the mob. And an angel appeared at my side. "You look a little nervous," said Leon Pitt, the only black reporter I worked with at UPI.

"Did you hear what that kid said?"

"What kid?"

"The little kid with the big gun – he threatened to kill me when the cops leave."

"So I guess we better get you out of here," said Leon, guiding me across Lennox Avenue to a bar where I was the only white face.

"You'll be okay in here," he said. "I'll get you a beer while you phone the desk."

I called in a description of how the scene had played out and the few quotes I got from the police public affairs officer who had been there. I didn't relate my encounter with the kid with the gun.

Leon and I had a beer and caught a gypsy cab back downtown.

Like I said, New York could be a scary place in the early seventies. But most of my day-to-day life, and most of my assignments, were in relatively safe neighborhoods.

The only other time I had felt really nervous during those three years as a reporter in New York was when I found myself after dark in the South Bronx without a ride – until Geraldo Rivera's crew saved my ass.

I arrived at Lincoln Hospital during daylight on July 17, 1970. A community group, abetted by the Young Lords Party – the Puerto Rican version of the Black Panthers – had taken over the city-run hospital, sent the staff scurrying, and declared themselves in charge, promising to provide better health care than the decrepit facility had to offer.

In most ways it was an easy story to cover. The occupiers were very PR conscious and cooperative, giving reporters a tour inside and handing out copies of their plan to improve the hospital's service to the community. Outside, an official from City Hall said Mayor Lindsay understood the complaints and would take action after the illegal occupation ended. And the cops on hand seemed calm and in no hurry to rush the joint.

I called in my story from a phone inside the hospital. Zumbo told me to hang around just in case the cops changed their battle plan, or somebody inside did something stupid.

As darkness enveloped the decaying neighborhood, I started to feel edgy. After Geraldo filmed his standup and his white working-class crew turned out their lights and started to pack up, I knew they were my last hope out.

"Can you guys give me a lift back to Midtown?" I asked the cameraman.

"Is the kid coming back with us?" he asked the soundman.

"Nah, he's staying here with *his people*," he snickered.

Geraldo had become a media darling as the mouthpiece – he was a lawyer – for the Young Lords. He was hired by WABC-TV to be part of its *Eyewitness News* team, structured to reflect the ethnic diversity of the city. The token Italian-American, Rose Ann Scamardella, was the inspiration for the Gilda Radner character, Roseanne Roseannadanna, on *Saturday Night Live*.

Geraldo's crew ridiculed him all the way back to Midtown. "This kid will never make it," said the cameraman. "You see how many takes it took just to do his wrapup?"

"Jeez," said the soundman. "Where do they get these kids?"

For a while in the early '70s, my regular beat seemed to be the airport named for the dead president. I probably got most of the assignments because I had a car and lived closest to JFK.

Friday nights were especially eventful, since the end of the work week appeared to inspire wannabe D.B. Coopers. By the third or fourth such occasion, the UPI slotman would call and say, "Hey, Ken, it's the Friday night hijack." I'd get in my car and drive to JFK.

These incidents could more accurately be called failed hijackings, some screwball looking for a free ride to Disneyland – not Damascus – who never got off the ground. The FBI would figure out a way to get the passengers off and an agent onto the plane. The troublemaker, armed with a water pistol or a Swiss army knife, would be hauled off in handcuffs.

One episode ended in a more dramatic fashion at JFK. It would gain great fame when it became the plot for the movie *Dog Day Afternoon*.

On August 22, 1972, I was at City Hall, where I sometimes helped out the reporter assigned there full time. I was checking in with the desk, when I was told, "Can't talk now. There's a bank robbery in Brooklyn, and it looks like they've got hostages."

"What bank?" I asked.

"Chase Manhattan, on Avenue P, at Third Street."

The desk editor hung up. I flipped through a Brooklyn phonebook, found the number for the bank and called it.

"Hello," a man answered.

"Hi," I said. "Who's this?"

"This is the bank robber."

"What's your name?"

"Sorry, I can't talk no more," he said, and hung up.

I called back – the line was busy – phoned the desk and reported my brief conversation with the robber.

"You want me to go to Brooklyn?" I asked.

"We've got it covered," I was told. "Just hang in there for now."

I followed the news reports on the radio until the desk called.

"You got your car?"

"Yeah," I said.

"Well, it looks like they might be leaving the bank soon, going to the airport. Get out there and see if you can follow along."

It didn't prove difficult. As night fell, it seemed like everybody in Brooklyn had piled into their cars and joined the convoy heading for JFK – led by the bank robbers and the FBI. Kids in convertibles were blasting music – *School's out for summer!* – honking their horns. It was like a pep rally for the robbers.

I knew my way around JFK and went straight to the press room in the main terminal. Some reporters were already there, and this was where we learned that one of the robbers had been shot dead and the other captured – fourteen hours after they entered the bank.

I usually did well on these stories, since AP would dispatch three or four guys, who would be fighting with each other over who would call it in while I dictated my story.

My worst day at JFK was in September 1970, when a DC-8 charter, operated by Trans International Airlines, crashed and burned on the runway. I got there – walked right onto the runway – when the wreckage was still smoldering.

"What's that smell?" I asked a fireman.

"Jet fuel," he said, "and burned flesh."

There had been eleven people on the DC-8, all crew bound for Washington where they would pick up a load of passengers for a flight to Europe.

News at an airport was usually bad news. You expect it. But do you hope for it?

That's the question I faced one night at JFK. I was working late at UPI when we got word of a plane coming in for an emergency landing. A Boeing 747 full of people had taken off from Geneva, where the tower noticed something wrong with the landing gear.

I drove to the airport with a colleague, Emil Sveilis – who had become a friend and soon would be my boss, in Canada. We found a vantage point overlooking the runway, climbed atop a small storage shed to get a better view, and stared into the darkness. The 747 was due in about 15 minutes.

"So," I finally broke the silence, saying what I knew we both were thinking, "do we want it to land safely or crash?"

It landed safely. No story.

CHAPTER 6
IS EVERYBODY HAPPY?

Allard K. Lowenstein was the architect of the ultimately successful campaign to dump Lyndon Johnson as the Democratic Party's nominee in 1968. The other half of his plan, to replace LBJ with a president who would end the Vietnam War, was less successful.

Lowenstein, a Democrat, had served one term in Congress, and had just lost his bid for a second, when I met him at his unpretentious two-story home in Long Beach, Long Island, on December 6, 1970.

Since I wasn't getting many assignments that first year at UPI, I figured the best way to get ahead, to get noticed, was to write features. I pitched ideas to the features' editors, and researched and wrote the stories on my own time.

I went to Lowenstein's home with a preconceived notion of what I wanted to write and what I wanted him to say: That political action was a waste of time, that the surge of energy that brought down LBJ died with

Bobby and was buried in the streets of Chicago, that we were all doomed to live the rest of our lives under Nixon and his ilk.

I figured the best way to go about the interview was to show up prepared – I knew the politics and the players of the previous three years and Lowenstein's part in the drama – turn on the tape recorder, start a conversation, and see where it went.

We sat at his kitchen table – the phone ringing constantly, kids wailing in the next room, jets flying overhead on their approach to JFK, his wife Jennifer interrupting with messages – and argued.

He wanted to talk about hope, his effort to find the best candidate, from either party, to bring down Nixon in 1972.

"What makes you think," I said, "that there is anyone – Democrat or Republican – who can go into that office and cleanse the political process to the point that you're not going to have deceptions and lies?"

"It's a matter of degree," he said. "I'm not trying to suggest purity. I'm just trying to suggest that there are some standards of public integrity which people in the country expect. Whether they are right to or not."

"You really believe that?" I asked.

"Yes," he said.

"Based on what?"

And on it went. Finally, exasperated, he said, "What's happening is you're pushing me into a situation in which, on tape, you want me to say things that I'm uncomfortable with, which, when taken out of context, are going to make it sound like I'm some Pollyanna."

"I wouldn't take anything you say out of context," I assured him.

"I don't know you," he said. "I can't take that chance."

Lowenstein was nearly twenty years older than me, a former congressman and graduate of Yale Law. I was a rookie reporter and a college dropout. One of us was better schooled in chutzpah.

After about an hour of close quarters verbal combat at the kitchen table, I turned off my tape recorder and stood to leave. Like two boxers at the end of an exhausting fight, we shook hands.

I asked about his kids and discovered our daughters had the same name. My Katherine had turned two years old the previous day. His Katharine – he spelled it the Hepburn way – was not yet a year old.

Suddenly, unexpectedly, he said, "You want to join us for dinner?"

It turned out to be a fundraiser, to help pay off his debt from the last campaign. It was at a restaurant in Great Neck, Fitzgerald's West Egg in *Gatsby* and home of my draft board. I stayed for cocktails, stood at the edge of the crowd, spotted the actor George Segal, and left.

My feature began:

NEW YORK (UPI) – Allard K. Lowenstein is: a) A deeply troubled man unable to accept the death of Robert Kennedy; b) A Pollyanna about rebellious students; c) An agent of Hanoi, or d) None of the above.

At this point in the nonstop, change-on-the-plane political life of the one-term congressman and

prime mover in the "dump Johnson" movement of 1967-68, the answer would appear to be (d). But he has been called all of these and more.

I had been exhilarated by the interview and not dissatisfied with the story. At UPI, we liked to think of ourselves as the writers' wire service. We could jazz the pants off AP with our leads and colorful language.

My multiple-choice lead had been an attempt at something different, to stand out. It was not discouraged. In fact, I received a note passed down from the big boss, H.L. Stevenson: *Fine piece. Cheers to kmb.*

I never spoke with Lowenstein again. Nothing personal. We just played our parts and moved on.

He would keep up the good fight, and was working for Teddy Kennedy's 1980 presidential campaign when he was shot dead, at the age of fifty-one, in his Rockefeller Center law office, by a deranged protégé.

I don't know whether he ever read my story. I'd learn not to care what the subject of a story thought about it and, in some cases, viewed a negative reaction as a sign I was doing my job.

But, in my early days with UPI, there was one story that caused an unintended fuss and personal rebuke. When my great-uncle, Ted Lewis, turned 80, I thought I'd do one of those where-are-they-now features. I knew where he was, of course – in his large and lavish apartment on Central Park West at 72nd Street, which I had visited many times as a child.

Ted Lewis was one of the biggest stars of the Jazz Age. Benny Goodman, Jimmy Dorsey and many others got their start in Lewis's band. He later became a celebrated solo act, coming on stage in his trademark top hat, asking, "Is everybody happy?" He would play his clarinet and croon his signature song, *Me and My Shadow.*

I pitched the idea to the features' editor, got the go-ahead and arranged to meet Uncle Ted for the interview in his apartment, where, growing up, I had met Sophie Tucker and Eddie Cantor, George Burns and Jack Benny.

We sat at his desk, in the same room where a genuine Las Vegas slot machine spit out silver dollars as presents for me as a kid.

The interview went well, I thought. He seemed old and tired – and bitter. He talked about how show business no longer had a place for him. I wrote the story as he told it.

NEW YORK (UPI) – Ted Lewis, who made "everybody happy" with his top hat and shadow during a career spanning six decades, spends much of his time reminiscing now that he's turned 80. But he'd much rather be out there on stage.

Interviewed in his memorabilia-filled New York apartment, Lewis said that he would like to perform but the offers have stopped coming.

"They think Ted Lewis is too corny. They probably think the parade has passed me by," he added. "If they threw me a couple of bones I'd grab them in a minute."

It went on to explain how he had tried a comeback in 1966, producing and starring in a show with his old friend,

Sophie Tucker. But the dream died with Miss Tucker before the show opened in New York.

It was a sad story about a sad man, and got a lot of play in papers across the country. Unfortunately, my Uncle Ted read it.

"He's very mad at you," my Aunt Adah called to say.

"Why?"

"Because you make him sound pathetic."

"I thought it might get him a job," I said.

"Well, it didn't," she said. "You should know better."

It was not long after that I got a call from the UPI desk early one morning – I wasn't due at work until later in the day. "Did you hear about your Uncle Ted?" my friend and colleague Peggy Polk asked.

"No."

"Well, I'm sorry to have to tell you, but he died this morning."

I didn't say anything.

"I've been asked to ask you if you want to come in and write the obit," Peggy said.

I did. And lost the logs. Rox – that's what we called AP, because its headquarters was in Rockefeller Center – kicked my ass on my uncle's obit.

A story that got a positive reaction – from one reader, anyway – was my coverage of a strike at the Willowbrook State School in the wilds of Staten Island. It was really not a school, more a prison without bars for fifty-two-hundred mentally disabled boys and young men.

The workers had walked out on Saturday, leaving the residents unattended and at risk of harming themselves or each other. The state put out an urgent call for volunteers.

I was among hundreds who showed up the next day, April 3, 1972. I was there to cover the story. But instead of standing on the sidelines taking notes, I joined four other young volunteers working on a laundry truck.

I wrote a personal account of my day, about *sorting mounds of stinking, feces-covered linens and green surgical gowns* with four other guys on Easter Sunday; about *the wretched dimly lighted barracks where the residents lived, how one put his head on my shoulder and called me 'mother,' and another in an old army jacket told me, "I'm the general."*

I had never written journalism in the first-person before, attempted to construct a narrative to tell a story. But, true to form, UPI gave me the freedom to try – or enough rope to hang myself.

I got mixed reviews from my editors and colleagues. I did get a letter from one reader in South Carolina, who described herself as a thirty-two-year-old state employee "who happens to have a mentally retarded son" at an institution in Georgia. She sent an expression of "admiration, appreciation, praise and a THANK YOU" and her "hope that you will be amply repaid and rewarded in some way."

There was nothing extra in my paycheck that week in 1972. But, all these years later, I still have the letter.

The big story that year was the presidential campaign, Nixon versus McGovern. Over the four years that Nixon had been in the White House, the country had become even more divided. The Republicans had frightened Americans into believing a Democratic victory would signal more student anarchy, more black rage, more violent crime, and Uncle Ho and Chairman Mao marching down Main Street.

Even my relatives, middle-class Jews, aunts and uncles who had voted for FDR, and cousins who adored JFK, were now in Nixon's corner. My mother was the exception, and she took a lot of heat and ridicule when she campaigned for McGovern in her Queens neighborhood.

Before '72, my election campaign reporting was restricted to local races. And, even then, it was usually a weekend assignment when the big guns were off.

In 1970, when New York's Republican governor, Nelson Rockefeller, was running against Democrat Arthur Goldberg, I was in a Manhattan television studio covering one of their debates.

What they said was not memorable – even then. But, as Rocky was leaving the studio, I got a first glimpse of what happens when a reporter catches a politician off guard.

I elbowed my way into Rocky's entourage as the governor got into a freight elevator. The governor was steamed. He hadn't done well.

As the door was closing, I raised my notebook and pen and asked Rockefeller a question.

"Who the hell are you?" he spat.

"Ken Becker – UPI"

"Get him out of here," the governor ordered. His bodyguards forced open the doors and pushed me out of the elevator.

My early assignments covering the president were less than auspicious, mainly standing outside a Manhattan hotel, watching Nixon and the White House press corps march past.

I'd run to a payphone, call the desk and announce, "Nixon entered the hotel at 8:42 p.m."

UPI then dispatched a bulletin advisory: *President Nixon entered the Waldorf-Astoria hotel in New York for a policy address at 8:42 p.m. EDT.*

I waited outside to complete my assignment: *Nixon left the hotel at 10:17 p.m. EDT.*

In '72, however, I did get a few cracks at the presidential campaign. I got within smelling distance of Nixon once – he smelled pretty rank, or maybe it was the garbage barge heading out to sea – during an event at the Statue of Liberty.

I got even closer to his vice president, Spiro Agnew, when he gave a speech at the Waldorf and reporters were allowed backstage after for questions. I don't remember what the nattering nabob said since I was focused on the man who had introduced him, Arnold Palmer, one of my sporting heroes, who was smashed.

I covered McGovern a few times. On the night of the New York primary, I sat in a hotel suite with his two-headed brain trust: pretty boy Gary Hart and the grizzled Frank Mankiewicz, who had been Bobby Kennedy's press secretary and the one who announced to the world when Bobby died.

We watched the returns on TV, though Hart and a young radio reporter, Connie Chung, disappeared into the bedroom for a while.

As the campaign dragged on, it was obvious McGovern was also a goner. He had lost his voice shouting about something called Watergate and other stuff no one was listening to.

Communication was also an issue for me. Anita and I didn't talk much. And, when we did, it seemed like we were speaking different languages. *Nicht sprechen Schweizerdeutsch.*

Perhaps we were doomed from the start. Two lonely people far from home in San Francisco. Having a baby within a year. The age difference. The cultural differences.

When we finally hashed it out, decided to separate, it was relief. But, if I was a loser at marriage, I was turning into a winner at UPI, with the best assignment of my now promising career.

CHAPTER 7
ROGUE COP

By the summer of 1972, my boss, Tommy Zumbo, and I had settled into a comfortable truce. He still didn't like me much – he told me so once, at a party, when he was loaded – but treated me as just another member of the staff and seemed to value some of my work, though he wouldn't come out and say it. Nor would I tell him that his tough-guy shtick had motivated me to be a more disciplined writer and better reporter. To seal the deal, he gave me the kind of assignment that only went to an ace reporter – a high-profile murder trial.

Bill Phillips, a New York City police detective, was charged with killing a pimp and a prostitute, and wounding her john, in a posh East Side apartment on Christmas Eve 1968.

A cop charged with such a crime would have been big news under any circumstances. But Phillips was also a celebrity of sorts, having been the star witness at the Knapp Commission hearings into corruption in the NYPD.

For days during the fall of 1971, Phillips testified, live on television, about his fourteen years on the force pursuing payoffs and perks to support his playboy lifestyle. He bragged of owning five airplanes, driving a fancy foreign sportscar, frequenting the hot nightspots and fine dining establishments on Manhattan's East Side, jetting off with stewardess girlfriends to ski weekends in Colorado and golf vacations in Palm Springs – all either on the house or on the proceeds of the graft he took from mobsters and other criminals – while his clueless wife in Queens thought he was out making cases as a police detective.

He admitted he would have still been shoveling in the cash if he hadn't been caught on tape trying to take protection money from an East Side madam – Xaviera Hollander, *The Happy Hooker* – and turned into an informant for the commission in exchange for immunity from prosecution and round-the-clock protection by U.S. Marshals.

Phillips said being charged with an old unsolved murder was a frame-up to get back at him for informing on other cops and to discredit testimony he was scheduled to give against them. He hired F. Lee Bailey, probably the best known and most flamboyant lawyer in the country, to defend him.

Considering the players and the case – rogue cop, celebrity lawyer, pimp and hooker shot in the head, on Christmas Eve, no less – it was a dream for my first murder trial.

It began in late June 1972 in a large, stately courtroom on the thirteenth-floor of the Criminal Courts Building at 100 Centre Street in downtown Manhattan. Behind the bench was State Supreme Court Justice John Murtagh, silver-haired and square-jawed, right out of Central Casting. For the prosecution was Assistant District Attorney John Kennan, wiry, combative, in an off-the-rack suit, looking every bit the honest and overworked civil servant.

Bailey, appearing older than his thirty-nine years, led the defense team, his ruddy complexion well scrubbed after a night of scotches and manly bravado, his chunky build packed into a well-tailored three-piece suit.

And then there was the defendant, forty-two-year-old William R. Phillips, every hair in place, fashionably long sideburns, conservative suit, Windsor knot in his silk tie, fresh shine on his Gucci loafers.

While they sat in the well of the courtroom, two press tables had been placed just behind the rail. The first day, I took a seat at the one on the left, behind the defense table, the better to keep my eye on Bailey and Phillips. Also at my table was Mindy Nix, a young and attractive radio reporter, whose straight blonde hair and miniskirt may have been the strongest lure to that side of the courtroom. Though the seats weren't assigned, we would return each day, for more than a month, to the same places.

It didn't take long to recognize that the seating arrangement would have a lot to do with how we reporters viewed the trial. During the many breaks in the proceedings, the lawyers – and even the defendant – would wander over to the rail. That made for a lot of off-the-record chats with Bailey, co-counsel Eddie Orenstein and Phillips, getting their take on how things were going, hearing their bitches about the prosecutor and the judge, establishing a relationship that would last throughout the trial and put me – and Mindy – in a position to set up an exclusive interview with Phillips after the verdict.

Meanwhile, the reporters at the other table would be talking to Kennan and his prosecution team during the breaks. On both sides, I suspect, this gave the reporters a rooting interest in the game, which inevitably leaked into our stories.

I had been told by one of the courtroom buffs – the rows of spectator benches were filled for much of the trial – that Bailey always slipped into his opening statement "the Perry Mason line."

Sure enough, after saying the state had charged the wrong man and suggesting the defense might soon produce the "real killer," he took a deep breath, puffed out his chest, looked straight at the ten men and two women in the jury box and began, "I know some of you may have heard of me, know my reputation. And I know most of you probably watch *Perry Mason*.

"Well, I'm not Perry Mason and this is real life, not TV. So don't expect someone to jump up on the witness stand and scream, 'I give up. I did it. I killed them.'" It was wonderful theater, and the jurors seemed to enjoy it, as I did.

The prosecution's case was based primarily on eyewitness testimony. Four prostitutes, who the courthouse wags christened "Hogan's Hookers" – Frank Hogan was the longtime Manhattan district attorney – each testified that Phillips had been a frequent visitor to the apartment of their pimp, Jimmy Smith, also known as James Goldberg. (Only in New York would someone named Smith use Goldberg as an alias.) They didn't say they saw Phillips on the night of the murders but that he'd come by occasionally – not for sex – that they knew he was a cop, and they assumed Jimmy was paying him protection money.

The doorman and another employee identified Phillips as the man who entered the building at 157 East 57th Street and went to Smith's apartment, 11-F.

Then Charles Gonzales took the stand. He was the forty-year-old john who had just finished having sex with nineteen-year-old Sharon Stango when the killer arrived.

Gonzales said he was sitting on a living room couch with Smith and Stango when the visitor pulled a .38 from his coat pocket, shot Smith once and Stango twice – both in the head – and fired a bullet through Gonzales's arm, into his gut, before walking out of the apartment.

Gonzales was a pathetic excuse for a man, a father of four who had spent Christmas Eve drinking with his buddies before going to have sex with a teenager. But, though Bailey at times seemed to shake the sweaty witness, Gonzales insisted that Phillips was the shooter.

The prosecution alleged Phillips killed Smith because the pimp was holding out on a $1,000 payoff. Why did it take three years to identify Phillips as the shooter? The prosecution said it was a lucky break, that the homicide detective on the case was watching Phillips on TV, testifying before the Knapp Commission, when he realized Phillips fit the description of the suspect in the Smith-Stango murders.

The defense countered that the detective was angry at Phillips for portraying the NYPD as institutionally corrupt, and fit Phillips for the frame. Bailey relied mainly on alibi witnesses – Phillips's wife and other family members – who said he spent Christmas Eve with them.

The main event came when Keenan cross-examined the defendant. Phillips freely admitted he'd been a crook with a badge, that he'd lied and cheated and abused his authority at every turn to feed his greed. But he never flinched when it came to the murders.

Didn't do it. Wasn't there.

It was an impressive performance by a truly repulsive man. I believed him.

If I was sympathetic to the defense, Murtagh's charge to the jury put me firmly in its corner. The judge appeared biased against the defendant in telling the jurors, "If he is found guilty, the consequences of your verdict will not be upon you, but will be the results of his own wrongdoing ... You will then return a just and true verdict, no matter whom it hurts."

Bailey was livid. So was the rest of the defense team. The prosecutors looked sheepish, if not embarrassed.

"No matter whom it hurts"? Who the hell could be hurt except Phillips?

From where I was sitting, the whole deal looked rigged against Phillips, from his arrest and indictment, to the trial and all those objections by Kennan that the judge sustained, and all those objections by Bailey that the judge denied.

After filing my story, highlighting the judge's "no matter whom it hurts," quote, I walked to Orenstein's nearby office.

Phillips and his family, his lawyers and a couple of other reporters from our table, were there. So was Bailey's very young and very pretty girlfriend Lynda – she'd be wife number three of four – who had sat in the front row on our side of the aisle throughout the trial, looking like a prom queen in a whorehouse.

"Tough day," I said to Lynda.

"Lee's really mad," she said.

The scotch was flowing, feeding the anger.

"That son of a bitch, Murtagh" said Orenstein, quickly adding, "I don't mind that you're here, but anything we say here is off the record."

"Sure," I said, "but our deal is still on? We get him for an interview right after the verdict."

"Sure, sure," he said, took a gulp of his drink and wandered across the room to absorb more of Bailey's aura.

Orenstein had done some minor legal work for Phillips years before the trial and had represented him when he was first questioned about the murders. Phillips had phoned Bailey's office in Boston soon after – nothing too good for our Billy – and Orenstein stayed on as second chair.

He's the one I approached about arranging a post-verdict interview with Phillips, thinking that once the trial was over, Bailey wouldn't be interested in anything except getting his fee, getting out of town and getting with his girlfriend.

It turned out we had to wait another day – and night. First, the jury came back with questions. Then, the jury came back to say it was deadlocked. But Murtagh kept sending them back. This pleased the defense, since Bailey said he believed the jury had voted eleven to one for acquittal.

"It's that fucking woman, the one that smiled at me every day," Phillips confided to me in Orenstein's office the second night of jury deliberations, as the empty scotch bottles piled up. "I told Lee not to trust any women on the jury."

Just before 11 p.m., we were told the jury was coming out again. By the time we returned to the courtroom, it looked like Times Square at 3 a.m. after News Year's Eve.

The spectator section was littered with discarded newspapers and food wrappers. The buffs were asleep on the benches, snoring while they secured their space.

TV reporters never seen during a trial were there too, including Geraldo, who'd brought a date – his waif-like child bride, Edith, Kurt Vonnegut's daughter.

Waiting for the verdict, I had called in two dummy leads – one for an acquittal, the other for a conviction.

Both were already set in tape, including the codes that rang five bells for a bulletin, with the correct one to be fed into the teletype machine and transmitted across the country as soon as I gave the word.

To get an edge on the AP reporter at the trial – she sat at the press table behind the prosecutor – I'd swiped the speaker out of the mouthpiece of the phone closest to the swinging doors of the courtroom.

But my plan crashed when the jury said it was hopelessly deadlocked and Murtagh declared a hung jury and a mistrial. I sprinted up the aisle, trying to rewrite the bulletin in my head as I ran, got in the booth, inserted the speaker, screwed in the mouthpiece, and dialed the desk.

"It's a hung jury," I shouted, "throw out the other leads."

"Okay, go," said the night editor.

AM-PHILLIPS
BULLETIN
By Kenneth M. Becker
NEW YORK (UPI) – A mistrial was declared late Wednesday in the double-murder trial of William R. Phillips, an admittedly crooked New York police officer accused of killing a pimp and his teenage prostitute on Christmas Eve 1968.
MORE

"OK," said the editor, "let me get this out."

I gathered my thoughts, and looked at the few notes I'd just scribbled in the courtroom.

"OK, go," the editor said.

AM-PHILLIPS
URGENT
1ST ADD PHILLIPS NEW YORK XXX EVE 1968.
"We are hopelessly deadlocked," the jury foreman told State Supreme Court Justice John Murtagh after 22 hours of deliberations over two days.
The judge, who had sent the jury back to try to reach a verdict earlier in the day, accepted the hung jury and declared a mistrial.
The packed courtroom in lower Manhattan erupted in groans.
The defense, which had said it believed the jury was leaning toward an acquittal, showed its frustration,

as the defendant raised his hands in the air and slammed them down on the table in anger.
MORE

"Get that out," I said to the editor. "And follow it with the background stuff I prepared. I gotta go."

From the phone booth, I spotted Phillips and Bailey in the corridor, in front of the TV cameras, and worked my way behind the defendant and his lawyer, where I could hear every word and not have to fight my way into the scrum in front and be jostled by the crowd – a trick I learned early and employed throughout my reporting days.

Phillips was going on about a "mockery of justice" and trashing the judge for being prejudiced against him. Bailey wasn't saying much, and looked like a man who had a ticket on the red-eye back to Boston – or maybe Barbados.

I called in some of Phillips's quotes to be worked into my story, told the desk I was done for the night and wandered over to Orenstein's office. The wake was already underway.

I had a scotch. Mindy and I confirmed with Orenstein and Phillips that we would be meeting the next day. I left and managed to find a cab willing to take me home to Queens.

Mindy had always been my bait. Phillips shamelessly flirted with her during the trial. I invited her to join in the interview because I knew Phillips couldn't resist the chance to have Mindy in his hotel room. My motivation was equally impure. I hoped the shared excitement of confronting a murder suspect in a hotel room would turn up the temperature between Mindy and me, since my marriage was a mess.

Mindy and I met in the lobby of a cheap motel off the West Side Highway and went up to Phillips's room. Two federal marshals greeted us, checked out my small tape recorder and Mindy's big one, and escorted us into the room.

"They got the five rooms on the floor around me," Phillips said of the marshals.

This was the first time I'd seen him dressed in casual clothes, chinos and a golf shirt – though he wore his Gucci loafers with no socks – but there were no other surprises.

For four hours, he speed-talked about his life of crime as a cop and how much he enjoyed the lifestyle he'd lived. He'd said much of this to the Knapp Commission and to other reporters. Though I kept trying to steer him back to the trial, he said little about it.

Finally, I got a quote I could use: "Do you think I'd blow it all for a lousy $1,000 and have two people dead. It's not my bag – $100,000 maybe, $200,000 maybe I could be tempted. Not for a lousy $1,000."

Back in the street, in the August heat, Mindy and I sucked in the fresh air and went to work. She to cut her tape at her station, WRVR. I returned to the office to write my story.

I saw Mindy once more. She invited me to her station – not her apartment – to hear her report on the interview, the same day my story hit the papers.

Last I heard from Mindy was five months later. She'd been laid off at the radio station, was living in Berkeley, and freelancing stories for the *National Enquirer*. In a letter dated January 15, 1973 she wrote: *I gave our friend the rogue cop a call ... He asked after you, and I told him you had split to Vancouver.*

CHAPTER 8
CROSSING BORDERS

In January 1973, I became a UPI foreign correspondent – in Vancouver, Canada. It may not have been one of the great capitals of the world, but it was foreign to me. Exotic even, in a backwater sort of way. Like Vladivostok. Or Reykjavik. The bonus was I didn't have to learn a new language – Canadians speak English, right? – or fly through turbulence to get there.

I drove my new blue Fiat 124 across the continent, taking a southerly turn to skirt snow and ice, following roughly the same route I had five years earlier. This time I was traveling with an American Express card and all expenses paid by UPI. One of my colleagues came along for the ride, making a vacation of my road trip.

We were in no hurry. The highlight was to be a stop at the Grand Canyon, where I'd booked two nights in the lodge at the South Rim. We arrived in the dark and awakened to snow on the ground – and the canyon filled with fog.

"Is the fog likely to lift anytime soon?" I asked a front-desk clerk.

"Never know," she said. "Sometimes it can be like this for days."

She explained that since it was always warm at the bottom of the canyon, a cold snap at the top – a mile higher – created fog. I canceled the second night and checked out.

Crossing the desert in California, I noticed the L.A. smog started to appear around Indio. Five years earlier, the air had been clear for another seventy-five miles or so, all the way to San Bernardino. I remembered flying into Los Angeles with Anita, the plane descending through a thick cloud of pea-green muck. I steered my Fiat around L.A. and stopped for the night near Santa Barbara.

The next day, we picked up Highway 1 at San Luis Obispo with great anticipation for one of the most beautiful drives in the world. The coastal road of hairpin turns, atop tall cliffs, affords unrivaled views of the Pacific all the way to Monterey. But, on this day, in thick fog – Was it following me from the Grand Canyon? – visibility was reduced to the rear bumper of the station wagon a few yards in front of me, which we followed for many excruciating hours at about 20 mph.

We spent the night in Mill Valley, with my old hippie friend, Barry Ginsberg. By this time he was married and had a kid, just a bit younger than Kate. I played with the kid. Barry and I had nothing to talk about. I was about to be a foreign correspondent and he was washing dishes in a restaurant in Sausalito.

The next day, I picked up Highway 101, followed it through the redwoods and into Oregon. We picked up a couple of hitchhiking hippie chicks in a rainstorm outside Portland.

We'd been on the road a little more than a week when we pulled up to the border in Surrey, B.C.

"What is the purpose of your visit to Canada?" asked the border guard.

"I'm moving here," I said.

"May I see your immigration papers, please."

I reached into my briefcase and pulled out the only document UPI had given me, a couple of lines typed on company letterhead.

> *To whom it may concern:*
> *Please be advised that Kenneth Becker is the new bureau manager for United Press International in Vancouver, Canada.*

"Where is your work permit?" asked the customs' man.

"This is all I got," I said, flapping the letter in his face.

"You'll have to pull over there," he said, pointing to a few parking slots beside a small one-story building. "Go inside to talk to an immigration officer."

I was pretty steamed, thinking these Canadians had some nerve deciding who could work in their country. It wasn't really much of a country, either, I thought, just a poor cousin on the other side of an arbitrary line. I'd visited Canada twice before, once driving to Halifax to see Anita's aunt and uncle and cousins, another spending a weekend in Montreal. Neither time had anyone questioned my right to enter the country.

But now I intended to stay, as evidenced by my baggage, which included a new, genuine U.S. Air Force Arctic Parka, guaranteed to keep me toasty in temperatures down to thirty-below. I was yet to discover that most days in Vancouver, year-round, were fifty-eight degrees and drizzling.

Still, my American ignorance did not override my American arrogance as I dealt with a condescending Canadian suggesting I couldn't go to my new job. "You need a permit to work in Canada," the immigration man said.

"Okay," I said, "give me one."

"I can't just write a permit for anybody who drives up to the border," he said.

"Why not? You let any draft-dodger into the country."

"Are you evading the draft?" he asked.

"No," I said, "I'm here to work, as you can see."

He retreated to an inner office. Evening dragged into night. I suggested he call my boss in Montreal – headquarters for UPI's small Canadian operation – who'd confirm my employment. He finally agreed and, after scolding my boss on the phone, wrote me out a work permit, good for one year.

The two American women, heading for some commune in the mountains, waited in my car throughout my interrogation. They had no trouble crossing the border since they'd lied, saying they were planning to spend only a few days in Canada.

By the time we drove into Vancouver, it was after midnight. The hitchhikers split when we arrived at my hotel, the Ritz, which hardly lived up to its name.

My transfer from New York to Vancouver had come about with remarkable speed. Emil Sveilis, the colleague I had stood with at JFK waiting for the 747 to land – or crash – had become Canadian news editor for UPI, based in Montreal.

We had kept in touch. He ended each conversation with, "When are you coming up to work in Canada?"

I'd laugh and say, "Who the hell wants to live in Canada?"

But when he called in late November, asking the question again and saying there was an opening in the Vancouver bureau, I asked, "Where's Vancouver?"

"Near Seattle," he said.

"I'll take it," I said.

By this time, Anita and I planned to split up, the only hitch being our equal devotion to Kate. Since I worked a lot of night shifts at UPI in New York, I'd spend days with our daughter, taking her to the playground or nearby Flushing Meadows Park, site of the 1939 and 1964 World's Fairs.

I took her to the U.S. Open tennis at Forest Hills, where my press pass gave us a place on the players' patio. After she insisted on going to the bathroom on her own, she emerged holding hands with Evonne Goolagong.

"Does this child belong to you?" asked the teenage Aussie star.

"Yes," I replied, "is everything okay?"

"Of course, we had a lovely chat."

Kate and I would often go to lunch at McDonald's – we were addicted to the fries and managed to choke down the cheeseburgers – or just hang around the apartment. Kate was hooked on a new TV show called *Sesame Street*.

By late fall, just shy of Kate's fourth birthday, the only question was when Anita and I would make the break. She wanted to go back to Bern. I didn't want to stay in New York, wind up spending obligatory Sundays at my parents' home, eating supper and suffering disapproving looks about my failed marriage. Vancouver, three thousand miles away, seemed the perfect solution.

While I served out the rest of my time at UPI-New York, I realized how excited I was about the move. I'd never stayed too long in one place and was itching for another adventure.

I figured I'd learned all I was going to from more experienced Unipressers. I had the self-confidence Zumbo and others had torn down before building it back up.

The most intimidating person I had encountered at UPI was Tom Corpora, a very cool dude not much older than me, who had earned his stripes as a war correspondent in Vietnam. I desperately wanted Corpora's approval but never got it.

A couple of times I'd go for drinks with him after work. The more he drank, the more he ripped me apart, saying I wouldn't know a story if I tripped over one and couldn't write it worth a damn anyway. I learned one important lesson from him, though – that every good story told could be a story written.

The point was driven home when Anita and I crashed with Corpora at his girlfriend's home in Washington during the Memorial Day weekend in 1972.

On Monday, Anita and I went to see the Phillips Collection of modern art. I parked out front. We walked to the front doors, opened them, and went inside the gallery. There was no one there.

In the entranceway, we admired a small Braque. We walked up a staircase and stood before Renoir's *Luncheon of the Boating Party* in its gilded frame. Not another soul around. Just the two of us and those Parisian partygoers, Renoir's chums from the 1880s, drinking and gabbing on a restaurant balcony overlooking the Seine.

We moseyed on, dawdled in front of paintings by Matisse, Monet, Picasso, Van Gogh, Gauguin, Cezanne, Seurat.

"This is weird," I finally said to Anita. "We could just take any of these paintings and walk out the door."

"What should we do?" she asked.

Since we were leaving Washington the next day and didn't know when we might return, we decided to spend a little more time with the paintings.

After about a half hour or so, we began to head out. "Let's see if we can call someone," I said.

We went back to the entranceway and found the reception desk. It had one of those sliding shelves where people often pasted lists of phone numbers. Sure enough, I found a list.

There was a number for a "Mrs. Phillips." I dialed it on the phone atop the desk. A woman answered.

"Mrs. Phillips?" I asked.

"Yes."

"My name is Ken Becker and I'm inside your gallery right now but no one else is here."

"Yes," she said, "we're closed today."

"But my wife and I just walked in. The doors were unlocked."

"That's odd," she said.

"Yes it is," I said. "What would you like us to do?"

No reply for a moment. "Well, I'll call our security company. If you wouldn't mind waiting there until they arrive …"

"No problem," I said, and hung up.

Anita and I stood inside the front door and guarded the Braque. When we saw a couple of rent-a-cops pull up and rush up the walkway, we met them outside.

"How'd you get in there," one snapped.

"We just walked in," I said, turning to demonstrate how I'd grabbed each handle of the double-doors and pulled. The doors opened.

"You're not supposed to do it that way," said the uniformed security man. He closed the doors, grasped only one handle, pulled, and the doors stayed locked.

I laughed. "You mean anybody with two hands can get in but you're counting on them to pull only one handle?"

He and his partner nodded. Doubling down on the idiocy. Obviously not amused.

They looked us over, apparently checking to see whether I had a Degas in my pants or Anita had a Klee in her purse, before dismissing us with a wave.

When we got back to Corpora's girlfriend's place, I told them the story. "Did you call it in?" Corpora asked.

"Sure, I told you I called Mrs. Phillips." He shook his head in disgust. Corpora had a habit of jiggling his leg when he was agitated. He was jiggling furiously.

"No" he snapped, dressing me down with his hard, hooded eyes, "I mean did you write a story and call it in to UPI?"

"No," I said, "I never thought of that."

"Big surprise," he said with a smirk.

While Corpora and I never got along, I did find acceptance, and friendship, from the best editor at UPI – maybe the best wire service editor ever.

I wasn't long at UPI when I began learning the legend of Lucien Carr, his early days in the royal family of the Beat Generation, with William Burroughs, Allen Ginsberg, Neal Cassady and Jack Kerouac; how he stabbed to death a homosexual stalker and served two years in prison for manslaughter; how he gave Kerouac rolls of teletype paper from United Press, which Kerouac threaded into his typewriter and pounded out *On the Road*.

Lucien was in his mid-forties when I arrived at UPI-New York. He was clearly The Man, sitting in the slot on the General Desk, handling all the top stories, rewriting cliché leads until they jumped off the page, plugging every hole, trimming all the fat, ensuring every sentence flowed into the next.

Every day, and especially when big news was breaking, this skinny guy in a white shirt, sleeves rolled up to his elbows, tie at half-staff, shit-eating grin under a scraggly mustache, calmly and quickly polished the stories that appeared on the front pages of newspapers across the country.

Everyone, including the bosses, looked to Lucien as the guiding force of the operation. And, at the end of the day, he would hold court at The Edison, on Second Avenue at 41st Street, knocking back glasses of vodka and Coke while we all sat around trying to keep up.

When his words started to slur, and his behavior became unpredictable – he could become syrupy sweet or dangerously menacing – he usually grabbed a cab to his home downtown. One night he dragged me along.

I went to his loft where I met his live-in girlfriend, a stunning black woman named Alene. I realized right away that Lucien was using me as a shield. Alene explained why. She said he had beaten her up the previous night and she'd been waiting for him to come home before she called the cops. I instinctively sprang to his defense.

"You know, of course, with his record, he'll go to prison," I told Alene.

"That's what he deserves," she said.

"You really want that?" I asked.

I pleaded Lucien's case further. She was softening. Lucien didn't say a word. Watched the show, slumped in a chair with a fresh drink.

I would have done anything for Lucien – he had that effect on me and many others – and that night I managed to persuade Alene not to call the law.

Months later, on a summer night, sitting on the roof above his loft, both of us half in the bag, he – now the sentimental drunk – turned to me, slapped my back and said, "You know, you saved my ass."

Just before I left for Vancouver, I visited Lucien in the hospital. He had been in a car wreck in Vermont, driving drunk, nearly killing himself and his new girlfriend, Sheila – tall, black, gorgeous and eighteen years old.

It was after visiting hours when I went to his hospital room – he'd been ferried by ambulance to Manhattan – smuggling in a bottle of Dewar's.

"Sorry," I said, "I prefer scotch to vodka," taking two paper cups from a brown paper bag and pouring each of us a generous shot.

Allen Ginsberg was in the room too, standing in a corner and looking forlornly at Lucien's battered body on the hospital bed.

After a few drinks – Lucien had started on vodka before I arrived – he turned to Ginsberg and said, "You know, this guy saved my ass."

He was a convicted murderer and a drunk who smacked around a woman. If he'd been a construction worker or a Wall Street banker I'd think he was a bum.

But he was what I wanted to be. A wire service pro. The coolest cat when the action got hot. He was my first – and last – journalistic hero.

CHAPTER 9
KRAUT EATS BRITISH NURSE

Early in my time in Vancouver, my phone rang in the middle of the night. It was the overnight editor on the Foreign Desk in New York.

"Ken," he said, "there's a ship going down off the coast of Labrador."

"Labrador is closer to you than it is to me," I said. "For Christ's sake, look at a map before you wake someone up."

My Canadian education began right after I accepted the job in Vancouver, when I looked at a map and saw where it was. Since my coverage area extended east to the Ontario border, and north to the Arctic Circle, I decided I should at least learn the geography, something about Canada's history – which seemed to be mainly about English and French fighting each other, the English always winning, and the French forever pissed off – and its parliamentary form of government, with its Liberals and Tories and the Queen still theoretically in charge.

UPI, though notoriously cheap, was surprisingly generous with my move, not only shipping all my furniture to Vancouver but all of Anita and Kate's stuff to Switzerland – she took the Beatles albums, I got the Simon and Garfunkel – and paying their airfare as well.

I spent about a month at the Ritz, where my best friend was a bartender named Joe, before finding a one-bedroom apartment in a modern three-story California-style building.

While I waited with the landlord for my moving truck to arrive, he asked, "Do you have a chesterfield?"

"No," I replied, "I smoke Marlboro."

My apartment, about a mile south of downtown, was only a few blocks from my office in the Pacific Press Building, which housed the city's two daily newspapers, the morning *Province* and afternoon *Sun*.

I'd been in Vancouver about three weeks when, one day, in the top-floor cafeteria, I stood dumbstruck at the north-facing picture windows. "Where the hell did they come from?" I shouted to no one in particular. I was talking about the mountains, beyond downtown, across the Burrard Inlet. I hadn't seen them before in the rain and gloom of my new hometown – did not know they were there.

The UPI bureau was two rooms, with a desk, two teletype machines and a couple of filing cabinets. One teletype constantly belched out the news from around the world, the other was for me to punch my stories onto a tape and feed them to the editing desk in Montreal. Since there was little news from western Canada, I did little punching.

Most days, I dropped by the office around noon with a fresh cup of tea from the cafeteria – in Vancouver, this hardboiled newsman gave up coffee – checked my messages and started thinking about the evening's social activities.

On Fridays, I filled a bottom file cabinet drawer with ice and beer and invited some of the reporters and editors from the Canadian Press – my new opposition – bureau next door to join me for happy hour.

Making friends in the community of journalists in Vancouver proved easy. I was a curiosity – the brash New Yorker unleashed among the genteel Canadians in the laidback Lotus Land of the Left Coast.

Vancouver was both the hippie capital of Canada and its financial hub on the West Coast. Stockbrokers would create their own little rush hour in the dark each morning to be at their desks before the opening bells of the exchanges in Toronto, Montreal and New York.

The seat of the provincial government, however, was in the capital, Victoria, across the Strait of Georgia, on Vancouver Island. Victoria was known as the place where British army colonels and their pale, doughy wives went to retire.

To get there from Vancouver, you could fly, but most people took the ferry from the terminal at Tsawwassen, about an hour south of downtown. The voyage took about ninety minutes.

The crossing could be quite civilized, I learned, reserving a place in the ferry's formal dining room. Seated at a window as the sun went down, cruising past small islands, at a table adorned with white linen, I dined on prime rib of beef with roasted potatoes, Yorkshire pudding and fresh vegetables.

We docked at Swartz Bay, named for John Aaron Swart, an original landowner in the 1870s. Somehow, a "z" – or zed, in Canadian – was added at the end of his surname. I called it Schwartz Bay, and decided it was named for my *landsman*, Tony Curtis, born Bernard Schwartz.

On my first trip to Victoria, to cover the provincial government's Speech from the Throne – the royal moniker was in deference to the Queen being the head of state, though the speech was much like a State of the Union, laying out the government's agenda for the coming year – I checked into the stately Empress hotel and made a beeline for the Bengal Room, a bar where the waiters dressed like lackeys from Delhi during the good old days of the British raj.

Dominating the room, above a fireplace, was a tiger skin, complete with head and tail. Sitting below it were a handful of guys – and one woman – drinking beer and laughing too loud. Obviously reporters.

I walked up to them, waited for a break in the conversation, and shouted, "Okay, which one of you sons-of-bitches shot that tiger?"

They looked up at me, sized me up, figured I was one of them, laughed, and introduced themselves. One, Joey Slinger of the *Globe and Mail*, would become a lifelong friend. I would enjoy the company of all, the business our bond, as were the hangovers we took to the legislature the next day.

For me, such assignments were otherwise a bore, provincial in every sense of the word.

Meanwhile, the biggest story in the United States was unfolding thousands of miles away. In the spring of 1973, the news flashes kept popping up on my office teletype:

H.R. Haldeman resigns.
John Ehrlichman resigns.
Attorney General Richard Kleindienst resigns.

Starting in May, and through the summer, I stayed home many days to watch the Senate Watergate hearings on TV. I followed the latest scoops from the Washington Post.

I would never be cut out for investigative reporting, combing through files, gathering a small piece here, another piece there. Didn't have the temperament, or the patience. Preferred the quick hit and move on to the next. Besides, the writing, not the reporting, was my passion.

In Vancouver, I mainly wrote features which I knew would merit space in U.S. papers. One that got tremendous play was on bald eagles, which were nearly extinct south of the border.

I drove across the Lions Gate Bridge and up to the small town of Squamish, where hundreds of eagles were feasting on salmon in the river off the highway.

SQUAMISH, B.C. (UPI) – The national symbol of the United States is alive and well in British Columbia.

But there was also some real news to report during my time in western Canada. The biggest and best story was a tale of cannibalism in the Far North.

Martin Hartwell was a German immigrant – Germans really love the Canadian wilderness – and professional bush pilot. On November 8, 1972, he was flying from north of the Arctic Circle to Yellowknife, capital of the Northwest Territories.

His passengers were Judy Hill, a twenty-seven-year-old territorial government nurse originally from Kingsbridge, England, and her patients: Neemee Nulliayok, a pregnant Inuk woman from Cambridge Bay, N.W.T., who was having complications from labor, and her fourteen-year-old nephew, David Kootook, suffering from acute appendicitis. Shortly after takeoff on the five-hundred-mile flight, they ran into a fierce storm. The small plane crashed, killing both women.

The boy was not hurt seriously. Hartwell had two broken legs. Thirty-one days later, the boy was dead and Hartwell was rescued. The story came out that he had survived by eating flesh he carved from the body of Judy Hill. The revelation was an instant sensation around the world.

One British tabloid carried the news under the headline: *KRAUT EATS BRITISH NURSE.*

I was not in Canada when the story broke, but went to Yellowknife at the end of February 1973 for the coroner's inquest, as did reporters from across Canada and Britain – Fleet Street couldn't get enough of it.

About a half dozen of us were booked on the same Pacific Western Airlines milk run to Yellowknife, with stops in Calgary and Edmonton, Fort Smith and Hay River, N.W.T., before finally arriving in Yellowknife.

It took all day on a chubby Boeing 737, with the stewardesses having to replenish the bar cart at every stop to keep the journalists from rioting. The entertainment was supplied by the pilot, Captain Carlson, who told stories on the PA.

"I'd like to tell you the one about the chicken and the pig," he began one. "Now the chicken, she contributes to our lives by laying eggs for our breakfast. But the pig, he sacrifices his life for the bacon that we have for breakfast. And that's just what my first officer and I are doing up here with you today. If anything goes wrong, we're on the same plate as you are."

If this wasn't disconcerting enough for a bunch of reporters on their way to cover the story of a plane crash and cannibalism, Carlson dedicated every takeoff and landing:

"This takeoff is for little Johnny Andreychuk, traveling with his mom, Hilda, to visit his aunt in Fort Smith."

"This landing is for little Suzie Simpson, who's taking her first flight, with her mom, Edith. And in honor of Suzie, I think I'll let the first officer take this one – he needs the practice."

An uneasy flier since puking and screaming on my first flight to Europe, my airborne anxiety kicked in each time the alcohol wore off. By the time we got to Yellowknife I wanted to carve up Captain Carlson and send a CARE package to Martin Hartwell.

We checked into the Yellowknife Inn, the only place in town that wasn't a flophouse. The inquest would be held in a ground-floor meeting room.

Each morning, I passed through the lobby, noting the locals and their kids assembled. The kids remained alone after the bar opened in the afternoon. When it closed, the adults staggered out, kids in tow.

Most evenings, in the early dark and arctic cold, after filing our stories at the telegraph office, we would trudge across the street to a decent steakhouse to eat and drink the night away.

My great triumph of the assignment came when the *Times* published one of my stories, though the bastards dropped my byline. It included the juiciest bits of a statement Hartwell had given to police – he did not appear at the inquest – which was read into the record by an inspector with the Royal Canadian Mounted Police.

"Did you eat or consume any part of Miss Judy Hill?"

"Yes, no one else did."

Did he and the boy discuss eating the flesh of the dead women?

"I asked him if he would eat their bodies," Hartwell said. "We had talked about it before but he stated that he would not eat them because his aunt had been so good to him."

So sad. So funny.

Most of the hilarity among the reporters focused on the fact that Hartwell dined only on the flesh of Judy Hill, ate only the white meat, that the Kraut got his pound of flesh from the Brits decades after Germany lost the war.

Early on, I got a kick out of every assignment having a punchline, that reporters would compete for laughs while covering even the most gruesome story.

Back in Vancouver after the inquest, with a lack of news to excite me, I began planning my days around when to start drinking and how to end the night with a woman in my bed. The hunt began in the early evening at the Vancouver Press Club, a hole-in-the-wall bar, with a pool table and pinball machine, across Granville Street from the Pacific Press Building.

As was the case in New York, nearly all of the people who interested me were journalists. We shared an instant and easy camaraderie, talked the same language, laughed at the same jokes, got turned on by the same things – booze, sex, adrenaline – read the same books and magazines: *Esquire, Rolling Stone,* everything by Hunter S. Thompson.

I enjoyed the company of men and women equally, though the etiquette became fuzzy on the occasions I had drinks with a guy at eight o'clock and slept with his girlfriend at midnight.

Casual sex was my birthright, having reached puberty at about the time The Pill arrived and collided with the free love mores of the Sixties. Married at twenty-one, I'd taken a pause, though not abstained.

But, once on my own, I was making up for lost time. Drink. Dine. Drink some more. Sex. The women, mainly fellow journalists, were on the same page. That was the life. I fell in and out of love a couple of times, and bounced back quickly.

My role was the worldly New Yorker, the adventurer just passing through on his way to the big time. To enhance my image as a foreign correspondent, I had bought a safari suit, a trench coat and a couple of turtleneck cashmere sweaters at Bloomingdale's before I left Gotham.

I further publicized my pedigree in a story I wrote for UPI, which was published on the op-ed page of the *Province*. It opened with an editor's note:

> *Kenneth M. Becker, United Press International bureau manager in Vancouver since last spring, previously had lived most of his life in New York City, which has one of the highest crime rates in the world. He was never mugged. This is an account of what happened to him during a trip to the wilds of B.C.*

I then told of an overnight hike with a fellow journalist to a remote lake where we camped overnight. I flexed my best gonzo muscles.

> *The only defense against bears, my mountain-man-of-a-companion decided, was to split a bottle of 151-proof rum – between us, not with the bears. But the fear of savage, hairy beasts breaking the tranquility of the night fought my rum-soaked mind – and won.*

I then detailed the hike back down the mountain to a parking lot off the highway.

> *Disbelief. It must have been the marauding bears come to the low country. The car was ransacked. All doors open, trunk broken into, battery gone, along with a set of golf clubs, a tennis racket and my baseball glove, a*

cherished possession from many memorable softball games in Central Park.
Drunk or sober, I thought, man is no match for marauding bears armed with wire coathangers and screwdrivers.

The piece concluded with a tow-truck driver arriving with a new battery.

"New York, huh," the driver said as he spied the license plates on my immobile Fiat. "I guess this kind of thing ain't new to you.
"Yes," I said, "it's the first time."

I'd learned Corpora's lesson, that anything can be spun into a piece of journalism. This was also my second first-person account for UPI, after collecting laundry during the strike at the Willowbrook school on Staten Island. I wanted to keep pushing my writing, but was not sure where to take it or how.

I was equally uncertain about where to go from Vancouver. I was tired of the lack of action – on the news front, anyway – and drained by the rain. Even on a clear day, it was the ugliest city in the most beautiful setting I'd ever seen – tall, snow-topped mountains rising from the sea.

But it seemed the same every day, chilly and drizzling, no tension or excitement in the air. Everybody looked the same too – the pasty white spawn of the British Isles.

If there were any black people in Vancouver I never saw them ... or him ... or her. If there were any Jews, I never met one. There were Chinese in Chinatown, but the Chinese food was third-rate, not New York Chinese food. No New York pizza either. And what was a New York steak?

I wasn't really homesick. There was nothing to go home to. I wasn't about to pack up and move three-thousand miles for an edible pastrami sandwich.

My parents came to visit once. I took them to the Cannery for Dungeness crab, and for eggs Benedict at the Rail Car with a couple of journalism cronies for our weekly Sunday brunch of drinking and shop talk. "Your friends are very nice," my mother said later.

I took them to Victoria, where they stayed at the Empress, and drove them across Vancouver Island. We stopped at a light in the pulp-and-paper-mill town of Port Alberni, the smog so thick you couldn't see across the street, so stinky you wanted to gag.

"I know," I said, "disgusting."

"To the people here, it smells like money," said my dad, a vice president of sales for Saxon Paper Company in New York, far from the mills that produced his product.

"No," I snapped. "To them, it should smell like cancer."

We didn't talk much after that. I couldn't wait to put them back on the plane.

Like I said, nothing to go home to.

About a year into my time in Vancouver, I'd moved into an old apartment house on Davie Street, between Howe and Hornby streets, downtown. Davie was a popular hooker stroll. My apartment looked down on a strip joint. It seemed the city fathers didn't mind sex for sale, as long as the bars stayed closed on Sundays.

Joining me in the Davie Street apartment was a cat named Jasmine I'd taken in when she became one animal too many in the menagerie of cats and dogs and kids often in residence down the hall with my pal David Wright, an editor at the *Province*.

I was awakened one morning by the girlfriend of the night before, who informed me, "There's a litter of kittens in the bottom drawer of a cupboard in the kitchen." David, if he knew, had not mentioned Jazz was pregnant.

I managed to give away the kittens and Jazz stayed with the apartment when I handed it over to Malcolm Gray, Joey's replacement as *Globe and Mail* correspondent in Vancouver.

I had kept in touch with UPI-New York, hoping for a transfer to Europe where there would be bigger and better stories to cover, and where I would be closer to Kate. But nothing was offered. I settled for an opening on the desk in Montreal.

At the beginning of September 1974, after a few farewell fucks and a going-away party at the press club, I climbed aboard the Canadian National, filled my private sleeping compartment with books and booze – and one night an elementary school teacher from Winnipeg – and rode the rail back east.

CHAPTER 10
TRICKY DICK AND TRUDEAU

On the editing desk in Montreal, doing my best Lucien Carr imitation, I handled copy from reporters in the other Canadian bureaus: Ottawa, Toronto and Vancouver. I'd done some editing in New York and found it made me a better writer – seeing the flaws in the copy of others helped me spot the holes and rough patches in my own stories.

But I still craved the glory of the byline, getting out of the office and back in the street. I did get to cover a couple of front-page stories in Montreal. One involved a fugitive murderer named Richard Blass; the other the prime minister of Canada, Pierre Trudeau, and his wife Margaret.

I had covered Trudeau several times when I was in Vancouver. I'd jumped on his campaign plane when he came west during the 1974 election, and also went along for the ride during a state visit by King Hussein of Jordan. The king had piloted his personal jetliner to the annual air show in Abbotsford, east of Vancouver, where he and his third wife, Queen Alia, hooked up with the Trudeaus. That evening, I sat in the bar of the Hotel Vancouver with the rest of the press corps while the middle-aged king and his young wife, and the middle-aged prime minister and his young wife, were upstairs in a suite, doing god knows what.

I was focused, however, on the TV in the bar, watching Richard Nixon live from the Oval Office. "I shall resign the presidency effective at noon tomorrow. Vice President Ford will be sworn in as president at that hour in this office."

"Good fucking riddance, you slimy piece of shit," I screamed at the screen. "I hope you wind up in Attica, you crypto-Nazi scumsucker – see how you like it taking it up the ass from some crazed three-hundred-pound junkie biker flying on smack,"

I'd read all of Hunter Thompson's pieces in *Rolling Stone* and, if I didn't have the freedom to write the words, I certainly could echo them in a crowded hotel bar in British Columbia.

My fellow reporters knew I was an American. I never hid it, never would, though I had been quick to lose the rougher edges of my New York accent. When confronted with anti-Americanism, I often told my Canadian friends that their only identity as a country was *not being American*.

I also brought to Canada a First Amendment attitude that the press was free to stick its nose into just about anybody's business, especially those in power. That's what led to my confrontation with Trudeau in the fall of 1974.

I was in the bureau when one of our reporters in Ottawa called with a tip that Margaret Trudeau was in the psychiatric wing of the Royal Victoria Hospital in Montreal, and that her husband was on his way to visit her.

I had witnessed Margaret on the campaign trail that summer, doing her best Nellie Forbush imitation. *I'm in love, I'm in love, I'm in love, I'm in love, I'm in love with a wonderful guy.* It was kind of sweet and sickening at the same time, this twenty-something standing at the podium in some small-town hockey arena asking people to vote for her man.

Personally, I found it a bit creepy that this good-looking young woman – younger than me – was sleeping with a guy my father's age. Their first two sons – Justin and Sacha – had been born on Christmas Day, twice giving the politician a nice front-page story on a slow news day.

I had covered Trudeau enough that he knew me. During the campaign, he would good-naturedly tease me about my habit of wearing my glasses on top of my head. So, when he arrived at the Royal Victoria Hospital with his two-man security detail – they stayed in the car – he knew the one guy waiting for him was a reporter.

"What are you doing here?" he snapped.

"How's your wife doing?" I responded.

"How would that be your business?"

"You're here and not working. That's the country's business."

He offered one of his best harrumphs, followed by a shrug of dismissal, all shoulders and arms and hands, palms up, as if to say, *You're not worth acknowledging.*

I followed him into the hospital lobby. "If you're here and not in Ottawa, you're not doing the country's business. The job the people pay you to do. The people have a right to know how you spend *their* time."

"Fuck off," the prime minister of Canada said.

"Is your wife seeing a psychiatrist?" My best comeback. He was approaching a bank of elevators. I kept pace. "How can you make important decisions when you have other things on your mind. Maybe you should step down until your wife's better. Don't you think the public has a right to know what's going on?"

This may have been the post-Watergate period in the United States, where the press was puffed up with its own importance and not taking any crap from politicians. But Canadians did things differently, tended to believe public figures were entitled to their private lives.

Trudeau disappeared in an elevator. I retreated to the street.

His two security guys were leaning against their plain blue sedan. The RCMP didn't constantly shield the prime minister in the same way the Secret Service did the U.S. president. I'd seen these two Mounties before and they seemed to know me. One gave me a wink. The other a nod.

I found a payphone. Called the desk and filed a bulletin advisory on the UPI wire, alerting all media that Trudeau was at the hospital. This was my reply to Trudeau's arrogance and expletive. I'd make sure every reporter and camera crew in Montreal got to the hospital before the prime minister could slip away, that he'd be forced to run the gauntlet when he left.

Two hours later, as was often the case, Trudeau surprised me. He *and* his wife emerged from the hospital and went for a little stroll while reporters shouted questions and cameras clicked and whirred.

Then he surprised me again. He guided Margaret to a scenic spot on the sidewalk, a lovely backdrop of just-turning leaves on a perfect Indian summer day, and nodded toward his wife, indicating she was ready to take questions.

How are you feeling? a radio reporter asked.

"I've been in the hospital for the past ten days," she said in nearly a whisper, "under psychiatric care for severe emotional stress."

What do you ask next? *Did you suffer a breakdown? How nuts are you?*

She looked very pale and seriously stoned. The prime minister had offered up a sedated and wounded kitten. Any question we'd ask would seem like blood dripping from the mouth of a jackal.

"I think I'm all right and on my way to recovery," Margaret added. "Thank you all for your concern and I hope you'll leave me alone for a while."

When the microphones moved toward the prime minister, he snapped, "it's her press conference," before the Mounties moved in, on cue, and escorted the couple back into the hospital.

I had to hand it to Trudeau. Trapped in the hospital, he'd figured out an exit strategy that would leave him smelling like the rose he always wore in his lapel.

Poor Margaret, suffering the stress of public life. Poor Pierre, all alone to run a country and a home with two little boys. That's the impression that would be formed that day, and it would stick for a while, even as their marriage came apart. I would be back on Maggie's trail a few years later, after she partied with the Rolling Stones and ran away from home.

Montreal was a pretty good news town. Though it was being surpassed by Toronto as Canada's most populous city and financial center, it was the capital of organized crime, Italian Mafia and French gangs. Which provided the other big story for me in Montreal.

Richard Blass was the most-wanted man in Canada. He was known as The Cat, because he had survived several shootouts with police and fellow gangsters, once getting out of a burning hotel room after being shot four times. He'd escaped from prison – twice. The media were counting his lives and the number was approaching nine.

At about 2 a.m. on January 21, 1975, I was awakened by a call from UPI-Montreal photo chief Gary Bartlett, who told me to get up, get a cab and meet him at a topless joint called the Gargantua on the north side of the city.

"I've already been to a bar tonight," I said. "Now, I need some sleep."

"Well, this bar is on fire," he said, "and we hear there are lots of bodies inside."

Montreal is not the most comfortable place to be on assignment in the middle of the night in January. When I arrived, it looked like a scene from the Ice Age, icy stalagmites rising from the pavement, frozen solid in seconds as water sprouted from fire hoses. The ruins of the building were still smoldering, the now familiar scent of roasted human flesh – after covering that airline crash at JFK – spicing the wind-chill. The spinning lights of police cars and ambulances added an eerie glow to the scene. As I stood there with my notebook and fast-frozen pen, the body bags kept coming out.

A couple of hours earlier, shortly after midnight, the bar manager, a waitress and eleven patrons had been in the Gargantua when a gunman – or gunmen – entered.

The manager was shot on the spot. The waitress and the rest were herded into a six-foot by eight-foot cold-storage room, and locked inside. A jukebox was pushed in front of the door to ensure their imprisonment. Then, the place was set afire. The bar manager died of the gunshot wound, the other twelve of asphyxiation.

Back in the office, I banged out a lead comparing the Gargantua to the St. Valentine's Day Massacre – worse, since thirteen were dead in Montreal and a measly seven in Chicago in 1929 – playing to UPI clients in the United States.

Later in the day, I added that police suspected Blass, who had busted out of prison three months earlier and implicated in a double-murder in the same bar.

After his escape, Blass taunted the cops by sending them photos of himself and "press releases" to the media, bragging he'd never be caught. That was enough to put Montreal's most feared and accomplished detective, Sergeant Albert Lisacek, on the case.

Lisacek had the reputation as a shoot-first-ask-questions-later cop who hated bad guys and loved the media – the tabloids called him Kojak, because he looked like the

Telly Savalas television character, a big man and a sharp dresser, with a shaved head.

I used to run into him in the convenience store off the lobby of my apartment building, where he once walked in on a robbery, drew his gun, scared off the lowlife, chased him into the street and shot him dead.

Lisacek was the natural choice to hunt down Richard Blass – which he did, three days after the Gargantua massacre. He and his cohorts, armed with submachine guns, found Blass in a cabin in the Laurentian Mountains, busted down the door at 4 a.m. and shot Blass twenty-three times, just to make sure he was out of lives. I wasn't at the scene, but wrote the story, with the lead: *Kojak killed the Cat this morning.*

The cops never proved Blass was responsible for the Gargantua massacre. The case was written off as many other murders were in the city in those days, as a *reglement des comptes*, an underworld settling of accounts, a synonym for that wonderful French phrase *laissez faire*, which, roughly translated, means: *the hell with work, let's go to lunch.*

Though I enjoyed such walks on the wild side of Montreal, there weren't enough of them to keep my juices flowing. And I wasn't getting enough time off the desk.

I decided the only way to get out of the office was to carve a niche for myself. With the 1976 Montreal Olympics coming, sports seemed to be the ticket.

I had already been writing stories about the serious construction delays on the main Olympic stadium and other venues. The labor unions in Quebec had a reputation for being confrontational and greedy. Both traits were coming into play on Olympic projects. Costs kept climbing as construction slowed down, all of which was big news in Canada and elsewhere.

Also, UPI needed better coverage of the city's two big league teams, baseball's Expos and hockey's Canadiens. Without a fulltime sportswriter in Canada, the games were left to stringers, journalistic hobbyists who were mainly interested in a free pass to the press box. They were not capable of covering big events or writing features.

I volunteered to take on the chore. My colleagues in the sports department in New York were all for it and, with their support, UPI signed off on the new position of a fulltime Canadian sportswriter based in Montreal. Me.

I had a lifetime of experience following sports, from early childhood in New York with three baseball teams, my Brooklyn Dodgers, the rival New York Giants and hated Yankees. I'd been a passionate fan of the New York's football Giants of Frank Gifford and Y.A. Tittle, the basketball Knicks with Walt Frazier, Willis Reed and Bill Bradley, and even the hockey Rangers of the Andy Bathgate era.

But my first love was baseball, going to games with my dad, once a star pitcher for his high school team and a legend on the city's sandlots. Before I was ten years old I'd seen Joe DiMaggio at Yankee Stadium, Willie Mays at the Polo Grounds, and Jackie Robinson at Ebbets Field.

But I never wanted to be a sportswriter. Too much serious stuff to report. My only sports-related assignment at UPI in New York had been covering Jackie Robinson's funeral.

On October 27, 1972 I went to Riverside Church in Manhattan. It was a perfect fall day. World Series weather. Bright sun, just a hint of a chill.

Ten days before he died of a heart attack at the age of fifty-three, Robinson, his hair white, nearly blind, had thrown out the ceremonial first pitch in the first game of the World Series between the audacious Oakland A's and the slugging Cincinnati Reds.

The celebrity mourners gathered that Friday morning in their Sunday suits, mostly middle-aged men looking like they were attending a banquet for an old-timers game.

I spotted Pee Wee Reese, the former Dodger captain from Kentucky who had befriended Robinson early on and helped him through the storm of breaking baseball's color barrier. Reese was standing outside the grand entrance to the church, being interviewed by Howard Cosell.

Roger Kahn, who chronicled Robinson's struggle in *The Boys of Summer*, was nearby, chatting quietly with another of Robinson's old teammates, Don Newcombe.

My press pass got me inside this VIP enclave, which was roped off and guarded by the NYPD. I was working, though my duties were uncertain.

I would not be the main man on the story. That would be the sports editor, Milt Richman. I was there to cover any "news" angles, though I was not sure what they might be. In this crowd, though, I felt more like a young fan – which I was.

A church office had been converted into a reception area. I went inside and wandered among my heroes.

There's Hank Aaron!
There's Willie Mays!

I wanted to go up to these guys and talk to them. But I really had nothing to say, nothing appropriate for this moment or any other. So I stood and gawked until it was time to file into the church.

The crowd, maybe three-thousand people, filled every pew. By happenstance, I sat next to Will Grimsley, AP's lead sportswriter, a large, florid man who introduced himself then sat scrawling notes on a large writing tablet. He picked up his pace when a young black preacher delivered the eulogy, his booming voice and theatrical style mesmerizing the crowd.

"In his last dash, Jackie stole home," said Reverend Jesse Jackson, pausing, before picking up speed, as if he was making the play. "Pain, misery and travail have lost. Jackie is saved. His enemies can leave him alone. His body will rest, but his spirit and his mind and his impact are perpetual, and as affixed to human progress as are the stars in the heavens, the shine in the sun and the glow of the moon."

It was a hard act to follow. And nobody did. As the widow, Rachel Robinson, and her family filed out behind the coffin, we all stood. Grimsley stretched and looked around the church.

He tapped me on the shoulder. "See that guy over there, that's Bill Veeck," Grimsley said, pointing to a man in baggy chinos and a ragged gray sweatshirt, standing alone in the back, sobbing into a handkerchief.

Veeck was known mainly as an outlaw team owner in Cleveland, St. Louis and Chicago, famous for such stunts as sending a midget up to bat – to draw a walk. But he had also signed the American League's first black player, Larry Doby, in 1947, and the next year gave Negro League star Satchel Page a chance to pitch in the majors.

Grimsley wandered off to talk to Veeck, while I went to find Richman and get my orders. "I want you to go to the cemetery," the sports editor instructed. "I've arranged space for you in one of the cars in the funeral procession. Call me when you can with notes and quotes."

I got into a car with a bunch of reporters and took a window seat in the back. We followed the hearse, taking the long, slow route to the cemetery in Brooklyn.

I'd heard that some schools in Harlem would be closing early so teachers and kids could line the procession route. But I was astonished at how many people turned out, at how universal was their respect for Jackie Robinson.

These were tough times in Harlem and the city's other black neighborhoods. Black-on-black crime, fed by drugs, was endemic, as was black rage at white society.

But none of that was evident as the hearse passed. Children in school uniforms stood at attention. Women sat on stoops. Old men leaned against lamp posts and wept. It was the same scene in Brooklyn, in the Bedford-Stuyvesant neighborhood.

By the time we reached Cypress Hills Cemetery, it was near dusk. The weather had changed. Dark clouds moved in as the pallbearers, Jackie's former teammates, Reese, Newcombe, Jim Gilliam and Ralph Branca – Doby and the basketball star Bill Russell – carried the coffin to the gravesite.

I stood beside a tree, apart from the scene, added some notes to the ones I'd jotted down during the drive, found a phone near the cemetery gate and called Richman before catching a ride back to Manhattan.

I was thinking about that scene when I went to find Duke Snider on Opening Day of the 1975 season at Jarry Park in Montreal. I'd seen Snider at the church for Robinson's funeral, standing alone, aloof, as he'd always appeared on the ballfield.

Snider had been my childhood favorite, probably because of the competition we kids imagined among New York's three centerfielders: Mickey Mantle of the Yankees, Mays of the Giants and Snider for my team, the Dodgers. I knew I drew the short straw with The Duke, but that did not diminish my adoration. He had been a great player, a prodigious power hitter and graceful fielder, though never the equal of Mays or Mantle.

As a newly minted UPI sportswriter in Montreal, I figured I'd do some kind of feature on Snider, who joined the Dodgers the same year as Robinson, 1947, and stood by his teammate and fellow southern Californian against the rampant racism of the baseball world at the time.

Snider was a broadcaster with the Expos, who sometimes coached the players. I found him in the concrete bunker that served as the team's clubhouse in the little makeshift ballpark.

"Hi Duke," I said, introducing myself. "Got a minute to talk?"

"What about?"

"Well, I was just thinking that we were both at Jackie's funeral."

"So?"

My boyhood idol was looking down at me like I was a cockroach that had scurried into his living room. He stood there, insolent for no reason I could imagine, shuffling his stockinged feet, baseball pants rising to a belt I couldn't see, somewhere below the huge gut that strained his white undershirt.

"Well," I finally said, "I just thought you might like to talk about the old days in Brooklyn, *Boys of Summer* and all that. I grew up in New York, watching you play at Ebbets Field. Maybe we could talk about what it was like in those days, with you in Brooklyn, Mickey in the Bronx and Willie at the Polo Grounds."

Now he looked at me as if I'd taken a dump on his spikes. "That's old news, kid," he said, turning to walk away, "I got work to do here."

I thought later that he was probably right, that there was no story in talking about the Brooklyn Dodgers, long gone and forgotten by many. I had approached Snider as a fan, not a journalist. I should have asked about the Expos batters he was tutoring, kids like Gary Carter and Larry Parrish, and then maybe steered him back in time. *Who of the guys you played with does Carter remind you of?*

But I hadn't prepared, just showed up like a kid looking for an autograph, thinking my baseball knowledge from the 1950s was enough to form a bond.

I'd yet to learn that you don't – don't want to – befriend the people you write about. Nor did I know yet that athletes were among the most narcissistic stars in the universe.

I stuck around Jarry Park that April day to watch the home opener. In the press box, the temperature was announced as eleven degrees Celsius – whatever that is – the Expos lost, and I wrote the game story.

But, after that, I left most of the day-to-day coverage of the Expos and the other Montreal teams to stringers. I was busy enough with the bozos planning to stage the 1976 Olympics.

My stories on the boondoggle of the Olympic project were getting great play in newspapers across North America and around the world. One, published in the *New York Times* – again with my byline stripped off – began:

MONTREAL (UPI) – What was the biggest snowbank in the city last month is now the biggest mud puddle. In a few months it even could resemble the site of the 1976 Summer Olympic Games.

It concluded with a line describing "the stadium site a circular series of blocks resembling England's Stonehenge."

I was starting to hear the tone I was seeking, knowing that sports could be written more from a point of view than news. Yet, writing for a wire service, you needed to please hundreds of masters.

First, I had to get my stories through an editor in Montreal, then through an editor in New York, then entice editors from Maine to Hawaii, from Newfoundland to British Columbia, to put my story in their papers.

One ex-Unipresser, Walter Cronkite, said the best way to approach a story is as if you're writing for a Kansas City milkman, the idea being that if you can interest him, you can interest everyone in the United States.

But I wanted a sharper edge. Since I was writing sports, I turned to Red Smith of the *Times* for inspiration. Smith was nearly seventy and was still getting a smooth, steady flow. Sometimes he'd write with a hammer, sometimes a feather. He could wield both in the same column.

I didn't try to imitate Smith, but thought that if I read enough of his stuff, something would rub off. It didn't. Better stick to what I can do. Maybe it would help writing under another name, which is what I was doing as a sportswriter. I changed my byline to Ken Becker, the name I'd gone by since about age six.

While I grew up a baseball guy – and to a lesser extent a football or basketball guy – hockey was the biggest story in Canada. That's why I covered Montreal Canadiens' home games in the 1975 playoffs.

For me, the scene in the dressing room after each game at the Montreal Forum was better theater than the play on the ice. Not being educated in the post-game interview, I had trouble understanding why the reporters were asking players about what had just transpired. Didn't they watch the game?

On my first visit to the Canadiens' locker room, I found it especially comical that all the Anglo reporters gravitated to goaltender Ken Dryden, the self-anointed hockey scholar and lawyer – the Cornell grad had a law degree from McGill University – who would offer an erudite, English-only critique of the night's proceedings.

Instead of exploring the Zen of Ken, I watched the French-speaking reporters gathered around Yvan Cournoyer. I didn't understand what they were saying, but the Q&A seemed serious. Perhaps they were discussing nuclear disarmament, or the difference between Brie and Camembert.

The scene of English reporters only talking to English players and French reporters only to French players was the picture Canadian writer Hugh MacLennan had painted in his novel *Two Solitudes*, the reality of a Quebec society where French and English lived together, though always apart.

It was something I recognized in my single solitude in Montreal, living in an English enclave near the Forum, speaking only English to the clerk in the English bookstore, to the barman in the Irish pub down the street, to the waiters in the upscale restaurants I frequented, to the people in my office and the other reporters from the English media.

I had a *bonjour-au revoir-s'il vous plaît-merci* vocabulary, just enough to be polite to the Quebecois, who were starting to get restless during my time in Montreal.

I didn't need another language to do my work. It never occurred to me to learn French.

I was starting to get that itch again, not satisfied with what I was doing. I was eager to again write in the first-person, to cut through the bullshit with a more personal take on a story, to get a clean narrative going.

I felt my writing was in a funk, had stopped getting better. I wasn't getting a lot of satisfaction from the sports beat, or from UPI either.

When I referred to Bobby Hull, the hockey player, as the "Blond Bomber" in a story, the sports desk in New York sent a message that read: *don't kno who 'blond bomber" is – psbly a roller derby star – but bobby hull the "golden jet."*

I replied: *Roller derby, hockey, wot's the dif?*

I hated making such mistakes. But I didn't give a shit about Bobby Hull's nickname. My body clock seemed to be telling me to move every two years, and that I had outlived my stay in Montreal.

I was bored with both my work and the city, where I mainly hung out in the press club in the Mount Royal hotel, where I'd sometimes see Mordecai Richler holding court at the bar, or a group of hockey luminaries, sportswriters and sportscasters, reminiscing about the 1955 Rocket Richard riot.

I often sat commiserating with my news editor, Dale Morsch – Emil Sveilis, the guy who coaxed me to Canada, had left to set up a bureau in Leningrad – who drank a lot to fight depression and only got more depressed.

I knew I was a constant contributor to Morsch's misery, since my instinct was to question authority, not respect it. But I guess I couldn't help myself. Nor could I stop my catting around.

I was sleeping with a Jewish woman from Long Island who was working with me in UPI's Montreal bureau. But I was also carrying on long-distance relationships with a woman in Vancouver and another in Boston, sneaking off to meet them for more intimate interplay.

At the same time, Anita and I were talking about getting back together. I'm not sure why, other than missing my daughter.

The first summer after I moved to Canada, I flew from Vancouver to Europe for a vacation in France with Anita and Kate.

In Paris, we were invited to spend a sunny day at a private swimming club where most of the women, adhering to the fashion of the time, paraded topless. During a poolside lunch of *salade nicoise,* complemented by a bottle of *Pouilly-Fuisse,* a club functionary scolded us for allowing five-year-old Kate to appear *au natural.*

When Anita translated the complaint for me, I went full-Yankee berserk on the Parisian prick. "You mean I have to look at these old ladies with their wrinkled, saggy tits, but you have a problem with a naked little girl?"

That set off a shouting match in two languages, with neither combatant understanding the other. I got in the last word when I raised a wine glass and threatened to smash it on the pool deck. "In America, we have the good sense to use plastic glasses outside."

Anita and our host, her friend Willy from Bern, a banker in Paris, did not come to the defense of the gauche American and did not put up a fuss when we were asked to leave.

From Paris, Anita and I and Kate drove south, stopping to see the sights in Avignon, Arles and the Comargue before following the Mediterranean coast, bound for Nice.

At the wheel, in the dark, on the windy road atop the cliffs running down to the sea, I opened a bottle of duty-free Dewar's and slugged it as far as Saint-Tropez, where I found a road that led to a beach and a dock.

We polished off the scotch and snoozed on the beach until dawn, when an elderly gent who looked like Ari Onassis appeared with his manservant, who told us to scram. *Propriete privee!*

Ari and his majordomo climbed aboard a cabin cruiser that had not been visible in the dark. We went back up to the road, stopped at a public beach – no sand, all rocks, of course – and doused our hangovers with a long soak in the salty sea.

The next night, having crossed the border into Italy, at a large seaside hotel in Ventimiglia, Anita and I had an epic brawl. This time, I smashed a glass – against a wall. We didn't exchange a civil word the rest of my vacation. I returned to Vancouver with a bottle of Chateauneuf-du-Pape and a tale of fear and loathing in Ventimiglia.

The next year, in the fall, I went back to Europe. But this time I traveled alone with Kate.

Anita's father, Hermann, let me borrow his second car, a Citroen Deux Chevaux, an ugly little beast that rattled and wheezed from Bern across the Alps, into Italy.

We drove past the beautiful Lago Maggiore and on to Verona and Venice. Kate was only six, but she never complained about our wanderings in the back streets of Venice, or my prolonged stop admiring Titian's *Assumption of the Virgin* in an off-the-beaten-track Franciscan church. She seemed happy with the reward of chasing pigeons while I smoked and drank in the Piazza San Marco.

By the time we got to Florence, however, she was bored – we said hi to *David*, raced through the Uffizi in about four minutes, hightailed it for the Mediterranean coast, and checked into the Grand Hotel in Viareggio.

These were the days when an American or Canadian could travel like royalty in Europe, when one dollar – U.S. and Canadian were about at par – bought four

Swiss francs, five French francs and eighteen billion Italian lire. My first Omega Seamaster cost about fifty bucks in Bern.

At the Grand Hotel, Kate and I spent the night at the bar. The bartender took a shine to Kate – she was a charming child – and kept the Shirley Temples coming while her old man ventured from Campari and soda to scotch. We probably ate dinner as well.

In the morning, we walked on the beach but it was a cold October day and we didn't get far. After more than a week on the road, the ugly little Deux Chevaux chugged back over the Alps to Switzerland.

As I mentioned, by the next summer, in 1975, after nearly three years apart, Anita and I were talking about getting back together. Kate was having a hard time in Switzerland, especially at school. A smart, precocious kid in New York was ostracized in Bern for not being a native and not speaking Swiss-German well enough.

Anita started to sound a little hesitant – and a lot weirder – as plans for a reunion got serious. Then, one day, on the phone, she told me she wasn't coming to Canada. She had joined the Children of God, and her future was in the hands of Jesus.

As soon as I got off the phone, I decided Anita could join the Manson Family for all I cared – we were done – but she wasn't surrendering my daughter to some cult.

I booked a flight to Switzerland. I talked to a colleague at UPI in Washington, who connected me with an official at the State Department.

"Do I have the right to take my daughter, a U.S. citizen, out of Switzerland, back to North America, against her mother's wishes, if need be?" I asked.

"You mean kidnap her?"

"If you want to call it that."

"The short answer is – no."

But the more we talked, the more he understood the circumstances, the more sympathetic he became, the more eager to help. It was implicit that our conversation was off the record, on the QT. Even post-Watergate, there was a kinship between the press and people in government.

Finally, he advised that if I got Kate cleanly out of Switzerland, he would arrange a "safe house" – yeah, he used that term – across the border in West Germany. He gave me a name and a phone number to call at the U.S. embassy in Bonn once I got across the border.

I phoned my parents to tell them what was happening. They had been aware Anita and I might reconcile. My mother called my sister Janice and the next thing I knew her fiancé, Steven, was coming along as "muscle" on my kidnap caper.

Steven Sherman was, like my sister, a painter. But he also played the streetwise New Yorker, the Dead End Kid with a degree in fine arts. He met me at the Swissair ticket counter at Montreal's Dorval Airport and we boarded a night flight to Zurich.

At Kloten Airport, I rented a car and drove the familiar hour-and-a-half route to Bern. We stocked up on snacks and drinks, bought a pair of cheap binoculars, and took up a reconnaissance position on a bank of the Aare, with a clear view of Anita's parents' house on *Altenbergstrasse* on the other side of the river. She was living in the same upper-floor rooms where we had bunked on my first visit.

We watched and waited. Waited and watched. Patience was never my strong suit. "Let's take a drive past the house," I said.

We climbed the hill, to the street where the rental car was parked. I drove around the block and crossed the little bridge over the river to *Altenbergstrasse*.

As we approached the house, on the narrow street, about a half-dozen hippies were walking in the opposite direction. I spotted Anita among them. And Kate. "Daddy!" she cried.

So much for the snatch and the clean getaway. I slammed on the brakes. Leaped from the car. Kate jumped into my arms. The cultists encircled us.

Steven, my muscle, tussled with a couple of guys. I took Kate into her grandparents' house. For the first time, Hermann and Elsa Schlumpf – Anita married me for my name and kept it – seemed happy to see me.

Kate and I went upstairs to her room. Anita, Steven and the cultists followed. Shoving and shouting ensued.

The cops came. Steven and I and the cultists – the ringleader was an American – were taken to the stationhouse. Anita was suddenly at my side – and on my side. So was her father, who powwowed with the *polizei*.

Hermann Schlumpf was a short, wiry, solid man who, Anita told me, looked like the actor Glenn Ford. He did. He was a career civil servant who had been in the army during the war, safeguarding the Swiss border from German invasion and keeping it secure for the importation of Nazi plunder.

Hermann seemed to know the cops involved and got us sprung quickly. He also managed to get Anita's passport back from the Grifters of God, who were ordered by the cops to stay away from the Schlumpf household. They had been crashing in Anita's apartment and been in the process of looting her bank accounts.

Steven flew home and I stayed in Bern long enough to find a lawyer and have Anita sign an agreement that said she would lose custody of Kate if she took up with any more predatory Jesus freaks or other crazies.

Anita seemed okay. But you never know. Being married to someone doesn't make her any less a stranger.

For the moment, everything appeared settled. I told Anita I'd take care of a legal separation agreement and the divorce. She seemed relieved and grateful.

I went back to Montreal. When an opening came up to take over UPI's Toronto bureau, I jumped at it. Maybe another change of cities would be the answer.

In September 1975, I got back on a train and headed west.

CHAPTER 11
SLEEPY TORONTO

Like Vancouver, UPI-Toronto was a one-man operation. And my first day on the job would be the busiest I'd have in the bureau. It was election day in Ontario, a big story for Canadian clients but not exactly a crank-turner for me.

But the day started with more exciting news, a shooting at the Royal York hotel. Like the Empress in Victoria, the Royal York was one of a chain of "railroad hotels" the Canadian Pacific and Canadian National built in the early 1900s. Each was bigger and more opulent than the next.

The twenty-eight-story Royal York, when it opened in 1929, was the tallest building in the British Commonwealth. It rose across the street from Union Station, so guests could walk from the train to the hotel, as could the porters pushing carts stacked with steamer trunks and suitcases.

On September 18, 1975, I got word that one person had been killed and two others wounded at the Royal York. By the time I got there, the hotel had been locked down while police searched every room – more than a thousand – for the gunman.

I huddled with dozens of other reporters, in a driving rain, outside. One was my friend from Vancouver, Joey Slinger, who had returned to the *Globe and Mail*'s home base in Toronto but by this time was working for the *Toronto Sun*, the first English-language tabloid in a major Canadian city.

Joey approached me while I was berating a police sergeant at the front door to the hotel, out of the rain, under the marquee, before the cop threatened to arrest me if I didn't get back behind the barricades with the rest of the reporters.

"Are all Toronto cops assholes?" I asked him.

"Why do you ask?"

"Because they could let us wait in the lobby instead of out here in the rain," I said.

"No they couldn't."

"Why?"

"Because they're assholes," he said.

Joey and I had many such discussions, which we played mostly for laughs. But he seemed to have an anthropologist's curiosity about Americans – New York Jews, in particular – how we took no shit from anyone, including authority figures, while I mocked the timidity of Canadians.

Playing the brash American would be my lifelong role in Canada, but it would also, probably, keep me from advancing very high in the hierarchy of Canadian journalism. Still, I entertained Joey and others when I sent back unsatisfactory meals in fancy restaurants or sparred with the law.

My first Christmas in Canada, Joey invited me to his family's home in Guelph, about sixty miles from Toronto. When we arrived at the railway station in his hometown, we were immediately cornered by a couple of cops.

"What have you got in the bag?" one asked Joey, who had stuffed Christmas gifts for his family into a large black trash bag.

"Why do you want to know?" I barked back.

The cops looked at me like I'd pissed on their brogues.

"We're asking the questions here," the cop said.

"No, you're not," I said, "not until you tell us what this is about."

After a brief staring match, the cop said, "Well, you two guys fit the description of a couple of suspects who robbed a Canadian Tire store."

I threw a puzzled look at the cops, first one, then the other, and pointed to the bag. "Does it look like we've got a tire in there?"

Joey broke up, explained to the cops that we had just arrived on the train to visit his family, that his father, Jake, was a prominent pharmacist in town, and that the bag was filled with Christmas gifts.

Then, as the cops walked off, Joey explained to me that Canadian Tire didn't only sell tires, but was more like Sears.

He told the story to his mother, Lucy, when she picked us up at the station. She seemed less amused that a visiting American had argued with Guelph's guardians of law and order.

My experiences with cops had been very different in New York. There, we seemed to be on the same side. The police issued our press passes, which allowed reporters to cross police lines. NYP (New York Press) license plates permitted us to park anywhere on city streets.

On a few occasions, New York's finest had let me slide after pulling me over for traffic violations, after I showed my red press pass, shaped like a police shield, and said something like, *I work with you guys all the time, can't you give me a break?* They did.

But I learned quickly that Canadian cops – outside Montreal, where laziness ruled – tended to be less secure. They had watched too many episodes of *Adam-12* and pretended they were under siege, patrolling the streets of big bad L.A. and not little Toronto the Good, as it was known when I hit town.

My day outside the Royal York ended when the cops concluded the gunman was gone and took down their barricades. I had spent about six hours standing in the rain – when I wasn't running across the street to a payphone at Union Station to call the desk in Montreal.

The story turned out to be that the hotel credit manager, a security guard and a city cop had gone to a room to confront a guest who hadn't paid his bill. The manager was shot dead, the other two were wounded and thousands of guests were riled about being cooped up in the hotel for most of the day.

That night, after I filed a story on the Ontario election, I found out that the gunman had been captured – in Colorado – long gone before all those hours the cops made me stand in the rain.

By the 1970s, Toronto was the center of the Canadian universe, its business and media hub. But it did not have the feel or the look of a big city. No bustle. No buzz. No great rivers spanned by towering bridges.

It was a sleepy and provincial place, with the same puritan drinking laws as Vancouver, the downtown sidewalks folded up after business hours and on weekends.

It had a Chinatown, where most of the food tasted like it came out of a Chun King can, and a Little Italy, where the pasta sauce tasted like it came out of a jar.

One night, on a subway platform, I was surprised to see a couple of black guys. Who were they? Where did they come from? What were they doing here? What was I doing here?

I lived in an apartment in the Beaches neighborhood, east of downtown, on Lake Ontario. There was a beach in the Beaches. But not much else. No bars. A couple of crummy restaurants. One small not-very-super supermarket.

Streetcars rumbled along the lone commercial strip, Queen Street, providing a twenty-minute ride downtown to the UPI bureau, a couple of small rooms above a branch of the Canadian Imperial Bank of Commerce at the southeast corner of Queen and Yonge Street, the city's main drag.

Joey introduced me to the social scene in Toronto – the press club above Hy's steakhouse. Growing up in New York, with corner bars in every neighborhood in the boroughs, and Manhattan chock-a-block with watering holes, I was getting used to Canadian cities with few places to have an after work drink or two, or twelve.

At the Toronto club, I got to know some of my fellow scribes and watched the sixth game of the World

Series, Carlton Fisk's walk-off home run for my Red Sox in Fenway, with Joey and a bunch of other baseball fans, including one who was introduced to me as Paul Anka's father.

Canadians invariably remind visitors of every native-born star in the American show biz galaxy. Besides Anka, they point to the likes of Lorne Greene (Pa Cartwright), Raymond Burr (Perry Mason), William Shatner (Captain Kirk), and the original "America's Sweetheart," Mary Pickford, born in Toronto.

Gordon Lightfoot and Joni Mitchell were among the new wave. And I caught up with them when the *Rolling Thunder Revue* rolled into Toronto at the end of 1975. This was Bob Dylan's show, with his old flame, Joan Baez, as co-star.

I covered the opening night on December 1st at Maple Leaf Gardens. The aged arena was packed and reeked of pot smoke.

Dylan organized the tour to promote his campaign to free Rubin "Hurricane" Carter, the ex-boxer imprisoned in New Jersey for a triple-murder. Dylan's song *Hurricane* was the show-stopper, but I got goose bumps when he and Baez did a series of duets, including *The Times They Are A-Changin'*.

All of the singers and musicians and assorted hands and hangers-on – there must have been fifty of them – were on stage for the finale, Woody Guthrie's *This Land Is Your Land*. Joni Mitchell took a turn on one verse, replacing "from California to the New York island" with the Canadian lyrics, "from Bonavista to Vancouver Island." As far as I know, Americans never felt the need to insert U.S. place names in any Canadian songs.

One of those on stage for the finale was my old friend Allen Ginsberg, dancing around with a tambourine. After the show, I found him backstage and renewed our acquaintance, talked about Lucien.

He invited me to a post-performance party at the Harbour Castle hotel. I dictated my story from the Gardens and drove down to the hotel on the waterfront.

The *Rolling Thunder* gang had taken over a floor of the Harbour Castle. All the doors were open, music was playing, voices were raised, dope was being smoked and alcohol consumed. I found Allen but the poet and I had little to say to one another.

I grabbed a beer, wandered from room to room, sticking to the fringes, as was my custom and preference on such occasions. I didn't see Dylan or Baez, imagined they were revisiting old times, and left.

The next day, I caught the second show of the two-night stand at the Gardens. Ginsberg had left me a backstage pass, so I watched from the wings. The perspective seemed wrong. I was an observer, not a participant.

Not working, my mind wandered. Why was it called the Gardens? Was there ever more than one garden on the site? And only one garden at Madison Square Garden and the Boston Garden? Or is it another Canadian thing, adding an "s," just to be different from the Americans?

Is that why Canadian football has three downs instead of four?

Why was the temperature outside minus-three degrees instead of twenty-seven?

Ken Becker

Why did my bank insist on me having a chequebook instead of a checkbook?

Why is Joni Mitchell, who lives in California, inserting Canadian lyrics in a Woody Guthrie song?

CHAPTER 12
CONGO OUT, TANZANIA TOO

Before I left Montreal, I told my UPI masters that I would return for the Summer Olympics, if they liked. I arrived before the Games started, assigned as a news reporter, not a sportswriter. This was okay with me.

As I traveled to Montreal a week before the July 17, 1976 opening ceremony, I wasn't sure what news might develop. But I was thrown right into the two big political stories of the Games. One involved the Canadian government, China and Taiwan. The other was a threatened boycott by black African countries.

The China issue had been simmering for months. Since 1970, the Trudeau government had officially recognized Beijing – or was it Peking? – as the one and only China. This, of course, pissed off Taiwan – or was it Formosa? – which severed ties with Canada.

Washington wasn't happy either, since the Nixon gang publicly hated the godless commies, even while the Trickster was planning a secret visit to Chairman Mao's place in 1972.

Trudeau and Nixon couldn't stand each other, which didn't seem to bother either of them. The year after Trudeau became prime minister, he famously expressed Canada's conundrum vis-a-vis its superpower neighbor.

"Living next to you is in some ways like sleeping with an elephant," Trudeau told the National Press Club in Washington in 1969. "No matter how friendly and even-tempered is the beast, if I can call it that, one is affected by every twitch and grunt."

The Nixon tapes would later reveal that he considered Trudeau a "son of a bitch," an "asshole," and, for good measure, a "pompous egghead."

By 1976, with Nixon banished and Jerry Ford in the White House, Washington's position on the China issue hadn't changed. Nor had Ottawa's.

Since Beijing was the only China that Canada recognized, and even though the People's Republic – Red China? – was not a member of the IOC and would not be sending a team to Montreal, Trudeau made it clear that any Taiwanese team would not be allowed in the country if it planned to compete, as it did, as the Republic of China.

A compromise was suggested, allowing the Taiwanese to compete as Taiwan, which seemed to please everyone but the Taiwanese. They went home and the controversy died, as Mao would a couple of months later, presumably raising the spirits a bit in Taipei.

The threatened African boycott was a lot more serious. These countries, many newly independent and black ruled, were starting to flex their muscles, winning support for more and more sanctions to isolate the apartheid regime in South Africa and the racist government in Rhodesia. They'd succeeded in getting South Africa kicked out of the IOC before the Tokyo Games in 1964 and had done the same to Rhodesia before Munich in '72.

In Montreal, they wanted New Zealand booted because that country had allowed its touring rugby team, the All Blacks – named for the color of its uniforms and not the color of the players' skin – to tour South Africa.

The New Zealand Olympic Committee said it had no control over a rugby team that had nothing to do with the Olympics. The IOC agreed. But that didn't satisfy the Africans. The boycott appeared to be spreading through Montreal like a brushfire. And it was my job to chase it.

"Talk to the *chefs de mission*," said sports editor Mike Hughes.

"Why would I want to talk to the cooks?" I deadpanned.

Mike looked at me like I was the Olympic village idiot. He had become sports editor after I left New York and supported my bid to become UPI's sportswriter in Canada. We hadn't met before the Olympics but had talked a lot on the phone.

Hughes had a limey accent, which traced to his exotic pedigree. He was born in India to an Irish-Italian father and Spanish-Portuguese mother, schooled in England, and was a veteran of the Royal Air Force before joining UPI in the 1950s.

He was about ten years older than me, but we seemed to get along well when we met in Montreal, killing a bottle of Johnny Red together before the Olympics began. I was intimidated by his worldly ways, but realized quickly I could get his goat, which I did with my crack about cooks.

Before he could scold my ignorance, I laughed, said I knew a *chef de mission* was the head a country's Olympic delegation, not its meal planner.

"I'm on it," I said, before leaving the press center and sprinting from office to office of the African teams.

My first stop was the *chef de mission* from Uganda. I really wanted to sit and chat about his president – "So, you know Idi Amin? Nice guy?" – or ask about the raid on the airport at Entebbe the month before – "Still pissed at the Israelis?" – but had no time.

"In or out?" I asked.

"We're going home," he said.

"Mind if I use your phone?"

"Be my guest," he said.

I called the UPI office in the press center.

"Uganda's going home," I said, and raced to the next office. It was the same all night.

"Nigeria's out."

"Tanzania's out."

"Ghana's out."

"Gambia's out."

"Kenya's wavering."

"Congo's out."

"Chad's out."

"Kenya's out now – for sure – going home."

I fed quotes to the desk and let them keep score. By the end of the night, more than twenty countries had pulled their teams out of the Montreal Olympics. I'd been on the story all day and night, and hadn't written a word.

I had no role in UPI's coverage once the Games started, having surrendered the sportswriter position I had angled for. I went to the opening ceremonies as a spectator.

The next day I flew to Toronto, changed planes and went on to Windsor, Ontario, and covered the Canadian Open golf tournament. It was a pleasant assignment, the press tent next to the pool at the Essex Golf and Country Club.

I had little interest in the circus in Montreal, which turned out to be a national sporting embarrassment as Canada became the first host country not to win a gold medal. The Games also ran up a $1.5 billion debt despite Mayor Jean Drapeau's boast that "the Montreal Olympics can no more have a deficit than a man can have a baby."

But more unnerving news for Canada was coming from Quebec. In November 1976, the separatist Parti Quebecois, under Rene Levesque, took power. That month, I turned thirty.

CHAPTER 13
FIGHTING THE WAR OF 1812

T he American bicentennial year of 1976 seemed an appropriate time for personal and professional reflection and assessment. Having always been among the youngest – in school, at work – I'd been in a hurry to grow up. I welcomed my thirties.

Anita and I now had a legal separation agreement and were on the fast-track to divorce. Kate was old enough to start flying unaccompanied to spend her vacations with me, so I didn't have to travel to Europe every year.

My Jewish girlfriend from Long island, via Montreal, had moved to Toronto to live with me. She found us a funky ground-floor apartment, still in the Beaches, but right on the beach. From our bedroom window, we could hear the waves slapping at the shore.

I don't believe either of us thought we would spend our lives in Canada. (She would as well.) But we were both working on building a resume, and opportunities were opening up in the country we happened to be.

For the U.S. Bicentennial, Canada gave the United States the gift of a book titled *Between Friends,* a collection of more than two-hundred photographs taken along the shared border – 5,525 miles, or 8,890 kilometres in Canadian – from Yukon and Alaska to New Brunswick and Maine.

Trudeau wrote the foreword and, Trudeau being Trudeau, it wasn't exactly a Hallmark card to the elephant next door. It read more like a lecture from a snooty cousin and included this:

> *Let no one seek to devalue the achievements of our friendship by glossing over its occasional difficulties. It is true that, as is not uncommon among lifelong friends, we have sometimes had serious differences of opinion, misunderstood each other, struggled against each other's competing ambitions. Long ago we even fought each other, usually in relation to the very boundary which this book illuminates.*

Jeez, I hate it when Canadians bring up the War of 1812. They say they won, though they were not Canadians then, they were British subjects. I was taught in school that the War of 1812 was a draw, which always seemed suspicious since we Americans only see things in terms of winning or losing.

A few weeks before the Fourth of July, sitting in my untidy office on Yonge Street, I interviewed Lorraine Monk, who edited *Between Friends,* as head of the still photography division of the National Film Board of Canada.

I had an enjoyable conversation with Monk. She inscribed my copy: *For Ken Becker, who understood what the book was all about.*

Maybe I did. Maybe I didn't.

Being a correspondent for UPI in Toronto, an hour's drive from the border, was no different than being a foreign correspondent anywhere else in the world. I was looking for stories that would interest American readers.

I covered the opening of the CN Tower, which was billed as "the world's tallest freestanding structure," taller than the World Trade Center. It was a phony comparison.

I'd watched the Twin Towers go up in New York. They were buildings, filled with offices, filled with people. The CN Tower was a communications antenna, a giant rabbit ear, a phallic mass of concrete with a gimmicky revolving restaurant just below the tip.

Toronto was also looking for bragging rights when it attempted to snatch the Giants out of San Francisco in 1976. I covered a news conference at which Labatt, the Canadian brewery, announced it had purchased the Giants and was moving the team to Toronto.

In Canada, getting a second major league baseball team was a big story. And a second National League team would have played well to the rivalry between Montreal and Toronto.

But the deal for the Giants got tied up in the courts in the United States, and, a couple of months later, Labatt and a couple of minor partners had to settle for an expansion American League team that would start play in the 1977 season.

The owners quickly chose the team's chief executive, Peter Bavasi, the son of Buzzie Bavasi, who'd run the Brooklyn and Los Angeles Dodgers. I interviewed Peter the day he was hired. We talked a lot about the good old days in Brooklyn, and commiserated about being Americans north of the border.

While Bavasi was assembling his staff – there were no ballplayers yet – the owners tried to interest prospective fans with a sham name-the-team contest. What the public didn't know was that Labatt had already decided the word "blue" would be in the name, since Labatt Blue was the brewery's most popular brand. Blue Jays was chosen, presumably over such options as the Toronto Blue–Winged Warblers, the Toronto Blue-Tongued Lizards or the Toronto Blue Balls.

Contemplating a move from UPI, I got an interview with the *Globe and Mail*, which, like the other Toronto papers, was looking for a writer to cover the Blue Jays.

The *Globe* fancied itself a national newspaper and Canada's answer to the *New York Times*. It had a reputation as whitebread and stodgy but also welcoming of young talent. I felt less than welcome as I entered the dark, austere office of the managing editor, Clark Davey.

"Why do you think I should hire you?" he asked.

"Well," I said, "I know baseball and I think I'd write it well."

"I'm not interested in baseball," he said.

"Okay," I said.

"What do you know about art?" he asked.

Art who? Garfunkel? Linkletter?

"I'm not sure what you mean," I said.

"I mean, have you studied art? What styles of art do you prefer?"

"I like the Impressionists," I said.

"Everybody likes the Impressionists," he said.

And on it went. From art, we moved on to wine, Bordeaux versus Burgundy, and classical music, of which I knew nothing.

"I prefer jazz," I said.

"Oh, who?"

"Charlie Mingus, Elvin Jones," I said, remembering the names of the bass player whose Cadillac I once rode around in, and the drummer who was a buddy of Lucien Carr.

"I don't care much for drummers," Davey said.

I had no comeback.

Finally, he stood to dismiss me.

"Don't you want to talk about baseball?" I asked.

"Not particularly," he said, "but what is it you want to tell me about baseball."

I blabbered about how I'd grown up with the game in New York, saw DiMaggio and Robinson and Mays play, how I understood and appreciated the game better than most – most Canadians, I wanted to say, but didn't.

When I left his office I wondered whether the other candidates knew more about art and classical music. In any case, I didn't expect to get the job. I never heard from Davey again.

Still, having been in the news biz for more than ten years, I figured I had it licked. I was a cocky reporter, comfortable enough, or arrogant enough, to walk up to anybody – prime minister, police chief, boyhood baseball idol

– and start asking questions. When I sat down to write, or even dictate on the fly, the lead seemed to jump out of my notebook. I'd rewrite leads as I drifted off to sleep. Write stories in my dreams.

I had no doubts about my ability or the quality of my work. So why couldn't I get along with my bosses? Or most of my Canadian colleagues? Was it because I was the only American?

One thing that had bothered me at the start in Canada was the animosity between my fellow grunts at UPI, members of the Newspaper Guild, and management.

The us-against-them mentality was corrosive. And I didn't feel I was on either side. I thought myself above my Canadian colleagues, convinced I was destined to return to the United States and take my place beside other great American writers – Mailer, Breslin, Hunter S. and the rest.

I had no respect for my bosses. They may have been real journalists at one time but demonstrated no ability to do any job other than pinching pennies and sucking up to *their* masters. Since I was not shy about expressing such views, I managed to alienate just about everybody at UPI-Canada.

Alone in the Toronto bureau, finding few stories that interested me, nothing I could turn into *The Armies of the Night* or *Fear and Loathing in Las Vegas*, I plotted my escape.

Pal Joey, who had been writing Sunday features for the *Toronto Sun*, got me an interview at the tabloid. I was offered a job as a city desk reporter, decided that it would afford me the chance to do more creative writing, and took it.

One of my last assignments for UPI was covering the Grey Cup, for the championship of the Canadian Football League, at the end of November 1976.

I'd never been as cold – and perplexed – as I was that Sunday in the press box at Exhibition Stadium. The chill off nearby Lake Ontario was numbing. But the opponents in the game – the Ottawa Rough Riders and the Saskatchewan Roughriders – were stupefying.

The CFL had seven teams and two had the same name. I never bought the explanation that one was one word, the other two words. Couldn't they come up with something original? The Saskatchewan Prairie Dogs? The Ottawa Bureaucrats? Better than naming two teams after Teddy Roosevelt's cavalry unit.

And why was it the Grey Cup and not the Gray Cup? To add to the confusion, the cup is named after Albert Grey, also known as Earl Grey, Canada's governor general from 1904 to 1911. Shouldn't it be called the Tea Cup?

Four days after the Rough Riders beat the Roughriders, I resigned from UPI and gave three weeks notice. The next day, I wrote a letter to H.L. Stevenson, UPI's editor-in-chief, in New York. It concluded:

> *I came to UPI as a snot-nosed 23-year-old, arrogant enough to think I should be made an instant foreign correspondent but not smart enough to know that I didn't have any of the basics of disciplined newswriting. Under the likes of Zumbo, Corpora ... and especially Lucien, I became a snot-nosed 25-year-old with a pretty good grasp of the game. Now, a snot-nosed 30-year-old, I can walk in anywhere and do the job.*

> *I think I stayed a couple of years too long. I let the Canadian operation frustrate me to the point that I wanted to either take it over in a bloody coup or ignore it completely.*
> *Because of this, and all the other times UPI waltzed me around, real and imagined, I thought I'd leave filled with rancor. It simply isn't there.*
> *Forgetting Canada, thinking of some of those incredibly talented people I worked with in New York, remembering the camaraderie, I can only feel good. I've been underpaid, over-worked, misused and misunderstood. What the hell ...*

I would be going to a non-union newspaper, which was fine with me, the rugged individualist. I used the Guild's notice boards to post a parting shot at my Canadian colleagues – union and management.

> *One recent resignation that will (but, then again my not) interest you: KEN BECKER is leaving UPI after seven years, nearly four of them with the Canadian operation, to join the Toronto Sun as a general assignment reporter. Ken's association with UPI began in 1969 when he paid his own way to Europe to accept a position in Switzerland that did not exist. Six months later, he worked for a month as a stringer in the Zurich bureau where he was told to return to New York at his own expense for a position in NX ...*
> *After three years of reporting for NXL and desking for NX-General, Ken was conned by his old buddy Emil Sveilis into an expenses-paid – Ken was wised-up by now – transfer*

to weirdest Vancouver, where he experienced 20 months of fear and loathing. From there it was off to HQ in Montreal, where he managed to antagonize everybody in the organization with his hard-nosed, know-it-all demeanor.

From there, he was exiled to Toronto, where he could only insult people by message or long-distance. About the only thing you can say about Ken Becker is that he never discriminated – he dumped on everybody, fellow-guildsmen (guildpersons?) and management alike.

Ken wishes you all what he wants most for himself: to be left alone to beat this bitch called writing.

Best wishes for the holidays,
Murray Burns, aka kmb

Murray Burns was the down-on-his-luck-but-obviously-smarter-than-everyone-else New Yorker portrayed by Jason Robards Jr. in both the Broadway play and the 1965 movie *A Thousand Clowns.*

At the *Sun,* I told myself, I'd be appreciated. And I was – for a while.

CHAPTER 14
NEW YORK STORIES

The inaugural *Toronto Sun* was published on November 1, 1971. That day's editorial began: *Our aim is to be an outspoken, independent voice for Toronto. We have no sacred cows, no editorial taboos. We are masters in our own newsroom, chaotic and unnerving as that cramped newsroom is at the moment.*

By the time I arrived on the first Monday in January 1977, the *Sun* had moved to a new building on King Street, just east of the downtown core. While the newsroom was no longer cramped, it remained chaotic. That was okay with me. I'd be able to do my thing, write what I wanted, since nobody seemed to be in charge or know what they were doing.

I knew when I took the job that the *Sun* wasn't exactly the *New York Times*. Though tabloid size, it wasn't the *Daily News*, either. The *Sun* was a mishmash and clash of newspaper styles. It published a daily pinup photo – a Sunshine Girl – alongside the usual police blotter fodder. The *Sun* really loved self-promotion pieces – reporters writing first person accounts of jumping out of airplanes with a *Sun* banner or playing softball in *Sun* uniforms against a team of showgirls from a road company of *Hello Dolly*.

But there was also some straight journalism from a small core of solid reporters and some fine writers, including my buddy Slinger and sports columnist Trent Frayne.

I was assigned a desk, in a group of four, with three other reporters who gave me the skinny on all the bosses. The editor-in-chief, Peter Worthington, stayed out of the daily news operation, concentrating on the editorial page; the managing editor, Ed Monteith, was mainly interested in making up the front page; the executive editor, Doug MacFarlane, sat in his corner office critiquing the previous day's paper and posting an assessment of what he liked or didn't like.

The day-to-day forces in the newsroom were assistant managing editor Paul Warnick, a Canadian veteran of the U.S. Marine Corps, and the city editor, Les Pyette. Warnick was a good guy and a good steady editor. Pyette was something else.

Soon after I started at the *Sun*, Pyette sidled up to my desk and said, "I'd like you to cover the Gary Gilmore execution."

"Lester," I said, using the formal name the other reporters did, talking to him as one would to a slow child, "it's in Utah. Tomorrow morning."

"Yeah," he said, "I don't want you to go there. I want you to write it from here, but pretend you're there."

"Huh?"

"You know, make it sound like it's happening now, when you're reading the paper tomorrow."

"How do you expect me to write it before it happens? And pretend that it's already happened?"

He smiled through his bristly moustache. "I know you can do it, baby," he said, slapping me on the back before dashing back to his desk to hatch his next harebrained scheme.

I checked the wires, which were filled with news about the execution scheduled at dawn Mountain Time the next day at a prison outside Salt Lake City.

There was enough information on the wires to paint a picture of what was planned for the execution. And, since I didn't want to totally piss off my new boss after fewer than three weeks on the job, I played soothsayer.

> **Check your watch now ... If it's before 9:49 a.m., you still have a chance to record in your memory where you were at the exact time Gary Gilmore got his death wish.**
> **While Toronto wakes up to a new work week, Gary Gilmore is waking up to the last day of his life.**
> **While you're breezing to work on the subway, or cursing rush-hour traffic, Gary Gilmore is preparing for a date with five anonymous men with rifles.**

It continued in that vein, with details about the firing squad, their weapons, the witnesses and the background of the murder case against Gilmore.

Maybe it was what Pyette had in mind and maybe it wasn't, but it was the best I could do to put the reader in the moment. I didn't feel too bad about scalping the wires either, since my UPI stories had been cannibalized by newspaper writers for years.

What I hadn't considered was that I was working for a newspaper now, not churning out a series of leads for the wire, which would be updated throughout the day and night. My story would be set in type at midnight, ten hours before the scheduled execution. I was reminded of that when I arrived at work the next day.

"I was up all night with your story," said Warnick. "There were appeals in the courts right up to midnight. I was going to kill the story, but decided to let it go."

He handed me a copy of the paper and opened it to my story on page three. "I added the line 'if all final appeals fail' in the second paragraph." Gilmore died at 10:07 a.m. Eastern Time, not that long after the scheduled execution.

It was the last time I would try to describe an event before it happened. It would also be a warning to steer Lester in another direction when he approached me with another goofy idea, as he did several weeks later.

"Ken," he said, "I'd like you to go to Newfoundland to kill a baby seal and write about what it's like."

"Yeah, sure, Lester, that's a good one," I said, laughing and walking away. He gave the assignment to another reporter, Kevin Scanlon, who was obviously wiser in the ways of Lester. Kevin went to Newfoundland and covered the annual seal hunt and the protests but never picked up a club, never considered it.

In March, I was assigned a racier story with a *Sun* twist. My old friend Margaret Trudeau had gone on the lam after cavorting with the Rolling Stones in Toronto. She was reported to be in New York and the *Sun* had aspirations of breaking the untold story of the prime minister's wayward wife.

Another young reporter, Jane O'Hara, and I were called into the boardroom, where all the paper's top editors were assembled.

"We'd like you two to go to New York," said one.

"To find Maggie Trudeau," said another.

"To get the real story on why she's run away from Pierre," said a third.

Jane and I just sat there. And waited.

The real story, we were told, was that she ran away because her husband tried to get her involved in a sex orgy at 24 Sussex Drive, the prime minister's official residence, with Michael Pitfield and his wife.

Pitfield had been appointed by Trudeau as the most senior civil servant in the Canadian government. They were known to be close friends. The *Sun* was also out to prove they were lovers.

In that first editorial, back in 1971, the *Sun* had declared: *We are neither right nor left; we dislike fanatics of any hue, and are prepared to tackle the arrogant left and the misguided right when occasion demands.* In practice, the *Sun* was unfailingly conservative, its editorials and columns consistently critical of Trudeau's Liberals.

In any case, these men around the boardroom table wanted Jane and me to hunt down Maggie, break her down, and get her to confess she ran away from her husband, the prime minister, because he wanted her to watch him have sex with his gay lover and have a lesbian romp with Mrs. Pitfield while the boys watched.

I didn't know what to say. Neither did Jane. Did these guys really think we were going to corner Margaret Trudeau somewhere in New York and get her to spill her guts?

Finally, I asked, "Where did you get this story about the orgy at 24 Sussex?"

"I've got a source," said one of the editors.

"Then why don't we get the story from him? I asked.

"Because he'll only confirm – on deep background."

Was this clown kidding? I'd read *All the President's Men*, saw the movie too when it came out the previous year. Now, some joker at the *Toronto Sun* was pretending he had a Deep Throat in Ottawa. But this movie wasn't over.

"I told my source," the editor went on, "that if we get the story, I'll call him and count to ten. If the story is solid, he'll stay on the line. If it's not, he'll hang up."

This was a line right out Woodward and Bernstein's book. Was this a gag? Should I be laughing? Was Allen Funt about to walk in the door?

The meeting broke up. Jane and I were told to pack and leave first thing in the morning.

Walking to our desks, Jane and I agreed this was the most ludicrous assignment yet. "Don't worry," I said, "we'll go to New York, check into The Plaza and order room service. I'll make some calls and we'll come home in a couple of days."

And that's what we did. We flew to Gotham, picked up a rental car, drove to The Plaza – as a New Yorker

I'd been awed by the grand hotel off Fifth Avenue but never got beyond a drink at the Oak Room bar – tossed the valet the keys and checked in. My room was a broom closet with a bed, a grimy window opening to a sooty airshaft, and furnishings dating to the Coolidge administration.

I ordered a room-service cheeseburger – the tab about equal to a week's pay – and called an old UPI colleague who was now at the *New York Post*. I found out that Margaret had been at the ballet the previous night, talked to reporters – didn't mention anything about orgies at 24 Sussex – asked to be left alone, and gone into hiding.

The scuttlebutt, he told me, was that Margaret was hiding out in the Central Park West apartment of Yasmin Khan, daughter of Prince Aly Khan and actress Rita Hayworth, or staying at the Hotel Pierre – aptly named – across the street from The Plaza.

Jane and I went for a walk and talked to the doormen – at the Pierre and at Yasmin Khan's apartment. I called the office with some inane quotes to be folded into whatever the wires had.

The next day, acting on another tip, we drove to Bedford, New York, an old-money town in Westchester, about an hour north of the city, where Maggie was supposed to be spending the weekend at a friend's estate. We had an address, but could not penetrate the gate or the stone wall surrounding the property.

I parked on the side of the rural road. We tromped into the bushes that skirted the estate, to some high ground overlooking the house.

"This is ridiculous," Jane said.

"I know," I replied, focusing on a back porch where some people were gathered. "Is that her, in the white pants?"

"Who can tell," said Jane.

Suddenly, there was a rustle in the brush behind us. Getting ready to explain to the cops why we were peeping at the residents in tony Bedford, a familiar figure emerged – Bob Reguly, a reporter with the CTV network.

It didn't take long for the three of us to decide it was beneath our dignity to spend another moment in the bushes and that we were not about to bang on the gate and demand to know whether the wife of the prime minister of Canada was in residence.

Bob and I arranged to have drinks at Costello's bar on 43rd Street, one of my old UPI haunts, that evening. We got in our rental cars and drove back to Manhattan.

Having decided this assignment was beyond stupid, I called the office and said we were coming back to Toronto. I was told to go to Ottawa instead. "We hear she's flying home."

Jane and I flew to Ottawa, checked into adjoining rooms at the Château Laurier, another railway-era castle, ordered room-service and awaited further instructions.

I finally caught up with Maggie as she walked from an Air Canada flight at the Ottawa airport, escorted by an RCMP security detail and surrounded by reporters. I walked alongside her for a while, asking dumb questions – "Do you plan to stay in Ottawa?" "Have you talked to your husband?" "How are the kids?" – while she remained mute all the way into the back seat of a government sedan.

While Woodward and Bernstein won a Pulitzer for the *Washington Post*, my walk alongside a young runaway PM's wife has been preserved for the ages in TV file footage replayed whenever another story crops up about the early exploits of Margaret Trudeau.

I never heard another word from my editors about the Pitfield-Trudeau connection, though the *Sun's* political cartoonist regularly drew a tiny Pitfield lurking in the shadows – often under a bed – whenever he penned a Trudeau cartoon.

I was back at The Plaza a few months later, assigned to cover a real news story, though with certain self-inflicted difficulties. The night before I went to New York to report on the capture of the serial killer known as Son of Sam, I had been engaged in my usual after work ritual with my *Sun* colleagues.

When the bars closed at 1 a.m., we moved to the house of a couple who had invited us back for a nightcap, which turned into an all night drunk. One of the partygoers, an assistant city editor who had left early – at maybe 2 a.m. – called to tell me Son of Sam had been nabbed in New York, and the *Sun* wanted me there to cover the story.

I was hopelessly bombed. I tried to steel myself to the challenge but knew I was doomed. I decided I needed a sidekick for this assignment, a gonzo photog to help me through the insanity and make sure I didn't pass out at a press conference.

I picked Kevin Scanlon out of the crowd at the party and said, "I have to go to New York on the first flight. You're my photographer. Let's go."

Kevin, who had taken Pyette's cockamamie seal hunt assignment, was not only a reporter, but a good photographer as well. He didn't have a camera with him, which was a problem. We went to the apartment of a *Sun* photographer, who had left the party early, woke him up and borrowed his equipment.

We went to my apartment, also nearby. I packed a bag and drove to the airport. We missed the first flight to New York, at 7 a.m. to LaGuardia, but caught a 7:10 to JFK.

By the time we touched down ninety minutes later, I was still running on no sleep, angry that the stewardess wouldn't give me a bloody mary for breakfast, and in total Hunter S. mode, referring to Kevin as my Samoan attorney/photographer.

"As my attorney, you should advise me to rent a Cadillac convertible," I said. The only convertible Hertz had was a T-Bird. We took it, lowered the top, and joined the rush hour on the Van Wyck Expressway. In the space of about three hours, I had driven drunk in two countries.

It was a steamy August morning, the heat and stinking auto fumes forming a nauseating mix for someone half hammered and half hung over. I cranked up the radio for distraction but my head hurt too much and we were getting some weird looks from the other drivers commuting to work.

I managed to make it to The Plaza without puking or crashing, left the T-Bird with the doorman, and marched purposefully up to the front desk.

"Becker and Scanlon from Toronto," I announced to the clerk.

"Do you have a reservation?" she asked.

"Of course we have a reservation," I lied.

She fussed with some papers on the other side of the counter, before saying, "I'm sorry, sir, but we don't have your reservation."

"That's outrageous," I said, much too loud. "My attorney here will confirm it."

Kevin, who, with his bushy dark hair and Pancho Villa moustache looked like the cool lead guitarist in a rock band, tried to suppress a giggle.

"I'm really sorry, sir, but we're fully booked," the clerk said, whispering, trying to lower my tone.

"What if the Queen of England showed up and wanted a room," I whispered back, leaning on the counter, hoping my breath would wear down her resolve.

"Well," she said," we'd certainly try to accommodate her."

"Okay," I shot back, "I happen to know her majesty is not coming, so we'll take her room." I wasn't sure who first told that joke but it worked.

She came up with one room, with twin beds, and a view of a bigger airshaft than the last time I was at The Plaza. But I knew we were in trouble as soon as we got to the room and turned on the TV. All the stations were all over the Son of Sam story. It was obviously unfolding faster than we could catch up.

I ordered some room service breakfast, including a pitcher of bloody marys – the tab was more than our airfare – before going down to the lobby to get the New York papers, which screamed Son of Sam headlines.

When I got back to the room, breakfast had arrived and Kevin had heard on TV that there was a press conference at police headquarters at eleven o'clock. I figured that gave me about an hour to eat, get some vodka in my bloodstream and get downtown on the subway. We didn't make it, arriving just as the press conference was breaking up.

I got a quick fill-in from a New York reporter I knew, headed back to The Plaza, gave the bellman twenty dollars to bring up every new edition of the afternoon *Post* as it hit the stand, turned on the TV and collapsed on the bed. A couple of hours later, I awoke to an alarm of anxiety, assuming I had slept through the *Sun*'s deadline.

Kevin assured me we had time to file and informed me that he had called the city desk to learn that our editors – and even the publisher – in Toronto were mad as hell that Kevin was in New York and demanding that he return home immediately.

Desperate to at least salvage the story, I started writing – stealing every fact and quote from TV and the New York papers. I knew the background of the story, that Son of Sam had been on the loose for more than a year, stalking young couples with a .44-caliber revolver, going after girls with long dark hair, killing five of them and one of their male companions, and wounding seven. I knew that New Yorkers, especially parents with daughters of dating age, had been terrified as the killings continued and became more frequent in recent months. I knew the killer had been writing crazed letters to the police and Jimmy Breslin at the *Daily News*, who had been impressed with the killer's proper use of the semicolon.

But that was all background. The news was the capture and the identity of the killer; that a $35 parking ticket issued near the scene of the last killing led police to the home of David Berkowitz, in Yonkers, just north of the city; that he was a twenty-four-year-old postal clerk who lived alone, had served in the U.S. Army and been an auxiliary police officer; that he surrendered to police, saying, "Okay, you got me, I'm Son of Sam"; that he took the name Sam from an elderly neighbor named Sam Carr; that he told police he communicated with Carr through the man's Labrador retriever, named Harvey; that police found the .44 Bulldog revolver in Berkowitz's possession when they arrested him.

As I wrote, in longhand in a notebook, I rationalized that all this stuff was in all the papers and on all the TV stations. It came from official police sources, not deep background conversations in underground garages. I was at least in the city where the story happened, not sitting in Toronto and trying to pretend I was in Utah.

As night fell, I called the desk in Toronto and began to dictate, sharing a byline with Kevin on a story that ran nearly a thousand words.

As soon as I got off the phone I crashed. My head spun with random thoughts. I remembered someone at the *Times* talking about what he called "the Afghanistan Principle of journalism" – the farther you were from your newspaper's home base, the less likely an editor would question the sources of your story.

I thought of Evelyn Waugh's *Scoop*, subtitled *A Novel About Journalists*, in which a London newspaper's nature essayist – William Boot – is mistakenly sent to Africa to cover a civil war, and gains fame filing fanciful dispatches from bits of gossip.

In Canada, there are laws prohibiting the press from suggesting a suspect is guilty of a crime. But there are no such constraints when reporting from another country. You could convict anyone from the get-go, as I, and everyone else, did Berkowitz.

I'd wrestled with cribbing the facts and some news conference quotes from other reporters. But my story was all my words, in what was becoming my own hard-boiled, over-dramatized style.

Besides, I thought, lying on my bed in The Plaza, the *Sun* didn't seem to have much concern with its reporters' ethics. That didn't mean I would bend the rules, as I knew them.

But I was working for a paper where I had seen a couple of unconscionable examples of plagiarism – one columnist copying a long feature, word for word, from *Newsday* and having it published under his byline, and a reporter starting a baseball feature with a nearly word-for-word opening paragraph of a Roger Angell piece in *The New Yorker*. Though we all knew it, none of the editors said boo.

In fact, when I returned to Toronto from New York, I was congratulated on the coverage, but called on the carpet for taking Kevin with me, running up extra expenses. The publisher, Doug Creighton, was especially angry and not talking to me, which was only mildly alarming, since we had barely spoken before.

One person who didn't seem disturbed by all this was Warnick, the assistant managing editor who had originally hired me and was becoming something of a rabbi for me at the *Sun*. Soon after I came back from

New York, Warnick offered me my own column. This was flattering and attractive, though hardly a big promotion. Most everybody at the *Sun* who'd been there more than a year, except the most junior reporters, had a column.

The most popular columnist was Paul Rimstead, who the *Sun* considered its answer to Breslin. Early in my tenure, working the night desk, I was asked to take Rimstead's column over the phone. Since it was evening, he was slurring his words and the phone connection to his home out in the sticks north of Toronto wasn't the best.

"Ready," he said.

"I can't hear you very well," I replied.

"The guy on the other end of the phone says he can't hear me very well," he said.

"Why are you repeating what I just said?"

"I hope you're taking all this down," he said.

"What?"

"Everything I say," he said.

And that was what the *Sun* printed the next day from its most prominent columnist, a narration of our phone conversation. Six hundred words of gibberish.

My editor told me to put it through, that Rimstead was a sacred cow, a close friend of the publisher and the editor-in-chief. I'd learn that all those who started the paper back in 1971 could do no wrong.

I wasn't sure how to handle my new column. Warnick made it easy. "Just go out and get stories that we don't necessarily cover or get a fresh angle on the big story of the day in Toronto. You can write from a point of view, take sides, but I don't want your opinions off the top of your head. It needs to be newsy, real reporting. In fact, it will be called 'In the News.'"

This sounded good to me. I would become Toronto's real answer to Breslin. Champion of the underdog. Over the next several months, I wrote about an ex-prostitute who'd cleaned up her life, only to have her past splashed in the media when she came forward to testify against her onetime pimp; a woman whose ex-husband kidnapped their four-year-old son and was hiding out behind the Iron Curtain, in his native Poland; a mother who wanted her homicidal teenage son locked away in prison forever; a man who tried to rob a bank, saying he was out to finance a plot to kill Idi Amin; a guy who was beaten by sheriff's deputies who came to his home to repossess a washer, dryer and TV; a Sikh temple that had been vandalized and its members attacked as they left evening prayers; a group that was trying to raise money to operate a halfway house for native ex-cons.

My trademark became trying to put a human face to cops-and-robbers stories. Here's the top of one:

> **HAMILTON – Mary Welsh and Larry LeBlanc aren't going to keep their wedding date tomorrow. They don't really mind, though. A couple of days ago, it looked like they'd never have any chance at a life together.**
> **Larry was in the Don Jail staring at a rap that could keep him behind bars for a very long time – first-degree murder. But it was a bum rap. Larry knew it. Donna knew it. Their families knew it.**
> **But, most important, the two Metro homicide detectives who arrested Larry two weeks ago**

suspected it ... A couple of cops with a good case bothered to take a second look, to admit that they might be wrong – and went out and proved it.

I may not have been Breslin, but I was the only streetwise New Yorker in the newsroom, at least I pretended to be, and cultivated the image. Nobody else in Toronto tossed out phrases like "bum rap."

Some of my colleagues said they liked my stuff. One, Jerry Gladman, teased me when he saw me banging away with two index fingers at my IBM Selectric. "You know you smile when you write?" he said. "You must really love the sound of your own words."

He was right about one thing. I did write with my ear. Still do. If it doesn't sound right, it probably isn't.

My biggest fan turned out to be one of the newsroom secretaries, Linda Bone. The first time we met, Kate was visiting and I was showing her my office. My precocious eight year old effortlessly struck up conversations with people. One of them was Linda.

"Where are you from?" Linda asked.

"America," Kate replied.

"North America? South America?"

"America, America."

"There's no such place."

"Pardon?" Kate was confused.

"We both come from North America," Linda said. "But the country you come from is called the United States of America."

She deserved a Bronx cheer for that. I walked away, thinking typical Canadian bullshit. But I'd admired her from afar. She was so damn pretty. Irresistible, really. Pale blue eyes, light brown hair. About my height with broad shoulders and a willowy walk.

I didn't have anything to do with Linda for a while. Then, one evening, a bunch of us were drinking after work at a Canadian Legion hall across the street from the *Sun*. There was no other place to drink near the office. And the veterans of the 48th Highlanders regiment made us feel welcome.

That evening, Linda and I wound up as partners in a game of pool. That was it. Our affair started that summer of '77 and stayed secret for more than a month. We left notes for each other in sealed, plain brown envelopes. Arranged rendezvous in stairwells at the *Sun* to smooch. Checked into hotels all over town. Necked in my shiny new silver Mustang when I dropped her off a few blocks from her house.

Linda was living with a guy – not in the news biz – in another part of town. I was still living with the nice Jewish girl from Long Island in the Beaches. I finally broke up with her after a terrible night of confession and recrimination at the Essex House hotel in New York.

Meanwhile, as word of our relationship leaked in the newsroom, I got some stern warnings from colleagues who wanted to protect Linda from this philandering American, this outsider. But they seemed to calm down when we moved in together in September of 1977.

But I still got the impression the bosses didn't approve of me taking up with a Day Oner, which is what everyone called those who had been at the *Sun* the day it began publishing. My work, my columns, weren't enough to cancel out my indiscretions. The *Sun* seemed to prefer more promotional material with screaming headlines.

Sun Man Swims With Sharks!
Sun Man Saves Tot From Burning Car!
Sun Man Kills Seal, Feels Its Pain.

I had no idea what Doug Creighton wanted when I was summoned to the publisher's office in the fall of 1977. This would be our first one-on-one conversation since he stopped talking to me because of Kevin's trip to New York.

He came right to the point. "Are you interested in becoming the *Sun*'s baseball writer?"

CHAPTER 15
THE GROSS MILE-A-WORD CALCULATOR

My first assignment as a baseball writer was to go to Hawaii in December 1977 for the annual winter meetings. The week-long getaway, usually held in a warm place, is attended by team owners, their executives and key staff, and a mob of sportswriters.

I caught an early morning flight from Toronto to JFK, where I boarded a United jumbo jet chartered by Major League Baseball. I found a seat in the belly of the 747 and passed a quiet time on the flight to Los Angeles, where we stopped to get fuel and pick up more passengers.

In the shuffle, I climbed up to lounge and laid claim to a comfortable club chair. My seatmates were the managers of the two New York teams, Billy Martin of the Yankees and Joe Torre of the Mets.

Martin was flying high on bourbon and being a World Series champion. Torre was nursing his amber liquid after a last-place finish in his first season as manager of the Mets. I was belting back beers, which seemed to amuse Martin, who'd occasionally roar in my direction, "Hey, Beer Drinker, how ya doin'?"

That was about all these men said to me. As the flight dragged on, the lounge filled with a standing-room-only crowd. I got into an argument with Mary Paul, the wife of the Yankees president, Gabe Paul. I don't know how the conversation got around to Howard Cosell but that was the detonator.

"Howard Cosell is the smartest man I know," Mary Paul told me.

"He's an idiot," said Beer Drinker.

"He is my neighbor and a dear friend and you have no right to talk about him like that," Mary Paul scolded.

"Just because the guy memorizes a bunch of ten-dollar words doesn't make him a genius," Beer Drinker said. "Half the time he's barely able to utter a coherent sentence."

"Well, I think you're a very rude young man," she said, and disappeared into the crowd before Beer Drinker could come up with another witty retort.

My working time in Honolulu was spent at a poolside bar or in the Blue Jays suite at the Hilton with the men who ran the organization, led by Peter Bavasi and general manager Pat Gillick, a shrewd judge of baseball talent who had been hired away from the Yankees.

The expansion team's second season promised to be as bad as its first. The 1977 Jays were an abysmal collection of castoffs and kids, with a league-worst record of 55-107.

From Honolulu, I filed stories to the *Sun* on what the Toronto team was up to. It wasn't much. A couple of seemingly insignificant trades.

Most of the other reporters hung around the press room or the hotel lobby, where baseball people spent an inordinate amount of time when away from home. I set up my little, lightweight portable Olympia typewriter at the pool. As a reporter, I favored being apart from the pack. And it seemed idiotic to travel from Canada to Hawaii in December and stay indoors.

One afternoon, at a nearby table on the patio, I spotted Ted Turner, a hot celebrity having recently bought the Atlanta Braves and launched a TV "superstation," TBS. I figured an interview with Turner would be worth some space in the *Sun*.

He was reading a newspaper and sipping from a tall drink. I walked over. "Excuse me, Mr. Turner," I said.

"I'm not Ted Turner," he replied.

"Yes, you are," I said.

"No, I'm not," he said.

"If you don't want to talk to me, that's fine," I said. "But don't pretend you're not Ted Turner."

"I'm not," he said.

"Not pretending? Or not Ted Turner?"

"Neither," he said, and raised his newspaper to create a wall between us.

In Honolulu, I didn't spend much time with the other Toronto baseball writers, Neil McCarl of the *Toronto Star* and Neil Campbell of the *Globe*, who must have known a lot about art and classical music to be hired by Clark Davey.

The Expat Files

My first day back at the *Sun*, my new boss, the sports editor, George Gross, ambushed me as soon as I arrived. He was pissed.

Gross was a silver-haired schmoozer, a Czech immigrant who was handed the editor's chair when the *Sun* was founded. His connections were as impeccable as his suits, his ethics as questionable as his writing ability. My fellow news reporters and I once counted up to a half-dozen mentions of American Airlines in a column about a junket he took to Arizona for an event sponsored by American Airlines.

Gross had welcomed me to his fiefdom, probably because Linda had once worked as his secretary and he treated all his attractive young secretaries much better than he did his writers and editors.

He also wanted me on the baseball beat because the reporter who covered the Blue Jays the first season wasn't fast enough to meet the *Sun*'s deadlines when the team was on the West Coast. With my wire service background, and during my time on the city desk, it was clear I could write quickly under pressure.

Gross called me into his office to dress me down after the winter meetings. "I expected you to write a lot more when you were in Hawaii," he told me.

"Did I miss any stories?"

"That's not the point. When we're paying to send you five-thousand miles away, I expect you to write five-thousand words a day."

After I left his office, I had a laugh considering the Gross Mile-a-Word Calculator and how it could be applied to the road trips I'd take during the season: Detroit equals

200 words; New York = 400; Kansas City = 800; Texas = 1,200; Anaheim = 2,000, and so on.

It would be yet another case – piled on the nonsense of killing a baby seal and getting Maggie Trudeau to confess to an orgy – when I would ignore the bosses at the *Sun*.

Thankfully, once spring training started in February, I would never have to be in the office. In the meantime, Gross kept me busy writing features.

One was on Debbie Van Kiekebelt, a young, attractive former track and field star who Gross was courting as a tennis partner. I met Debbie at the Underground Railroad, a soul food restaurant a few blocks from the office on King Street. A couple of Americans, former CFL players, owned the joint. They and their staff were about the only black people I saw in Toronto in those days.

Canadians didn't talk about the issue of race. Yet that was where my interview with Van Kiekebelt quickly drifted. She told me about her family's disapproval of her relationship with a Pakistani squash player.

About a week later, I was face to face with bigotry that struck me personally. Harold Ballard, owner of the Toronto Maple Leafs, was a powerful and influential member of the Canadian sporting scene. Never mind that he was an unabashed blowhard with a reputation as a bully.

Gross had arranged the interview, suggesting a profile piece. But the sports editor told me not to mention Ballard's fraud conviction or prison time – so I saved it for last.

I met Ballard in his office/apartment at Maple Leaf Gardens. A jowly, florid-faced man in his mid-seventies, he was eager to impress a visitor with the secret of his success. "Do you know what B-B-B stands for?"

Big Braggart Ballard?
Bigmouthed Bastard Ballard?

"Nope," I played along.

"Bullshit baffles brains," he said with a flourish, as if he'd unlocked history's greatest mystery.

He went on to tell me how his special brand of bullshit baffled all his rivals, especially smartass "sheenies." I knew the word was a slur for Jews.

I hadn't been to synagogue since my bar mitzvah. I was never religious or a believer. I wanted to wash Ballard's mouth out with soap – or gefilte fish.

But, what was the point of picking a fight with a stupid old man I'd never see again? Instead, I asked him about his stretch in prison, and his boast that it was like a vacation in a motel, with color TV and steak dinners.

"Didn't George tell you I don't want to talk about that?" he blustered, his face reddening.

"Yeah," I said, "but this is my interview."

I wrote the story, heavy on his prison time, let the ex-con gasbag be a gasbag, and prepared to leave for spring training in Florida.

Linda and I had settled into a comfortable life in the upscale Moore Park neighborhood north of downtown. We rented the top floor of a house, near one of the ravines that provides a country atmosphere in the city. In the early months of 1978, we set a date to marry July 29, a year to the day after the game of pool that sparked our romance.

I knew I'd be getting the occasional break from the baseball beat and our wedding would be one of them. I'd miss a trip down the road to Detroit – only two-hundred words away.

In Florida, I'd arranged for the *Sun* to rent me a one-bedroom condo near the Jays spring training camp in Dunedin, a short drive from Tampa airport. Linda would be coming down for about ten days, and Kate, now nine years old, would be flying in from Switzerland.

I spent the first couple of weeks in Florida on my own, or with a *Sun* photographer crashing on the pullout couch in the living room. I went each morning to little Grant Field, sat in the sun, on the grass along the right field foul line – the other newspaper reporters, the two Neils, preferred the tiny press box – and watched the players put through their paces.

I talked most days with the manager, Roy Hartsfield, a fifty-two-year-old Georgia cracker who'd never made it in the big leagues as a player. He was a safe choice, a good company man, to lead the fledgling Jays.

I focused most of my stories on the new Jays, those who had signed since the previous season. One was Luis Gomez, the new shortstop, who came to me one day and asked about Hartsfield. "Why does the skipper talk to me so slow, like I'm a moron?"

"Because he thinks you don't understand English." I laughed.

"Shit, man." He spat, "I went to UCLA."

During the early days in Dunedin, I was invited to a get-to-know-you dinner by Pat Gillick. We went to one of those mammoth Florida restaurants that seats a couple of thousand sunburned tourists. This one, in Tarpon Springs, was called Pappas. Gillick recommended the stone crabs. Baseball people, who spend so much time going from city to city on expenses, tend to know some of the best places to eat and what's choice on the menu. They eschew exotic fare, preferring the staples of steaks and seafood.

Gillick, all nervous energy and good manners, was a pleasant dinner companion. He complimented me by seeking my counsel on a sensitive subject. Since I was a fellow American who had been in Canada for five years, compared to his one, he asked, "Do you think the people in Toronto would accept a team that is more black than white?"

I knew immediately what he was driving at. This was a time when race was still a consideration in the way Americans viewed baseball and all other sports. Teams had concerns that too many blacks and Latinos on the field drove white fans from the stands.

Gillick was looking for an edge. If Toronto was a place where race didn't matter, he could scour the baseball universe for the best players.

"I don't think people in Toronto care," I told Gillick. "I think they just want to be winners." Under Gillick's guidance, a crop of black and Latino stars would lead the Jays to two World Series championships in the early '90s.

Later in spring training, I took a drive to Winter Haven, the Florida home of the Boston Red Sox. I had a rooting interest in the Sox since a visit to Boston in the fall of 1967, when they won the pennant on the final day of the season.

I fell in love with their star, Carl Yastrzemski, who seemed to come to bat in every crucial situation and come through with a home run or a game-winning double off the wall. I was disappointed when the Sox lost that 1967 World Series but also elated that I was engaged in baseball for the first time since the Dodgers left Brooklyn.

In Winter Haven, I watched Yaz in the batting cage, working up a sweat in the gloom of a foggy morning, under the watchful eye of the great Ted Williams. "This is probably the best hitting team I've ever seen," Teddy Ballgame told me.

I received the same appraisal from the Sox manager, Don Zimmer, when I joined the Boston writers in his office that morning. Zimmer, a little Popeye look-alike, was derisively nicknamed "the gerbil" by his hippie-dippy pitcher, Bill "Spaceman" Lee.

Zimmer had been one of my dad's favorite players, a hard-nosed little spark plug who didn't mind getting his uniform dirty when he played the infield for Brooklyn. On this day, the Sox manager was spitting confidence his powerful lineup would win the pennant after losing it to the damn Yankees the past two seasons.

I reckoned he was right. But, being a Sox fan, I assumed they'd find a way to blow it.

CHAPTER 16
BAR TALK

Flying north from Florida with the Blue Jays, I was anxious to get the season going. Spring training seemed like a vacation. It was time to get to work.

Our traveling circus of players, manager, coaches, road secretary, trainer, broadcasters and writers piled onto a wide-bodied Lockheed L-1011 TriStar in sunny Tampa and got off in chilly Detroit. A charter bus picked us up at the airport and deposited us at the Westin in the new Renaissance Center complex.

In 1978, Motown was not a place for sightseeing, unless you enjoyed the sight of buildings still burned out from the 1967 riots or wanted the thrill of being robbed at gunpoint. So the baseball lifestyle of hanging around the hotel seemed like a good idea.

After opening day was rained out, I spent a lot of time in my room, watching TV, reading, talking to Linda on the phone and ordering room service. The next day, the season began in warm sunshine at Tiger Stadium, filled to the rafters with kids and grownups playing hooky. The game, though, pretty much set the tone for the rest of the season – the Jays lost.

As for my major league debut, I followed the other writers on their appointed rounds. The pregame ritual included hanging around the cage during batting practice, chatting with the coaches and the managers; setting up my typewriter at my assigned spot in the press box; joining my fellow scribes in the private dining room for the complimentary pregame meal.

During the game, I dutifully kept score in my genuine baseball writer's scorebook – shipped directly from the genuine baseball writer's scorebook company in Cincinnati – ate the available free snacks and drank the free beer and listened to the wisecracks of the hometown Detroit writers – mainly going on about cleanup hitter Rusty Staub, speculating on his sexual predilections.

After the game, I dashed down to the clubhouses, talked to Hartsfield and the pipe-smoking Tigers' manager Sparky Anderson, went back to the press box, wrote my story and handed it page by page to the gofer who delivered it to the Western Union operator for transmission to the *Sun*.

All of these chores would become routine, some more onerous than others, depending on the city and ballpark. On my first trip with the team to Texas, I bought a new pair of cowboy boots because it was the style of the day and all the cool baseball folks wore cowboy boots. But the footwear also proved practical for the postgame walk to the clubhouses, which were down the outfield lines at the stadium in Arlington, requiring a walk through the stands. After the fans were gone, giant cockroaches moved in to feast on the litter of ballpark chow.

I began the season hoping to get along with the people I was writing about. At thirty-one, I was older than most of the players, but not by much. At first, they seemed to accept me more than the other writers.

I'd been a decent athlete in my youth and could still handle a glove and a bat without looking like a klutz. During pre-game warm-ups, I'd play catch or shag flies in the outfield.

The only player I socialized with was pitcher Dave Wallace. He was different from the others, more thoughtful and a lot smarter. I was about a year older. We'd both been born and raised in the Northeast. He was from Connecticut, and had graduated college. We'd talk about baseball but also about other things, books and movies and life.

Early in the season, on a day off in Oakland, I rented a car and took Wallace to Sausalito. I'd called my old hippie friend, Barry Ginsberg, who met me in the No Name Bar while Wallace had a look around the town. Thankfully, after Barry described in great detail being abducted by aliens, he had to go to work, as a chef at the nearby Trident restaurant.

Wallace joined me at the No Name and we settled in for the night. An attractive woman, a blonde about our age, sidled up to us at the bar. "You look like baseball players," she said.

"He is," I said.

"I hate baseball players," she said.

"I don't like them much either, except this guy," I said, pointing to Wallace.

She was really drunk. And really wanted to talk. She said she was a stewardess for United Airlines and sometimes worked on charters for major league teams.

On one late night flight, she told us, at thirty-thousand feet, her crewmate had been dragged into a lavatory and raped. She said the airline insisted her crewmate not press charges, that nobody believed her, that everyone assumed she had initiated the event and only cried rape later.

I believed her story. I asked some questions, trying to identify the rapist. But she kept shaking her head and guzzling vodka. "That's why I hate ballplayers," she concluded, before staggering off into the night.

Wallace and I were quiet on the long drive back to the hotel in Oakland. We didn't have a chance to talk much after that night. He was released by the Jays and, when no other team gave him a chance, he retired at the age of thirty. The cerebral Wallace would go on to have an accomplished career as a major league pitching coach. I would turn the flight attendant's tale of rape into the plot of a novel.

Any fraternization I had with players ceased after I chronicled an incident that would get outfielder Rick Bosetti fined. Earlier in the season, I could have been mistaken for Bosetti's press agent. In my setup story for opening day in Toronto I wrote: *Bosetti is a truly free and refreshing spirit. A flamboyant dresser – the other day he was wearing a rabbit-skin fur coat and shiny knee-length boots – Bosetti seems to cheer up a room with his chatter.*

But, as the season went on, I couldn't help noticing Bosetti was a serial sleaze. We all know ballplayers play with themselves on the field, in front of thirty-thousand spectators and TV cameras. But at least most keep their privates in their pants.

Bosetti bragged that he regularly unzipped during a game, that his quest was to piss in every outfield in the American League. I was also told by a flight attendant on a Jays' charter that Bosetti – she pointed him out – was fondling himself on the darkened DC-9 as she passed him in the aisle.

I didn't write these stories, since I didn't know them to be true and believed a player's conduct out of uniform, unless criminal, was probably his own business. But that summer at County Stadium, I witnessed something shameful and wrote about it.

> **MILWAUKEE** – Rick Bosetti proved yesterday that he can be just as rude and vulgar on the road as he can be at home.
>
> Bosetti, who earlier this year at Exhibition Stadium cursed and made an obscene gesture at an adult, yesterday made an equally disgusting remark to a group of kids seeking autographs.
>
> Seated in the visitors' dugout before the Blue Jays-Milwaukee game, Bosetti was asked: "Sir, could I have your autograph please."
>
> Apparently unaccustomed to a polite request, Bosetti responded in his usual manner: "There ain't no fucking sirs in here, kid."

After word of my story got back to the team the next morning, Hartsfield phoned my hotel room and said he wanted to talk to me when we got to the ballpark. I didn't have to ask what it was about.

We had moved on to Minneapolis, billeted at the rundown Leamington hotel, which I recognized from some night shots on the *Mary Tyler Moore Show*. I was to meet Hartsfield in the visitors' clubhouse at ugly old Metropolitan Stadium. But I first ran into some angry players. When I entered the locker room, and Bosetti saw me, he let loose with a stream of expletives and charged toward me. He was tackled and held back by a couple of other players, notably Roy Howell, the red-headed third baseman.

When things calmed down, Howell cornered me. "You showed some guts walking in here," he said. "But nobody in here trusts you any more."

The code of the clubhouse says that a writer who criticizes a player in the paper is required to stand up to that player and his teammates before the next game. I really didn't care what Bosetti thought, but I hadn't expected his teammates to condone his behavior. I was wrong. "You can't take money out of a player's pocket," Howell went on. "You're messing with people's careers – their lives – when you write stuff like that."

Hartsfield and I huddled in the tunnel between the clubhouse and the dugout. "Are you sure you got it right?" he asked.

"Yeah," I replied. "I wrote exactly what he said."

"Okay," Hartsfield said.

"Did he get fined?" I asked.

"Yup – two-fifty," Hartsfield said.

In 1978, the minimum salary for players was $21,000. While the Reggie Jacksons were raking in about a half-million a season, players like Bosetti were making about the same salary as a newspaper reporter.

After the game in Minneapolis, as usual, I retired to the bar in the hotel. The Jays had a rule that barred players from drinking in the hotel bar, which provided a sanctuary for the managers and coaches and the other adults who traveled with the team.

On the road with the Blue Jays, I usually hung out with the other writers, travel secretary Mike Cannon, and the broadcasters, Tom Cheek and Early Wynn, the radio voices; Tony Kubek and Don Chevrier, the TV guys.

For me, Early Wynn – everybody called him "Gus" – and Tony Kubek were the perfect post-game drinking companions. They were both basically small-town guys, Wynn living in rural Florida, Kubek from rural Wisconsin. But they had been big-time players.

Kubek appeared in half a dozen World Series with the Yankees; Wynn in two, with the Indians and White Sox. They'd played against each other during the impressionable years of my childhood, in the 1950s. I enjoyed egging them on and, in turn, they would tease – "rag" as the ballplayers said – each other.

"So, Gus, how'd it feel losing to the Yanks every year?" I'd start the conversation at the bar.

"We didn't lose every year. Beat 'em in '54 when I was in Cleveland and in '59 when I was with the White Sox."

"How many World Series you win?" Kubek piped up.

"None," Gus said.

"You win any, Tony?" I asked, knowing the answer was three.

"Yep."

"Not all," Wynn countered. "Guess you don't remember Mazeroski."

"And Lew Burdette – and Koufax," I added.

And on it went, with one game, one name, tripping into another memory. Talking baseball with Early Wynn and Tony Kubek was heaven.

But on the night after I learned Bosetti had been fined, back in the Leamington hotel bar in Minneapolis, I wasn't talking baseball. I was talking newspapering with Neil Campbell of the *Globe*.

"My paper is really pissed at me about that story," Neil said.

"What story?" I said.

"Your story, about Bosetti," he said. "They want to know why I didn't get it."

"You weren't there," I said. Neil looked miserable. I ordered another round of drinks.

"You know what they want me to do?" he said. "They want me to sit in the lobby every night and write about who comes in after curfew." The players were supposed to be in their rooms by 1 a.m.

"That's ridiculous," I said. "That's not news. Who cares?"

I thought back to a night in Kansas City in April, when I rode up the hotel elevator with young Willie Upshaw and a couple of clinging farm girls. He seemed embarrassed to see me, but I just smiled, thinking the kid deserved a reward for knocking the winning hit in the late innings of a wild game. What could I have reported, anyway? *Willie Upshaw probably got laid last night.*

"They seem to think," Campbell went on, "that if a player comes in late and has a bad game the next day, it's news."

"What if a player comes in late and has a great game? You going to write that?

"I don't know what to do," he said.

"What are you supposed to do, smell their breath?"

"I don't know," he said, falling deeper into the dumps.

"You going to do it?" I asked Campbell.

"I don't know," he said.

Campbell would finish the season – and his career as a baseball writer, a job he truly loved – by stealing a bunch of documents from Bavasi's desk, going into a bathroom and copying the information in his notebook. He got caught and the documents turned out to be boring insurance forms. But the *Globe* had made him crazy, trying to convince him that covering baseball was like covering Watergate. Maybe he should have written about art or classical music.

My season as a baseball writer would also end that fall. But not until after a breathtaking pennant race between the Yankees and my Sox, which went down to the last game – and one more.

CHAPTER 17
BILATERAL RELATIONS

My predecessor on the baseball beat at the *Sun*, Paul Palango, wrote a memorable line describing Alvis Woods, who was black, and his attachment to his bat, which was black. *Al Woods came out of the shower swinging his big, black bat.*

Being a sportswriter was a peculiar occupation, considering the amount of time spent interviewing naked men. I happened to be in New York the night some women joined us – and changed the profession forever.

Nearly a year earlier, *Sports Illustrated* reporter Melissa Ludtke filed suit against Major League Baseball, the Yankees and the City of New York, saying they had discriminated against her by not allowing women access to locker rooms at Yankee Stadium during the 1977 World Series.

On September 26, 1978, a federal judge ruled in Ludtke's favor and the Yankees opened their clubhouse to women before and after that night's game against the Blue

Jays. Ludtke was not there, but a handful of women reporters, most from local TV stations, entered the smelly locker room to find the Yankees in various stages of undress. To mark the historic occasion, a couple of giggling naked men – Yogi Berra, the fifty-three-year-old coach, his dick somewhere beneath his pale gut, and Cliff Johnson, a six-foot-four-inch, two-hundred-and-twenty-pound backup catcher, swinging his big black bat – streaked from the shower and circled the room to the amusement of the rest of the Yankees.

I stood back from the pack to assess the scene, since the story of the women in the clubhouse was more interesting than the Jays ninety-seventh loss of the year.

I watched one of the TV reporters interviewing a naked Willie Randolph, trying to make eye contact but constantly stealing downward glances. I talked to another of the TV reporters, Linda Sutter, about the experience.

"I'm delighted to be here," she said in my sidebar story that night. "Unfortunately, I got off to a bit of a bad start. I was standing outside the door and this guy came up behind me, grabbed me, and dragged me in here. I didn't know who the hell it was – it was Jay Johnstone – I didn't know him and I feel that if I'm going to be in here, working, I should know who I'm dealing with. That's what Reggie (Jackson) told me. 'If you're going to be working in here, you'll have to gain the respect of the players. And you'll get that by knowing them and asking intelligent questions.' Right now, my biggest fear is asking a dumb question."

I wanted to wise up Sutter, tell her Reggie Jackson didn't know an intelligent question from a fungo, that all he did was suck up to the network TV types and treated anyone who couldn't advance his career like shit. I'd witnessed Jackson's shtick with a young radio reporter in Toronto, deliberately saying fuck every third word so the interview tape was useless.

I asked Sutter why she would want to cover sometimes hostile, usually naked, and always foul-mouthed ballplayers. "Look," she said, "this is my game. When I was ten years old, I wanted to be a shortstop when I grew up. I stopped playing baseball only because they wouldn't let me play Little League. I grew up in New England and I've always been a Red Sox fan. Last week, when the Red Sox were here, I read a piece about how they reacted to their losses. It described how Yastrzemski sat at his locker and sobbed into a towel, how Remy sat with his head hung low. I thought to myself, damn it, I'd like to do that story. I'd like to be here to see it and describe it."

I'd witnessed the locker room scene she was talking about, when the thirty-nine-year-old Yaz and his mates sank into despair. It was heartbreaking. Boston had collapsed over the summer, their fourteen-game lead over the Yanks evaporating in the heat of August and early September.

Since the Jays played their last twelve games of the season against the Yanks and Sox, I had a press box seat for the closing act. Boston had regained its form to close within one game of the Yanks entering the final game on the schedule. When the Indians beat the Yankees and the Sox beat the Jays, Boston and New York were tied for first place. The division title would be decided in a one-game playoff the next day at Fenway.

While the Jays' players and coaches flew back to Toronto to clean out their lockers and begin the off-season, I returned to the Sheraton hotel and called home. "I'm here another night," I told Linda. "I've decided that if the Sox win, I'll keep going and follow them in the playoffs and the World Series. When they lose, I'm done."

We'd discussed before that this would be my last assignment as a baseball writer and my last with the *Sun*. I was tired of the beat and couldn't see myself returning to the paper, either writing sports by the mile for George Gross, or going back to the city desk and being asked to kill seals for Les Pyette.

Cover to cover, the Sun was an embarrassment, with its cheesy photos of buxom girls – one photog bragged of getting blowjobs in exchange for putting some bimbo's picture in the paper – self-promotion and lame, punny headlines.

Linda would stay at the *Sun* and I'd give freelancing a shot. My young bride was very understanding, sensitive to my restless nature and ambition.

We married on July 29, 1978 in the International Suite at the Hotel Toronto. We invited about thirty guests, my family and one friend, all from New York; Linda's family and one friend, all from Toronto.

Kate stood with us during the ceremony, performed by an American, John Hanley Morgan, a Unitarian minister and president of the Canadian Peace Congress. I wrote our vows, which were pretty schmaltzy. While my Uncle Sidney kibitzed from the sidelines, Linda and I pledged our love would overcome the differences in our nationality and religion.

I was once more marrying a foreigner and a Christian. While Anita Schlumpf was born in 1940, a Protestant, the eldest of four children, Linda Bone was born in 1950, a Roman Catholic, the youngest of six. Ten years apart, both had gratefully taken my surname.

The New York Jews and the Canadian Catholics seemed in tune as the ceremony concluded, the bar opened, and the sunset provided a warm glow to the thirty-second-floor suite.

The families would get along the few times they met over the years. Linda's widowed mother, Edith, a great lady, sent my parents new year's cards on Rosh Hashanah. Linda's sister Brenda and my Aunt Fay got smashed and giggly on Dry Sack sherry one Christmas at our house in Moore Park.

I'd politely correct other in-laws when they reminisced about the "sheenie man" – that word again – who pedaled junk in their neighborhood growing up, or the occasions when they "Jewed downed" a salesman.

Linda and I continually worked out our Canadian-American differences. I learned that wieners were hot dogs, serviettes were napkins, and a toque was a stocking cap. She learned to understand what a mensch was.

She tolerated me crossing the street against the light. I waited for her on the other side while she stared at the DON'T WALK sign until it gave her permission.

"What a good Canadian," I'd say to her and others who obeyed every rule.

Q: How do you get a bunch of Canadians to get out of a swimming pool?
A: Say, "everybody out of the pool."

After our wedding, Linda and I spent a couple of days at her brother Tom's cottage on a lake in the Haliburton area a few hours northeast of Toronto. But then it was back on the road with the Jays.

By the time the season was over, I'd flown more than seventy-thousand miles, taking only a few days off. I still loved baseball but hated the view from the inside. The baseball world was not the real world. Not my world, anyway.

I remembered being in the boarding area at Logan airport in Boston with the rest of the Blue Jays. I spotted John Kenneth Galbraith also waiting for our flight to Toronto. I turned to the person next to me, coach Harry Warner, and said, "That's John Kenneth Galbraith."

"You mean the guy with Pittsburgh?" Warner asked.

"Short guy with a moustache, right?" added player Bob Bailor.

Another day, before boarding a charter flight in Seattle, one of the pitchers confided that he had brought along a bag of pot for the long ride back to Toronto. I sometimes smoked dope in the back of the plane with this pitcher and another player on flights within the United States.

I suggested to the pitcher that it might not be wise to be in possession of the baggie when we went through Canadian Customs. He had to be reminded that such laws applied to athletes. He got rid of the contraband.

The most comical trip through customs was thanks to a Jays' pitcher named Balor Moore, twice afflicted as a lefty and a Texan.

"How long have you been out of the country," the customs' inspector asked.

"I dunno."

"Where have you been?"

"I dunno."

"What flight did you arrive on?"

"I dunno."

"What airline?"

"I dunno."

I couldn't imagine spending another season following the bores of summer.

Now, in Boston, after the final Jays' game of the season, I knew my days in the big leagues nearly over. That Sunday night, I went to the Union Oyster House with some other writers from Toronto, including the *Sun*'s sports columnist, Trent Frayne, and Alison Gordon, a friend who, within a year, would become the first woman baseball writer in Canada, with the *Toronto Star*.

We spotted Dewey Evans, the Sox rightfielder, at another table. I joked that poor Neil Campbell, now removed from the beat, would have felt compelled to go over to Evans's table and check out what he was drinking the night before the big game.

I told Frayne that I'd be quitting the *Sun* if the Sox lost the next day, and asked if he'd mind covering the playoffs and World Series on his own for the paper. Ever the gentleman, ever compassionate, he said he understood, though I don't think he did.

We had a wonderful dinner, fresh, steamed lobster and lots of wine, and retired to the Sheraton in high spirits. The next morning, I caught a cab outside the hotel and asked the driver to take me to Fenway.

"Going to the game?" he asked.

"Yeah, it's my job," I said. "I'm a writer."

"Which paper?"

"One in Toronto," I said.

"Tough season for Toronto," he said.

"Yeah," I said. "Last place. Another hundred losses."

"What do you think of the Sox chances?" he said.

"I'm a Sox fan," I confided, "so I guess I expect the worst and hope for the best." He laughed in recognition.

We pulled up to the press entrance to Fenway. I checked the meter and reached for my wallet.

"Forget it," said the cabbie. "I like you guys from Toronto. It was nice talking to you."

It was a perfect New England day, blue sky, bright sun, a hint of fall in the air.

I found my assigned spot in the press box, dumped my typewriter and scorebook on the table, and went to the dining room. There was a choice of baked cod or roasted veal. I had the veal, with roasted potatoes and a salad.

The New York writers were there, of course, so the volume in the room was turned up a notch or three. By this time, after five years in Canada, I thought I'd lost my New York accent, a mission I'd been on since I left home in

1968. Somehow, I found it more seemly to be a know-it-all New Yorker without saying *caw-fee*.

I certainly didn't want to be associated with loud-mouthed New York sports fans, especially after seeing big-haired women at Yankee stadium coated with makeup, wearing painted on designer jeans and tight T-shirts that read *Boston Sucks* or *Yaz Has VD*.

Fenway was full early for the Monday afternoon playoff game, 32,925 crammed into the little ballpark. Yaz, ever heroic, hit a home run in the second inning and Jim Rice knocked in another in the sixth to give Boston a 2-0 lead.

But in the top of the seventh, the Yanks had a couple of runners on with two out when their most anemic hitter, Bucky Dent, came to the plate. He hit a fly ball toward the thirty-seven-foot-high Green Monster in left. Yaz, playing left field, seemed prepared to make the catch and end the inning. But the baseball gods, ever Yankee fans, lifted the ball over the wall.

That put the Yanks ahead and every Boston fan from Fenway to Fiji knew the game – and the season – was over. Sure, the Sox rallied a bit. But Yaz popped out, with the winning runs on the bases, to end the game and any suspense.

I watched that last half-inning from the stands, behind the seats along the third base line, sharing the inevitable pain with the Fenway faithful. Littered copies of an extra edition of the *Boston Globe*, distributed earlier in the ballpark, were illustrated with a six-inning linescore under the front-page headline: *SOX AHEAD*.

I made my rounds of the two clubhouses, the champagne and euphoria in the winners' room, the beer and gloom of the losers. My story in the next day's *Toronto Sun* was a Sox fan's lament.

> **BOSTON – It wasn't supposed to end that way. It wasn't right to break the hearts of the people of New England, just when their spirits were starting to rise, just when their expectations were at their highest.**
> **October in New England offers the promise of two things: The leaves changing colors and the Red Sox playing for the world championship of baseball. Now, one is dead.**

I whined on from there and closed the story with a quote from Yaz. "The last three weeks, with our backs to the wall, we played like champions. But now, there's just tremendous disappointment."

The next day, I flew home to Toronto, called Gross, quit my job and packed the car. Linda and I drove to the coast of Maine to look at the damn leaves.

CHAPTER 18
TRAVELS WITH YAZ

Journalists are scorekeepers. We chronicle what other people do and say, tally it up, glorify the winners, deride the losers. I thought I had more to say, something that came from *my* head and *my* heart.

The first thing I wrote after I quit the *Sun* was a piece for *Toronto Life*, the city magazine, about my year on the baseball beat. It was titled *Your Toronto Blue Jays: The brats of summer* and recounted much of the bad and brainless behavior of the players.

I also recalled a ride through Harlem, from our midtown hotel to Yankee Stadium, the first time I'd been in Harlem since the shooting at the Black Muslim mosque.

I heard the ballplayers in the back of the bus. "Look at that old pitching coach," one of them said, pointing to a derelict lying in the gutter. "Bunch of southpaws," said another, the bus passing a corner crammed with junkies. "How 'bout that for a slice of dark meat," a third reacted to a hooker in a red shift.

Then, I turned the focus to John Mayberry, a black player from Detroit who knew the faces of poverty and degradation. I described him as "the team's fiercest hitter and gentlest man," and "the most intrinsically decent human being I'd met in my year of covering baseball."

Yet, Mayberry did not react to the cracks of his white teammates on the bus. Perhaps had not heard them. More likely he was shuttered from the world around him as he prepared for another baseball game.

During the last homestand of the season, I met Mayberry for a drink in the bar at the Hotel Toronto, his home away from home. We had enjoyed a comfortable professional relationship. He had not turned on me, as others had, after the Bosetti incident.

"I'm quitting, John," I told him.

"Aw, man, what you wanna do that for?"

"Gotta get back to the real world," I said.

Mayberry shrugged. Sipped red wine. "Well, guess a man's gotta do what a man's gotta do." He would have four more seasons in the big leagues before retiring at the age of thirty-three.

As I said, I needed to get back to the real world. And nothing could be more real than a visit with my old rogue cop friend Bill Phillips, now a convicted murderer doing life inside one of the most notorious prisons in the United States.

Phillips had been tried again after I left New York. The second time, without F. Lee Bailey, the ex-NYPD detective had been found guilty of killing pimp Jimmy Smith and teenage prostitute Sharon Stango.

In February 1979, Linda came along for the ride as I crossed the border near Niagara Falls and headed east on the New York State Thruway. It was a cloudy, gloomy, cold day. The drive took a little under three hours.

I parked in the visitors' lot below the great gray walls of Attica. I was surprised how easy it was to get into a maximum-security prison. I wasn't frisked. Or grilled by the guards. Simply ushered through several sets of barred doors. As each closed behind me, I worried about some colossal screw-up – being mistaken for a prisoner, and never getting out.

Phillips had arranged my visit. We'd exchanged a few letters the previous month. *As you can well imagine,* he wrote, *being a cop in jail has its disadvantages, to say the least. Things have not been easy for me these last four years.*

I hadn't considered Phillips a cop during the time I knew him. A crook with a badge was more like it. But not a killer. A con artist.

His letter went on: *I know that we will have a lot to talk about, and I will be looking forward to meeting you again, and discussing all the past and present things that have happened to both of us.*

His last letter before my visit set off alarm bells. *Have been thinking about writing the article you spoke about and in jogging my memory I have a tremendous amount of tapes that have not been made public concerning my personal investigation in my case ...*

Who is writing the article? Does Phillips think I plan to collaborate on whatever comes from our meeting?

That was his deal with a book called *On the Pad*, which came out in 1973, the year after his first trial. The title was cop slang for accepting regular payments from criminals – putting them on the pad – to protect them from arrest. The book was written by Leonard Shecter, *with William Phillips*. Shecter, an accomplished magazine writer and author who died a year later, paid Phillips $30,000 for his part in the book.

Is that what Phillips had in mind for me? To be his ghostwriter? I was looking for a quick, down and dirty piece about Bill Phillips' life in prison. I certainly didn't want to get dragged into his "investigation" of his case.

We met in the large visiting room under the watchful eye of the guards. They didn't object to me turning on a tape recorder or taking notes. There weren't many visitors on a weekday. Like most state pens, it was far from the cities where the prisoners came from.

Phillips looked beaten down, if not beaten up for being a cop. Always the sharp dresser with a fresh haircut, he was wearing rumpled khakis and needed a shave. The same nervous energy was there. But the interview veered wildly into tangents about his case, his appeals, his lawyers, the prosecutors and cops who he said had framed him.

I quickly realized there was no story here for me. Not now, anyway. I'd have to spend too much time on a piece to be written on spec, and had no clue who would be interested in publishing it. I had no contacts with newspapers or magazines in New York, the only place where Phillips was well known.

I was relieved when our time was up. And more relieved when the last gate slammed behind me and I was back outside the walls of the wretched fortress called the first "big house" when it was built in the early 1930s.

I would not see Bill Phillips again. He would rot in prison – suffer a stroke and cancer that cost him an eye – before being paroled in 2007.

As a freelancer, which is generally considered a synonym for unemployed, I started writing regularly for *Maclean's,* Canada's newsmagazine.

In my six years north of the border, I had joined a fraternity of Canadian journalists who travel the country for major news events. Some of them had moved into positions to give me work. A couple were editors at *Maclean's,* which had just switched from a biweekly to a weekly and needed freelance writers to churn out copy.

Again, as an ex-wire-service guy, I could be depended on to be fast and proficient. Having jumped from news to sports – and not forgetting my stint as a movie critic for the *Livermore Herald & News* – I was also a jack of many trades.

Over the next year, I wrote more than a dozen pieces for *Maclean's*. I did a cover story on Canada taking in thousands of Vietnamese "boat people." I wrote a piece on Detroit, after it was chosen to host the 1980 Republican National Convention – when Reagan and Bush were nominated – spent a day riding around in mayor Coleman Young's limo, listening to him complain about the knock outsiders put on his city.

During one stop, Young's driver confided, "The mayor loves Toronto. He goes up there when he wants to hang loose, have some fun and not be recognized." I would discover that many black Americans visited Canada to get a break from the alienation of racism they felt in their own country.

My story in *Maclean's* highlighted Detroit's efforts to recover from the devastation of the 1967 riot that left forty-three people dead and more than a thousand injured, mostly poor and black. But I saw little hope for a renaissance in a city where the black majority distrusted its cops of any color.

I traveled to Parris Island, South Carolina, to do a story – which would be under the headline, *Dressed to kill and scared to death* – on the Marine boot camp, at a time the corps was catching a lot of flak for its drill instructors beating recruits. Linda came with me, as my photographer – we'd bought a new Nikon and were hoping she would eventually leave the *Sun* and secretarial work and we might develop into a husband-and-wife team. *Maclean's* picked up some of the tab for the trip, which was mainly spent playing golf at Pinehurst, North Carolina, and Hilton Head Island, South Carolina.

As an American writing for Canadians, I felt a greater freedom to spin controversial yarns from places like Parris Island and Detroit. Maybe it was cowardly, avoiding the scrutiny of my compatriots, the people I was writing about, since few of them would see the story. It never occurred to me to pitch Canadian stories to American magazines. Didn't think anyone south of the border would be interested.

I preferred writing American stories, anyway. And, since *Maclean's* seemed to like what I was doing, I kept doing it. I was also getting a steady stream of assignments from the magazine's sports editor, Hal Quinn.

Hal and I met playing a board game called APBA, American Professional Baseball Association. We were among the six members of what we called the Fireside League, since each of our homes had a fireplace and we would gather for games only in the wintertime.

Hal's brother Warren was the only non-journalist in the group. The others were Alison Gordon, a rookie baseball writer for the *Star*; Bryan Johnson, the drama critic at the *Globe*, and Marty O'Malley, a columnist for the *Star*'s Sunday magazine run by Pal Joey.

We took great care in creating our team names. Someone came up with the idea of basing the names on the streets where we lived. Hal, who lived on Roselawn Avenue, was the Roselawn Undertakers, or 'Takers, for short; Warren, the Quebec (Avenue) *Separatistes*, or 'Seps; Bryan, the Chateauneufs du Pape (Avenue), or 'Neufs; Alison the Simpson (Avenue) Studs, and Marty, taking exception to the street theme, was the North End Greens. I was the Hudson (Drive) Rivers, an homage to my hometown, a city with real rivers and magnificent bridges.

We drafted teams of major league players – Yaz, of course, was my first pick – and met on Monday nights. We'd roll dice to get the result of a play and keep score. The night would always begin with a case of twenty-four beers. Often, it wasn't enough.

Hal and I became fast friends and drinking buddies. He'd invite me to lunch to discuss story ideas. We'd eat Chinese food – I'd adapted to the Toronto variety – drink beer, laugh a lot, and emerge from the restaurant after dark.

With *Maclean*'s as the backbone of my freelance business, I was doing okay. Naturally, I started getting restless.

I quickly tired of going to meetings with editors to pitch stories, the personal PR.

I was also tired of living in Toronto and of the flat, boring landscape of southern Ontario. Though I'd spent nearly all of my thirty-three years in cities, I had a notion that life would be simpler, maybe more satisfying, in a small town on the ocean or a mighty river, or with a mountain view. Maine was my first choice – Linda and I had gone to the coast of Maine three straight autumns – but I didn't know what I'd do when we got there. It was time for a little recon.

"You know," I told Linda, "I really don't have to be in Toronto to do freelance stuff. We could live anywhere."

Over weeks and months, this discussion eventually led me to suggest, "Why don't we buy a camper and just wander around? I could write stories from the road and maybe a book, like *Travels with Charley*."

This inspiration came not only from Steinbeck, but from my dog. Like Charley, he was a black standard poodle. Like his masters, his father was American, his mother Canadian. We got him as an eight-week-old puppy in the fall of 1978, after the baseball season. Naturally, I named him Yaz.

On April 1, 1980, with a small nest egg and a lot of dumb optimism, we left Toronto in our new fourteen-foot Mini Cruiser we called Fenway. I'd traded my '77 Mustang for the little motorhome in New York. It had a large bunk over the cab, another bed that could be assembled from the seat cushions and the dining table, a two-burner stove and small fridge, and a bathroom that doubled as a shower. It would be our home for a while, since we gave up our Moore Park apartment and put our furniture in storage.

The plan was to ramble west across Canada, pick up Kate at an airport somewhere in early July, drop her at another airport a few weeks later, drive down the coast to L.A., east to the Grand Canyon, north to Yellowstone, and then bolt across the northern states to arrive in Maine at our usual time, early October. I'd take a job on a paper, maybe in Portland or Bangor. We'd rent a little house on the ocean. I'd practice journalism, write a book, maybe call it Travels With Yaz, in my spare time and quit the paper when a New York publisher handed me a six-figure check as an advance against the inevitable bestseller royalties.

Meanwhile, we'd finance our adventure with stories from the road, stories nobody else would get because they were anchored in cities, not floating free across the continent. I had my Olympia portable and a list of editors who said they'd take the stories I found. Linda had the Nikon, three good lenses and darkroom supplies to develop film in Fenway's tiny bathroom.

Before we left, Americans told me, "Have a great time." Canadians said, "Have a safe trip."

I kept a journal. Filled it with ruminations and observations. Some themes emerged, starting with the first entry, the first night, camped in a snow-covered parking lot off a frozen lake a couple of hours north of Toronto:

April 1, Algonquin Park, Ontario
We're finally on the road. After months of talking and planning, we're doing ... After seven years in Canada, seven years of calling myself a New Yorker and feeling more and more Canadian, I feel like a traveler, passing through, unlikely to return.

April 21, Kenora, Ontario

Three weeks of camping. Needed a break. Checked into a Best Western motel, $34 for a king-sized bed and Jacuzzi. Had dinner in a restaurant next door. Filled up on drinks and appetizers and salad bar. Sent back two steaks. Chef came out to have a look at the complainant. We talked. He deducted my dinner from the bill.

April 26, Riding Mountain National Park, Manitoba

News on the radio from Iran – the U.S. raid to free the hostages was aborted, eight U.S. airmen killed ... And yet, when the day was over, all I could think about was the bears Yaz treed on our walk around the lake. Bunch of Germans in our campground. Told they're soldiers, training at the military base at Shilo, south of here. What can Canadians teach Germans about war?

April 29, The Pas, Manitoba

Had dinner in a motel restaurant. Sent back both our steaks. Overdone. Served two more steaks. Raw. Sent them back as well. Refused to pay.

May 8, Saskatoon

Went to a movie. Neil Simon. Chapter Two. Good movie. Bad choice. James Caan plays a New York writer, living in a New York townhouse. Taking taxis. Wearing different clothes every day. And me? I'm some fucking Okie driving across the prairies in a covered wagon, tin plates clashing in the back. Who the hell am I? So much of me is that New York writer with a house on the West Side. Going to restaurants. Playing softball in the Broadway

Show League. Going to Knicks games. That's me, right? But I don't want to live in that place. I don't want to live here, either. What the hell am I doing in Saskatchewan? SASKATCHEWAN!!! Maybe one day I'll reconcile my hate for big cities and my scorn for the sticks. Maybe one of these days I'll stay in one place long enough to know it and write about it ... When do I get out of this transitional stage? I'm almost 34 years old.

May 10, Saskatoon
Checked into the Park Town Motor Hotel, five stars in the Saskatchewan travel guide. Dinner in the Four Seasons lounge. This time I sent back the fish.

May 13, Drumheller, Alberta
After weeks in the Prairies, we're now in the Badlands. Found some little fossils. Lady at the makeshift museum said they were dinosaur bones. Took a little pull-ferry across the Red Deer River. Only a few minutes to cross, but enough time for the ferry operator, Bob – his name stenciled on his hardhat – to tell us that Albertans don't give a shit if Quebec separates and then tripped into the standard western rant about French being crammed down his throat. He wanted to know what we Americans were going to do about all those Cubans in Florida. I suggested we send them to Quebec to become trilingual.

May 20, near Kamloops, B.C.
After a week in the Rockies, heading to Vancouver. The radio says the "no" people won in Quebec – referendum on separation – where saying "no" means saying "yes" to staying in

Canada. Does this mean everything stays the same? Fucked up and hopeless for poor, confused Canadians.

May 23, Vancouver
Went to dinner at the Keg. After we filled up on booze and salad and bread and wine and appetizers, I declared our entrees inedible. The manager apologized and ate the check. Am I turning my New York attitude into a Canadian racket?

June 7, Larrabee State Park, Washington
Crossed the border today. The U.S. Customs guy was really confused yet arrogant. American man? Canadian wife? (He didn't see Yaz.) New York plates? Where's your home? I said: "Here. Or New York. Or Toronto. Take your pick." He finally waved us through. Immediately, I started looking for differences between Canada and the U.S. The freeways are nicer here. The supermarket in Bellingham was nicer — cheaper too — and it sold beer and wine. The lady at the checkout asked Linda for ID. Then she asked me. She said she was just following orders. Maybe Americans and Canadians aren't that different.

June 11, Olympic National Park, Washington
On the ocean, at a campground, surrounded by Washingtonians and Californians. People are quite friendly, in that superficial, suburbanite-on-vacation way. I feel like a Canadian here and an American in my own country ... WHAT AN ERROR ... I meant, an American in Canada. More comfortable set apart, looking in.

June 23, Okanogan Lake Provincial Park, B.C.
Heading back to Alberta to pick up Kate. Maybe the guys at the Edmonton Sun will give me some work.

June 26, Edmonton
Went straight to the Sun and straight into managing editor Kaye Corbett's office. He has given me some work, two features, and will give us some money up front. We need it to pay for Kate's ticket. I hate admitting that we're in such a bad way, but what the hell. Getting good at being poor.

July 3, Edmonton
KATE DAY. Got the kid. She looks wonderful. Grown up, though not yet twelve, yet the same. We're stuck here another day, waiting for a check from the Sun. Also sold a story to Pal Hal at Maclean's on an oldtimers rodeo.

July 9, Kootenay National Park, B.C.
Took Kate to Jasper, our favorite park in the Rockies, and Banff. Now exploring a new park. Made a desperate call to Hal today for money. He was in rough shape after his bachelor party but said he'd come through. Know he will.

July 11, Somewhere in the Bugaboo Mountains, B.C.
Had dinner with Rick and Ronnie and their three boys, Kurt, Erik and Brett, from Suffolk County, Long Island. We all looked like the Waltons sitting around the picnic table. Hal came through with payment on

the rodeo story. He and Kathy are getting married tomorrow. Sent them a telegram saying "wish we were there." Wish we were.

I didn't make note of Rick showing me his .357 Magnum, which he'd smuggled into Canada in case there was a showdown with a grizzly. Or, that I'd never understand why so many of my fellow Americans found the need to pack heat on their way to McDonald's.

My journal entries ended a few days later. Once Kate was aboard, there didn't seem to be time to write every night and I never again picked up the thread. But the odyssey continued. Back to Vancouver Island, down the Oregon coast, through the redwoods. We put Kate on a plane in San Francisco for her trip back to Switzerland.

In August, we spent a couple of nights with friends in Santa Barbara. I crashed on the couch and watched Teddy Kennedy fail to wrest the Democratic nomination from Jimmy Carter. Later, walking around the trendy town, I wandered into a trendy saloon.

"What'll you have?" the barmaid asked.

"Beer."

"Any special kind?"

"Whatever's good and cold."

She reached into a fridge and came out with a bottle of Moosehead. "Ever had this?" she asked.

"No."

"It's Canadian," she said.

"So am I," I said.

Heading south, we stopped at the Norton Simon Museum in Pasadena to visit with Picasso, Van Gogh,

Modigliani and others unlikely to encounter in a campground. Matisse's *Odalisque with Tambourine* would come along for the rest of the journey. Unlike at the Phillips Collection in Washington, there was no opportunity to swipe the original, so a poster had to suffice.

Leaving civilization and culture behind, we headed east across the Mojave. Camping on the California-Arizona border, a chatty neighbor told us about the upcoming Snake Dance on the Hopi Reservation in northern Arizona. Not about to pass up the chance to write about Indians dancing with snakes, that was our next destination.

But, when we got to Second Mesa – Or was it First Mesa? Or Third Mesa? – the warnings against drinking and photography nearly sent us packing. Still, we followed the crowd, climbed a ladder to the roof of some Hopi's house and stood under the noonday desert sun.

Pale-faced spectators filled the rooftops on both sides of the sandy, narrow street where the ceremony would presumably be performed. Some were lounging in lawn chairs, with coolers and picnic baskets at their side.

We'd been told by other visitors that Hopi priests would dance down the street holding venomous rattlers. But none of the locals I encountered so far would talk to me. I figured I'd wait until the dance was over and corner the snake handlers. So, we waited for the show to begin. And waited. And waited. And waited.

"I've had enough," I said to Linda after a couple of hours.

"Me too."

We climbed down the ladder, out to the dusty lot where Fenway was parked. Yaz needed a drink – so did we – and a walk. We heard a bit of a commotion – apparently the dance had begun – coming from the village but didn't bother to go back. We left just as a bunch of Hopi boys were releasing gopher snakes – not deadly diamondbacks as advertised – among the tourist vehicles in the parking lot.

We camped that night in leafy Oak Creek Canyon and visited nearby Sedona, a small western town with a few trinket shops and not many tourists. We drove the two-hundred-plus miles, four hours, around the Grand Canyon to the North Rim, my first glimpse into the abyss free of fog.

At dinnertime, I cooked chili, my specialty, in a cast-iron pan over a campfire. We sat on a boulder at sunset, watched the canyon's colors turn from yellow to orange to pink to purple. After dark, the dancing flames in the fire pit provided the entertainment, the scent of burning juniper an aphrodisiac.

We'd been on the road for five months. Rambling from the boreal forests of the Canadian Shield to the Rockies and the Pacific, down the coast to big cities and into the desert of the Southwest. Sticks to cities. Cities to sticks. But not all cities, or sticks, are created equal.

We went north into Utah, where we hiked among the red-rock spires of Bryce Canyon and spent the Labor Day weekend in Zion National Park, where much of *Butch Cassidy and the Sundance Kid* was filmed.

We were fit and healthy and awed by the landscape of the canyons. We were skilled campers, always prepared with firewood, food, water and beer.

David Cobb, a friend and editor of a magazine called *Today*, a weekend supplement in newspapers across Canada, kept us going with a $2,200 check for a story I'd done on looking for a hermit on Vancouver Island. It was enough to get us home, if we didn't linger anywhere too long.

Driving north, heading for Yellowstone, I got a speeding ticket on the Interstate outside Salt Lake City. Nice view of the Mormon Temple while the highway patrolman wrote out the summons. Didn't tell him I'd never pay the fine.

We spent a couple of nights in Yellowstone and the Tetons. Old Faithful was predictable. Enjoyed a long walk on a trail beside smaller geysers and unfathomable holes of boiling mud. A fleet of trumpeter swans buzzed us, trumpeting time to head south. After we got stuck on the road in a bison jam, and paused to photograph a bull moose in full antler feeding at the shallow end of a large lake, we headed east, the home stretch.

We stopped at Mount Rushmore to thank Teddy Roosevelt for all the national parks we had visited. Spent the night at another one, Badlands, where I found a pristine rattlesnake skin to add to our collection of souvenirs: the small dinosaur bones from the badlands of Alberta; moon snail shells from the beach at Denman Island, the Matisse poster from Pasadena.

From South Dakota, we stuck to the Interstates and crashed with family: Linda's sister Lois and her husband

Jim in Port Huron, Michigan; my sister Janice and Steven, who was teaching art at Penn State; my parents in Queens.

As planned, we arrived in Maine in early October. I walked into every newspaper office – Portland, Augusta, Waterville, Bangor – changing into a suit in the back of the motorhome. All the editors thanked me for dropping by. All said they had no openings. Besides, they said, I was probably over-qualified for a reporter's job and wouldn't be happy at their little papers.

We turned tail and went back to Toronto and moved into a small apartment. I fought with the neighbors, who played their music too loud. Everything was too loud – the subway, the buses, the trucks, the people, the whole damn city. Linda got a job with a PR firm. I went back to freelancing, again writing for *Maclean*'s, mainly sports on assignment for Hal – stories on such thrilling subjects as a gymnastic meet in Toronto and a new indoor soccer league.

One top *Maclean*'s editor, Bob Marshall, took me to lunch that winter and said, "You know, you could be making a good living just working for us. You're one of the few guys who can tackle just about everything, do it fast, and do it well."

"I know," I said, "but that's not what I want to do."

"What do you want to do?" he asked.

"I wish I knew," I said.

The next summer, I got a call from Tim Bragg, managing editor of the *Morning Sentinel* in Waterville. "You still interested in a job?" he asked.

"You bet" I said.

So we packed up again, and moved to Maine. On my first day at the *Sentinel*, the city editor, Glenn Turner, told me, "The guy you're replacing got a job at The AP in Baltimore. He's moving right up the ladder."

"I know," I said, "I passed him on my way down."

It was meant as a joke. He wasn't amused. And the joke would be on me.

CHAPTER 19
SAVED BY PETER, PAUL AND MARY

I never understood how anyone could be "over-qualified" for a job in journalism. You'd think every newspaper, from the *New York Times* to the *Waterville Morning Sentinel*, would want the best reporters, the best writers, the best editors available. When I was at the *Times*, I was told that Homer Bigart, the paper's most distinguished reporter – he had won two Pulitzers – was making more money than the managing editor, Clifton Daniel. I didn't know whether it was true, but it seemed right. If Bigart was better at his job than Daniel was at his, he should be paid more. If all news outlets did this, they would produce a better product. As it was, and has always been, a brilliant reporter had to take a management position to move into the next tax bracket. And, more often than not, first-rate reporters became third-rate editors. If the Peter Principle wasn't born in a newsroom, it flourished in most.

Moving to Waterville in July 1981 turned out to be my pipe dream. It would end in tragedy with the death of our first child two days after he was born.

What I hadn't considered in accepting the job was that Waterville was not the Maine we had visited every year. Our Maine had been the coastal affluence of Kennebunkport and Bar Harbor, of charming country inns and lobster suppers in the crisp fall air. The Maine we moved to was the inland poverty of decaying mill towns, of people living in shacks, hoping to stock the freezer with enough venison or moose meat to get through the long bitter-cold winter.

Linda found us a two-bedroom house in the woods for rent in the hamlet of Clinton, about a fifteen-minute drive from the office. It was far enough from town that we had no cable TV, only a couple of snowy channels tuned in with rabbit ears. I listened to Sox games on the radio. I couldn't decide which I missed more, TV or takeout Chinese food.

Fenway was our only vehicle. An oddity during the past eight months in Toronto, the little motorhome seemed less out of place here, except for the New York plates. I drove it to work each day, and often on assignment.

There were three other City Desk reporters. Terri Stanley a bit older than me, a grownup with kids, had turned to journalism later in life. She worked very hard, was very insecure about her writing and didn't want her reporting to offend anyone in her community. Bill Nemitz was younger, from Massachusetts, with a good grasp of the basics of journalism but no flair as a writer. He was the star reporter on the paper – before I showed up.

Brigitte Raquet was a kid, twenty-two, right out of school, Waterville's Colby College.

I started out doing routine work, covering meetings and going to the police station to check the overnight log of petty crime. I also hung out with the cops, listening to their stories and gripes. It seemed to me they were an unhappy bunch. I quickly convinced them to go on the record. What resulted was a front page story that began:

The Waterville Police Department is in crisis, a state of discontent that has working cops openly criticizing their superiors, publicly questioning their own safety and the safety of the citizens they're charged to protect.

I quoted seven cops, some with their names attached, others who would only speak with the promise of anonymity, plus two former Waterville officers who were anxious to tell why they left and taken jobs with other departments.

I presented the allegations to the police chief and the Republican mayor and printed their responses. They insisted the claims were exaggerated, that the rank-and-file was always grumbling about something.

It reminded me of the reaction to a story I'd done for the *Sun*, relaying the complaints of inmates in isolation at a maximum-security prison in Ontario. Some suggested I had been conned by the cons. My reply was that we always report what people in power say, some of which prove to be lies. Why not apply the same standard to the powerless? Let history sort out the liars.

My story on the Waterville cops was published on July 29, 1981, our third wedding anniversary. It was also the day Prince Charles and Diana Spencer married, obviously having picked the date to emulate the Beckers.

I was proud of the police story. Only later would I consider the message I was sending to my colleagues and bosses. I had been at the paper for less than a month. I was an outsider, a hotshot New Yorker from Toronto. If there was such a big problem in the police force, why didn't anybody break the story before? Were the *Sentinel's* reporters incompetent? Were they in bed with the mayor and the police chief? Were they unwilling to stir things up in their community? Had I taken the job on a lark? Was I planning to continually show up my colleagues before going back to the big city?

I knew right from the start that I was the best writer and most experienced journalist at the paper. That included my editors. I never stopped to think that others would not appreciate me waltzing into town with my big-city swagger and my tall tales about covering a terrorist trial in Zurich, *Dog Day Afternoon*, the rogue cop and F. Lee Bailey, the Kraut cannibal of the Northwest Territories, the Olympics and Major League Baseball.

I thought they enjoyed hearing my war stories over a beer and were inspired when I talked about writing. A few did. Most didn't.

In early February 1982, after I had been at the paper for six months, I was called into managing editor Tim Bragg's office. City editor Glenn Turner was there too, though he didn't speak.

"This is not working out," said Bragg.

"What's not working out?" I replied.
"Your work."
"My work?"
"Yes," he said, "we're not satisfied with your work. You've been here six months and your performance has not been what we hoped it would be."

I was dumbstruck. I had dominated the front page with stories no one else on the paper had the guts to get or the skill to write: on the plague of alcoholism in the community; on the case of a fifteen-year-old boy who shot and killed his ten-year-old sister; a three-part series on a new home for abused children.

Local politics never got my adrenaline pumping, whether it was in Livermore, Toronto or New York. I left the city councils and the school boards and the rest to the other reporters, who seemed committed to those beats. UPI had taught me to write stories that might interest every man and woman everywhere. I'd traveled throughout the state of Maine in search of such stories for the *Sentinel*.

I went to Bangor for a trial on a book-banning case. The school board in the tiny town of Baileyville, near the New Brunswick border, had removed the nonfiction book *365 Days*, by Ronald Glasser, from its high school library because the wounded Vietnam vets quoted used profane language. Federal judge Conrad Cyr insisted that "fuck" and all its derivatives be replaced with "the word" in all testimony in his court.

During the two-day trial, in December 1981, I interviewed three writers who had chronicled the war and were called to the stand to defend Glasser's book: Pulitzer Prize-winning author Frances Fitzgerald; Ward Just, one of my favorite novelists, who had covered Vietnam for the *Washington Post*, and former *New York Times* Vietnam correspondent Gloria Emerson.

It was a good story but a thoroughly depressing experience for me, since I wanted to be one of them, not a reporter for the Morning Fucking Sentinel of Waterville Fucking Maine. Sorry, Judge Cyr.

Yet here I was a couple of months later, sitting in the office of the managing editor of the Waterville Fucking Sentinel and being told I hadn't made the grade.

"Do you want to keep working here?" Bragg asked.

"Yes," I said, thinking that Linda was pregnant and due to have our baby in June, that I had no clue what I would do or where we would go if I was suddenly out of a job.

"We're prepared to give you one last chance," said Bragg, "assuming you'll shape up." I had no idea what that meant or how I might shape up. But I didn't want to argue, gave no reply. Didn't say I was the best damn reporter the *Sentinel* ever had and that it was lucky to have me.

Instead, I said "thanks" and got up to leave.

"Peter, Paul and Mary saved you," Bragg said. "Before that story, I was ready to fire you."

A few weeks earlier, I'd gone to South Blue Hill, near Bar Harbor, to interview Paul Stookey, of Peter, Paul and Mary fame.

The trio had split up in 1972, cut a reunion album in 1978, and just about to release another. I had read a bit about the breakup, which was blamed mainly on Stookey's born-again Christian awakening. But I hadn't found much on his side of the story. That's what I was after when, on a cold January day, I went to see Stookey at his home above Blue Hill Bay.

Stookey had called himself Noel when we talked on the phone to arrange the interview, so that's what I called him. I found out Noel was his first name, Paul his middle name. The group, he said, became Peter, Paul and Mary because it required fewer name changes than "Neter, Noel and Nary."

I was a big fan of Peter, Paul and Mary. I'd first seen them in the early '60s from a front row table at the Bitter End in the Village, with a girlfriend who had straight, blonde hair just like Mary, and again at Forest Hills with another girlfriend, after they were famous. I had several of their albums and played *Leaving on a Jet Plane* over and over before the first time I left Kate behind in Switzerland.

But it had been a long time since I'd been awed by a celebrity. When I had the notebook, I was driving the conversation.

Stookey and I talked in his home office/studio, a four-story henhouse that he had converted into a multi-media workplace he called Neworld. As I often did in an interview for a profile, I took him back to his childhood in Baltimore, his high school and college years in Michigan, his early years in New York where he met Peter Yarrow and Mary Travers.

I knew where I was going – to the story of the Jesus freak breaking up the beloved folk group – but I wanted it to come out slowly, chronologically, hoping for anecdotes along the way.

"Part of my search for God began in 1963," he said, "when I realized that having a million dollars and a townhouse in New York wasn't enough for me." He rambled. I prodded him back to the breakup of PP&M. "What happened was, here was this Jesus freak and they couldn't resolve how to deal with a Jesus freak. But we were all going through changes. Peter was very political. Mary was a feminist."

We talked for a couple of hours. I knew I had my story. The next day, back at my desk in Waterville, I worked the phone to track down Peter Yarrow and Mary Travers.

Peter wouldn't talk to me about the whole Noel-Paul-Jesus thing. But Mary was sweet and chatty. She went back through the origins of the trio and how it all fell apart. "One night, he (Stookey) got up on stage and did a whole thing about 'The Man, The Word and The Book.' We were playing Forest Hills, a mostly Jewish audience. Our musical director actually walked out. He said, 'I didn't come here to listen to Billy Graham.'"

I brought her around to the reconciliation. Mary told me Stookey was now "less strident, had his sense of humor back. He admitted, 'I lost it there for a while.'"

My story, which ran a few thousand words and filled two pages, appeared in the *Sentinel*'s Saturday supplement on January 30, 1982. It was the cover story, titled: *Peter, Paul, Mary, and Jesus, Now in Concert*. I inserted my approach to the interview in the body of the story.

> *He hadn't expected to be questioned about the rise and fall and rise again of PP&M, he said after the interview. But he answered questions forthrightly, with ease and good humor.*

For me, that was the key. To get him to talk about what I found interesting and newsworthy. I'd write it and move on. Probably never see Noel Paul Stookey again. That was okay with me.

CHAPTER 20
THE CELEBRITY INTERVIEW

Journalists spend much of their time talking with people the rest of the world sees only on TV – presidents, prime ministers, movie stars – or pays to see in person: musicians, comedians, athletes. For a reporter, it's tough, at first, not to be star-struck or to think you have a relationship with these people.

My first close encounter with celebrity was when I was in New York working with Richie Havens on his story – if you can call it that – for *Changes* back in 1969. The next year, during my first visit to Paris with Anita, we noticed that Havens was playing at the Odeon theater and went there to get tickets. Instead, we ran into Havens, who was arriving to rehearse.

"Remember me?" I asked him. "New York. *Changes* magazine. Last year?"

"Yeah, man," he said. "Why don't you come on in with us."

Anita and I watched Havens and his two band members rehearse, and then sat around and shot the breeze for a while, talking about home, and the differences between living in the United States and Europe.

Havens told an American in Paris story about his bass player, who was sitting with us. "So this cat is down in the lobby of the hotel and he sees this pair of shoes in a glass case. He wants a pair of those shoes, so he writes down the name of the store and goes out into the street and jumps in a taxi and hands the driver a piece of paper with the name of the store on it. The driver makes a U-turn, stops across the street, says 'ten francs,' and that's it. The store was right across the street."

It was a good story and a warm moment with three Americans at a time when I was an innocent abroad. Havens got us a pair of tickets for the concert that day – in one of those ornate boxes looking down at the stage – and we said goodbye.

Years later, in Toronto, this time with Linda, we went to see Havens at a small club downtown. I took Linda backstage between sets, showing off for my new girlfriend. Havens pretended to remember me, was very polite. But we really had nothing to say to each other. By that time, I should have known better. I'd already had some perplexing encounters with celebrities.

There was the rendezvous with Xaviera Hollander in her room at the Bayshore Inn in Vancouver, where fugitive Howard Hughes had taken up residence in the penthouse in 1972. She was in the city pushing her book, *The Happy Hooker*, and a new line of sex toys. She greeted me at the door in a loosely tied bathrobe, her considerable charms spilling out. I took a seat in a chair, she on the bed a few feet away.

When I was in New York with UPI, I'd heard a story about Hollander riding in a car with a young reporter and masturbating him with her bare toes while he was driving along the West Side Highway. Since I was not averse to mixing business with lechery, I waited for her move. At one point, she sat at the edge of the bed, leaned forward to give me a better view and planted her foot on the seat of my chair, between my legs. Then the phone rang.

She answered it, said "I'll be right down," cut off our interview, went into the bathroom, and told me to see myself out. Since I didn't have much of a story, I decided to catch up with her later in the day at the sex trade show where she was appearing. When I approached her booth, she cut me with a cold glance, said much too loud "are you following me?" and walked away. I left before she could return with a security guard, or a cop.

A few years later, in another hotel suite, in the Royal York, I had a strange encounter with Richard Pryor. He was in Toronto shooting a movie, *The Silver Streak*. I knew I could get a story out of the comedian who had won a couple of Grammys and made a big splash into movies, in *Lady Sings the Blues*. He invited me to watch him eat breakfast, at 2 p.m.

I arrived just ahead of the room-service waiter who wheeled in a cart topped with white linen, real silverware, platters of eggs, bacon, sausage, homefries, a stack of toast, pot of coffee, and one pitcher of milk, another of fresh orange juice.

Suddenly, the living room of the suite was filled with people, two women in various stages of undress, a couple of little kids, me and Pryor, who was wearing silky black pajama bottoms and a white T-shirt. The women and kids filled plates with food and retreated to the bedroom. Pryor began wolfing down eggs Benedict.

I pulled up a chair, put down my tape recorder, sat there and watched him eat for a few minutes before he said, "You can turn that thing on. We can talk. I only got about half an hour."

So we talked. About his albums, about the movie he was making and about how he went from being a potty-mouthed pariah to a Hollywood celebrity.

He told me he'd recently bought a house in North Ridge, on three acres in the San Fernando Valley. "But they didn't want me moving in," he said. "They stole my fence, stole my dog, cut the wires on my car. They even threatened my housekeeper, a nice old lady who wouldn't hurt anybody. It must be because I'm black. I haven't done anything. I've hardly been there. Man, can you believe this in 1976?"

He mopped up the last of the eggs with a piece of toast, took a sip of coffee, got up, said "be right back" and disappeared into the bedroom. About 20 minutes later, he came back, with his shirt off and a case of the sniffles.

"You still here?" he said.

"You said you'd be right back."

"Yeah, well," he said, a sly grin spreading beneath his trademark moustache, "sorry, but I really needed a blowjob."

One of my first assignments as a freelancer was to go back to the *Sun* newsroom to meet with actor Ed Asner. At the time, Asner was starring in the highly rated television show *Lou Grant*. He had moved the character from the *Mary Tyler Moore Show*'s TV newsroom to the city desk of a fictional Los Angeles newspaper.

Linda was still working at the *Sun* and had shown me an "appointment notice" that appeared in the newspaper: *J. Douglas Creighton, publisher, is pleased to announce Mr. Lou Grant has accepted the position of Senior City Editor.*

Of course, it was a one-day stunt, a typical piece of *Sun* self-promotion. What intrigued me was why Asner would go along with it. I did some research and found that Asner had recently been a speaker at a conference of editors and publishers in the United States. Why would they ask him? What could an actor tell real journalists? And why would Asner presume to take the stage in front of a roomful of real editors? Did he think he was the city editor of a real newspaper? Those were the questions I wanted Asner to answer. I pitched the story to a *Maclean*'s editor and he bit. I called Asner's agent in Los Angeles and arranged to meet the actor at the *Sun* newsroom.

Lou Grant's arrival at the *Sun* in March 1979 was marked by great fanfare and much enthusiasm from all the paper's staff, from publisher Creighton down. Local TV cameras caught the standing ovation and the gushing by the real editors and the fake editor pretending to be a real editor. When things calmed down a bit, I sidled up to Asner and introduced myself.

"Yeah, yeah, the magazine writer," he said, still in character.

"These guys think you're really Lou Grant," I said, summoning my most pronounced American accent. "Doesn't take much to fool these Canadians."

"Where you from?" he said.

"New Yawk," I replied.

"We'll talk later," he said, with a wink.

His first obligation at the *Sun* was to go to a morning editorial meeting. There had been no such meetings when I was at the *Sun* only a year earlier. But, I guessed, the same editors who mimicked dialogue from *All the President's Men* in giving Jane O'Hara and me the Maggie Trudeau assignment were now following the script to include the movie's scenes of Ben Bradlee's daily meetings with his top editors at the *Washington Post* and similar scenes from *Lou Grant*.

I stood in a corner and watched the show in the boardroom. Monteith went around the room, asking the assembled editors what was on the agenda that day. It was the usual collection of cops and courts, no mention of the Ayatollah Khomeini, who had just returned to Iran and was acting seriously scary, or Quebecers cooking up a referendum on separation.

Asner asked whether there were any plans to cover Pinochet cracking down on dissidents in Chile or the farmworkers strike in California. Faced with blank stares, the meeting moved on. When it got to my old boss, George Gross, he talked about hockey, went on to curling and baseball spring training and some rumor about some tennis player nobody ever heard of.

"What about the basketball?" Asner asked Gross.

"Basketball?" said the sports editor.

Asner swiveled in his chair and looked at me. Then at Gross.

"Why don't you ask Ken?" Asner said.

Everyone in the room, all my former bosses, turned to me. None was a fan of the guy who quit the paper a few months earlier.

Since I had the floor, I took it, trying not to smirk but not succeeding. "The Final Four," I said. "This weekend."

No one in the room, except Asner, seemed to know what I was talking about. The actor and I continued our conversation.

"Whodaya like?" he asked.

"Gotta like Indiana State and Larry Bird," I said.

"I'll take Michigan State," Asner said. "Gotta love Magic Johnson."

I felt like I was sticking it to Gross. No love lost there. Soon after, the meeting broke up. Asner still had several hours left of playing Lou Grant at the *Sun* and going to lunch with the bigshots. I wasn't invited.

I arranged to meet him at the main entrance to the *Sun* at 3 p.m. I got there just as he was leaving with Peter Worthington, my former editor-in-chief. He had arranged the charade with Asner and was acting as chauffeur. Asner invited me along for the ride. I climbed in the back. Asner was in the passenger seat.

Worthington drove while Asner and I talked some more about college basketball, which tripped into the NBA – he was a Lakers fan and I was a Knicks fan. When we got to his hotel, the august Windsor Arms, off Bloor Street, Toronto's Fifth Avenue, I got out and watched Asner say goodbye. Worthington watched my pal Ed and me go inside the hotel.

When we got to his suite, Asner excused himself, went into the bedroom, and returned wearing only boxer shorts and a T-shirt. I was just about to wonder whether I would have to fend off some Hollywood gay blade when he whipped out a bottle.

"You like single malt scotch?" he said.

He got two tumblers from the bar in the living room, poured a couple of fingers into each. "You gotta drink this stuff neat," he said. I nodded approval.

We slouched into comfortable chairs, sipped scotch and talked until after dark. He talked about growing up Jewish in Kansas City. I talked about growing up Jewish in New York. He talked about his father. I talked about my father. We talked about baseball, and Jackie Robinson, and the JKF and Bobby Kennedy assassinations, and Nixon and Watergate, and *All the President's Men*. Every time I tried to steer him to Lou Grant, he went elsewhere, about his admiration for Cesar Chavez and the farmworkers.

At about nine o'clock, the bottle empty, he got up and announced, "Time to go."

"Yeah," I said, "I should be getting home."

"Nah," he said, "come on over to my trailer. I've got another bottle."

He got dressed, grabbed another bottle of Glenlivet and we walked the two blocks to his trailer. He was in town to film a made-for-TV movie called *The Family Man*. He was the title character, who was fooling around with Meredith Baxter Birney. On this night, he would be shooting a scene with Anne Jackson, who played his wife.

He opened the bottle of scotch, poured two paper cups full, handed me a script and said, "I need you to help me run my lines. You read Anne's part. She's Maggie."

We sat at the small table in the motorhome in a no-parking zone on Bloor Street, protected by off-duty Toronto cops assigned to the movie location.

Asner got in character and I got drunk. When an assistant knocked on the door, and called him to the location across the street, he rose steadily. I less so. He gave me a big hug and a kiss on the forehead.

"I need to talk to you again – for the story," I said. "I don't have much."

"Call my girl," he said. "She has the shooting schedule."

The next day, I found out that Asner would be on the set in a warehouse on the waterfront. I showed up and waited for him to finish a scene. I sat down next to him on the sidelines.

"What do you want?" he said, obviously annoyed.

"I told you I needed to talk to you more, for the story," I said.

"Haven't I given you enough of my time?" he spat, and walked off.

I never wrote the story for *Maclean's*.

CHAPTER 21
DEATH IN A SMALL TOWN

In May of 1982, as a thirty-five-year-old ace reporter for the *Waterville Sentinel*, I received a UPI New England Newspapers Award. It wasn't much of a story and I was less than thrilled with a second place prize in a limited-circulation category. It was hardly a Pulitzer.

But, recalling my first interview with UPI, with foreign editor Jack Fallon in New York in 1969, it was ironic that my former employer was giving me a plaque for a story that opened with a quote.

I also took some satisfaction in being the only one on the *Sentinel* staff honored, considering my situation had not improved since I was told my work did not measure up. By this time, I knew that a cabal – reporter Nemitz, editors Bragg and Turner, and the paper's photo chief, Dick Maxwell – wanted me gone.

Everybody at the paper seemed to know what was going on, even the outdoors columnist, a courtly old gent named Gene Letourneau, who was rarely in the office.

"People around here don't exactly welcome newcomers," he confided.

But, with a baby on the way, I wasn't going anywhere without a fight. I just kept finding stories, commanding space on the front page. One person who seemed to be on my side was Bob Moorehead, the general manager, the big boss at the *Sentinel*, which was part of a small chain that included papers in Portland and Augusta.

Moorehead and I seemed to hit it off the first time we met, when he shook my hand, looked at my watch and asked, "Is that a Rolex?"

"Omega," I said.

"Good," he said with a laugh, "I don't want anyone on my staff wearing a more expensive watch than me."

He was just a bit older and had been a reporter and editor before moving up the ranks. We shared a love of the Red Sox and good writing. (He gave me a copy of Roger Angell's book, *Late Innings*, when I left the paper.) He was the one superior who congratulated me on my story on the Waterville cops, and regularly sent me notes praising my stuff. He didn't seem to want to get involved in newsroom intrigue, so I decided not to go to him unless Bragg and the boys tried to fire me.

When I won the UPI award, Moorehead said the paper would pay my way to the banquet in Framingham, Massachusetts, and that he'd drive me there and attend as well. We chatted easily during the ride south, until I said, "You do know what's going on with me, right?"

"Don't worry about it," he said.

"Maybe we'll talk after our baby is born," I said. "It's not a great situation."

"I know," he said.

Sean David Becker was born at 8:47 p.m. on Sunday, May 23, 1982 at the Mid-Maine Medical Center in Waterville. He arrived a couple of weeks early, but seemed to be a healthy six-and-a-half pound boy. I called our families and friends in New York and Toronto and spread the news.

I took Monday off and spent most of it with Linda and our baby. The new mom in the next bed was fifteen years old. Her mother, the new grandma, was Linda's age, thirty-one.

On Tuesday morning, at about six o'clock, alone in bed in the house in the woods, I got a call from Linda in the hospital.

"Is everything okay?" I asked.

"No," she said.

"Are you okay? The baby?"

"I heard them screaming 'Code Blue' in the middle of the night. I didn't know what it was. The nurses told me he wasn't breathing."

"Is he okay?"

"I'm not sure. They took him to Portland."

I rushed to the hospital. Linda was getting dressed. I found out Sean had gone by ambulance to the Maine Medical Center in Portland, where he was in the only neonatal intensive care unit in the state. That's where we found our tiny baby hooked up to machines, his eyes closed, barely moving, except for the occasional spasm.

His doctor, Douglas Dransfield, escorted us to a small, private room. He gave us the prognosis. Sean, he said, had stopped breathing the previous night in the nursery in Waterville. He had been resuscitated, but not soon enough to prevent brain damage. After arriving in Portland, he had had seizures. His vital signs were very weak.

If he lived, Dr. Dransfield said, our son's mental capacity would be negligible. But, he said, it was unlikely our baby would survive more than a day if taken off the ventilator that was breathing for him.

"Does that mean he's basically brain dead?" I asked.

"Yes," the doctor replied. He said it was our call.

Linda, who had given birth fewer than forty hours earlier, sat in a chair and cried. I held her and asked the doctor to give us some time to talk. We didn't have much to say. We knew what we would do. We told the doctor we wanted Sean taken off the ventilator. He suggested we find a hotel and someone would call us when the time was near.

"It could be hours," Dr. Dransfield said. "It could be days."

We checked into the Hilton. I called my parents in New York and Linda's mother in Toronto and told them the situation. I didn't phone anyone in Waterville. We went to the hotel bar, had a drink, telling the front desk to route any calls for us there. We were back in our room after ten o'clock when the hospital phoned. I answered.

"We think you should get down here," the nurse said. "Do you want us to call a priest to administer last rites?"

"No, of course not," I said. "Why would I want my baby to have last rites?"

Linda, raised a Catholic, burst out crying.

"Yes, please call a priest," I told the nurse.

We jumped in a taxi and went to the same small room we had been in before. It was very dark. A nurse brought Sean in and placed him in Linda's arms. She held our baby. I held her.

Sean hardly moved, barely seemed to be breathing. The nurse came back a couple of times to check his heart and respiration. The third time, she shook her head and said, "He's gone."

We sat there a while, a sad little family, our baby dead. It was 11:30 p.m., Tuesday, May 25, 1982. Our son had lived fifty hours and forty-three minutes.

Linda fell back on her Catholicism, God's will. As a nonbeliever, I had nothing to hold on to and nobody to turn to. I paced the halls of the hospital, went outside and screamed into the night.

Dr. Dransfield, who had been incredibly kind and inspired great confidence, had stayed the night with Sean. He came back to talk with us after our dead baby was taken away.

"You did the right thing," he said.

"I know," I said.

Linda didn't say anything. She was weak and totally spent, going from new mom to grieving mom in two days. I gave Dransfield permission to order an autopsy. We both wanted to know what killed Sean. We never found out, the results deemed "inconclusive."

I phoned the *Sentinel* and dictated Sean's obit to my colleague Terri Stanley. I could hear her sobbing while she typed. I didn't miss a beat, though she corrected me when I referred to Kate as Sean's "stepsister" not "half-sister."

My parents flew in from New York. The next day, we all went to Brooklawn Memorial Park and watched the tiny white coffin placed in a tiny burial plot. We stayed another night at the Hilton and then went back to Waterville. We knew we wouldn't stay long.

When I next went to the office, on my desk, I found a notebook that had disappeared before Sean was born. It contained all the notes I had from a day I spent on the campaign trail with Dick Pierce, a Maine state senator from Waterville who was running in the Republican gubernatorial primary in June.

I assumed it had been stolen by one of my bastard colleagues to sabotage my work, to provide an excuse to fire me. I guessed they reconsidered their plot after Sean died. That's how I interpreted the notebook's reappearance, anyway.

Generally, a great wave of sympathy rolled over Linda and me. Linda had worked at the paper too, part-time on the night sports desk, taking in scores of games. Being a Canadian, when she was given the score for a UConn game on the phone, she typed "Yukon," not knowing that UConn was the short form for the University of Connecticut.

Despite the difficulties during my ten months at the *Sentinel*, a lot of people in the community appeared touched by our tragedy. More than any other place I had worked until then – or later – readers responded to what a reporter wrote. I was constantly getting letters and phone calls from people who enjoyed one of my stories, even from people I wrote about. When Sean died, many of them expressed their sympathy in cards or letters.

One, in graceful penmanship on pale blue stationery, was professionally satisfying.

Dear Ken Becker,
I am a stranger to you but I feel as if I know you through your fine and sensitive reporting. It's to this person within the writing that I offer my most heart-felt sympathy ... I pray that you and your wife will find strength and hope.
Very sincerely,
Frances Sandmel

Another handwritten note, from the new Democratic mayor of Waterville, Nancy Hill, included a line I have since borrowed in similar circumstances. *My Irish ancestors have an expression used regularly when words cannot be found to express your feelings. "Sorry for your troubles" says it as well as any words I can find.*

Also in the mail was a bill from the ambulance service that took our dying baby from Waterville to Portland. I called them and told them to stuff it. "In Canada, they don't prey on the sick and the dying," I said and hung up.

A letter of condolence from Dick Pierce, in a bold script on his state government stationery, in fountain-pen blue ink, noted: *Winning and losing is so unimportant compared to what goes on in real life.*

My story about the day I spent with Pierce, written after my notebook resurfaced, was published a few days before he lost the primary election. It was the last story I wrote for the *Sentinel*.

Linda and I packed up our house in the woods. We knew we'd be moving to Toronto, the only home we knew. But first we went on another road trip, this one all about R and R, to a place we'd never been.

CHAPTER 22
UNDERSTAND NEWFOUNDLAND

On June 22, 1982 I steered Fenway out of our driveway in the sticks of Maine for the last time and headed north by northeast. Linda was still recovering from giving birth. She still sobbed when she was lost in thought. I didn't cry. I never cry. But I felt an empty place where my son was supposed to be.

We would camp that night on the ocean and remain within the sight and scent of saltwater for more than a month. During all my time in Canada, I had never traveled to the Atlantic provinces. Neither had Linda. Or Yaz, who had enjoyed the freedom of woodsy living but seemed happy to be with us on the road again.

We relaxed for a few days on the far north coast of Maine, in Cobscook Bay State Park, roughly the easternmost point in the United States. The sunrises were spectacular. Seals announced their presence when they floated in with the tide. When the tide went out, I dug clams. We dined on steamers one night. Linda made spaghetti with clam sauce another.

We crossed into Canada briefly, to check out FDR's place on Campobello Island, before making a more lasting break from the USA into New Brunswick. We spent a windy Canada Day at Fundy National Park and a hot sunny Fourth of July at Kouchibouguac National Park, on the Gulf of St. Lawrence.

Then, it was down to Nova Scotia to pick up Kate at Halifax airport. She was flying in from New York, after visiting with my parents. The board in the terminal said her plane had landed. We waited in the baggage claim area. And waited. And waited.

I questioned people fetching their luggage, people who looked like New Yorkers on vacation. *Were you on the New York flight? Did you see a thirteen-year-old girl with red hair?*

Most shrugged. One nodded. Another mistook me for a mugger.

When all the New Yorkers were gone, I accosted one of the commissionaires – the geriatrics who guarded the gates to security areas at Canadian airports – at the door to customs. "I need to find my daughter," I said.

"You can't go in there," he said.

"Then you go find her," I ordered. "She's thirteen. Has red hair. Her name is Kate Becker. She was supposed to be on the flight from New York."

"I can't leave my post, sir."

"Then get out of my way," I said, sidestepping the geezer and pushing through the door – right into Kate and a customs' officer.

I hugged my kid. "I take it you're the father," said the customs' man. "Would you come with me, please."

"Where?"

"My office."

"Why?"

"I have a few questions."

"About what?"

"About this young lady."

"What kind of questions?"

"Sir," he said, "if you don't come with me I'm not going to allow your daughter to enter Canada."

It was the same old bullshit, another brush with a tin-badged Canadian authority figure trying to push his weight around. The upshot was he thought my child looked like a teenage drug mule or some similar hippie undesirable.

"Do you have any evidence or cause to detain my daughter?"

"No."

"Then," I said, rising from a chair in his office and taking Kate's hand, "we're leaving." Which is what we did.

That night, in a campground on the ocean east of Halifax, I grilled a couple of porterhouse steaks Kate had brought – smuggled in? – from New York. For dessert, we had chocolate she had brought – smuggled in? – from Switzerland.

As she did during our 1980 trip, Kate slept in the high bunk, over the cab, with Yaz. He was happy to see her. We didn't talk much about the baby brother she would never meet.

We pushed on to Cape Breton, hiked some inland trails, dined on cod bought from a local fisherman, and made bonfires on the beach. On Bastille Day, we took the 11:45 a.m. ferry from North Sydney, Nova Scotia, to Port aux Basques, Newfoundland. Seven hours on the high seas. Sat on deck as the sunshine turned to fog and back again. Breaching pilot whales welcomed us to The Rock. As did a lone fisherman in a fast skiff, showing off his catch, hoisting a large cod with a smile – the smile was on the fisherman, not the cod.

The next day, driving up the west coast of the island province, we passed the town of Stephenville and its abandoned U.S. air base, opened during the Second World War, when Newfoundland was still a British colony. It did not become Canada's youngest province until 1949.

Outside of Corner Brook, we stopped at a visitor center where I added a lasting lesson in my continuing Canadian education. "How do you pronounce the name of your province?" I asked the nice lady behind the counter.

She smiled. This was obviously not the first time the question was asked. "It rhymes with understand," she said. "So the trick is – understand, Newfoundland."

I understood. And never forgot it.

I also quickly understood that this was like no place I'd ever been in Canada, or anywhere else. It was rocky and mountainous, bleak and barren. There were peaceful fjords in one direction, wild ocean in the other. Little pastel-colored houses perched on hillsides.

Some of the people were as alien as the place, spoke with an accent difficult to understand. Understand,

Newfoundland? Sure. Understand Newfoundlanders? Not so much.

And, it seemed, they found us odd as well – the Canadian-American couple with the Swiss-American girl, the giant black poodle and the little motorhome with New York plates.

One day, we stopped at a picnic ground in a village off the highway to have lunch. Dozens of children, from tots to teens, came out of their houses to watch us eat ham and cheese sandwiches. When I tried talking to them, asked if they wanted to pet Yaz, their faces went blank. Maybe they didn't understand New Yorkese.

We made our way up the coast to Gros Morne National Park, with its mountains rising out of the sea and picture-postcard fjords. Our neighbors in the Shallow Bay campground were a couple from California, roughing it in a motorhome the size of a Greyhound bus.

On Saturday night, we all went into the nearby metropolis of Cow Head for a drink at the only tavern in town. When a rock band started to play, and the noise became unbearable, we moved into an adjoining restaurant, which was closed. The manager, however, assigned a waiter to our beck and call after the Californian flashed a wad of Yankee greenbacks. Eventually, a bottle of scotch was left on the table.

On July 23, two months after Sean was born, we took the overnight ferry, sailing from Port aux Basques back to North Sydney. We gained back the half-hour we lost on the first crossing, since Newfoundland has its own, weird time zone.

On July 25, two months after Sean died, we were on Prince Edward Island. We bought hake, a fish I had never heard of, from a fisherman at the dock in Murray River. He filleted the hake and told us to fry it in breadcrumbs or batter with lots of spices. Not bad.

As I had all through Atlantic Canada, I inquired where we could get lobster. Every time, the reply was the same, "It's not in season here."

"When's the season here?" I would ask.

"Last month, and next month."

"Where is it in season now?"

"Somewhere else."

I never figured it out. In Maine, year-round, a seafood market on my route home from work had live lobster, delivered daily. It was cheaper than steak and always delicious.

On P.E.I., camping in Panmure Island Provincial Park, the clamming was good. (I'd bought a clam hoe in Calais – pronounced callous – Maine, before beginning our latest Canadian adventure.) We had our fill of steamers and spaghetti with clam sauce.

One night, after dinner, after Linda retired early and Kate and I sat around the campfire, a Korean gentleman from Toronto wandered over to show off his gigantic clam shells. "Your wife is very nice," he whispered to me, nodding toward my thirteen-year-old daughter.

We arrived "home" in Toronto on July 29, our fourth wedding anniversary. Kate flew back to Switzerland. Linda and I bunked in her mother's apartment in Thorncliffe Park, an unsightly collection of highrises overlooking the Don Valley Parkway.

I hadn't thought much about work, or an uncertain future, during our five weeks on the road. I just wanted to keep busy, keep moving, keep Linda from drowning in grief.

Linda went to work as a secretary in the corporate headquarters of Labatt's, the giant brewer that owned the Blue Jays. I started to get a freelance business going again.

We found a large, three-bedroom apartment on the ground floor of a duplex just west of midtown Toronto. The neighborhood was okay. But I hated the name of our street – Watford Road. Who'd want to have a mailing address on Watford? Wretched-sounding word. Now that we had a place to live, we needed our furniture and the rest of our stuff.

I rented a big mother truck, not as big as an Allied Van Line but not exactly a U-Haul either. Drove the Trans-Canada Highway to Montreal, followed the freeway to Sherbrooke, crossed the border at Woburn, Quebec-Coburn Gore, Maine, and followed a familiar route through mountains, past lakes, down to Waterville. The ten-hour drive took more than twelve hours in the big mother truck.

That night, I slept in the truck, in the driveway of the three-bedroom house of a former *Sentinel* colleague and his wife. "Thanks for the hospitality," I said before turning in.

My New York sarcasm never played well in Waterville. Neither did Jewish humor. I'd written a story for the paper on a lecture delivered at Colby College by Stephen Whitfield, a professor of American studies at Brandeis University. The subject was American Jewish humor.

There were some delightfully clever quotes in the story, including the stated aim of his lecture: "To be more attentive to *What Makes Sammy Run* than to what makes Saul bellow."

An editor placed the piece below three photos of Whitfield, with the headline, *Funny, he doesn't look Jewish* ... Funny, he did.

It was about what I'd expect from a Maine hick who didn't know Sammy Glick from Sammy Davis Jr. When I awoke with the sun in the cab of the truck, I could hardly breathe. Or, more accurately, I could breathe just fine but every breath hurt like hell. Can you break a rib sleeping?

The host of the driveway was kind enough to let me use the phone. I'd never been to a doctor in the area. The only ones I knew were Linda's obstetrician and Sean's pediatrician for the day and a half he was alive in Waterville.

I called the pediatrician, Dorothy Eisengart, a Jewish doctor. We had corresponded after Sean's death and she knew I was going to be in town. She had asked that I stop by. When I phoned her office that morning I was told to come right over.

Dr. Eisengart was still awaiting the final post-mortem report on Sean. But she diagnosed my ailment in a few minutes – pleurisy, an inflammation of the lung tissue. She gave me a prescription, and enough antibiotics and painkillers to get me home.

Properly doped up, a couple of kids helped me load the truck at the house in the woods in Clinton. I was okay to lift and carry, as long as breathing wasn't involved. I hauled pillows and blankets and the like. They did the rest.

I was on the road in early afternoon. Followed the same route back through the Maine woods, about three hours to the Quebec border at Woburn, a shack and two customs' guys. I had all my papers ready, an inventory of our belongings and my immigration documents.

Yes, I was emigrating from the USA. Once I got across, I'd be what was called a "landed immigrant" in Canada. After Sean died, after I quit the *Sentinel* and we knew we were going back to Toronto, Linda and I had gone to the Canadian consulate in Boston.

Just as I had sponsored her for a green card in the United States when we moved to Maine, she sponsored me as a landed immigrant in Canada. (UPI and the *Sun* had gotten me work permits before.) My application for immigration had been approved and the documents were at her mother Edith's house when we returned from our trip to Atlantic Canada.

So, all I had to do was drive the big mother truck a few more feet and I was landed.

"You cannot cross here," said the border guard, a young skinny guy with a moustache and a French accent.

"Whattaya mean?"

"We cannot process your papers here."

"Why not?"

"There are only so many ports of entry for immigration."

"Why the fuck didn't somebody tell me that before I drove all the way up here?" I was steamed. My chest hurt. I wanted a cigarette, but knew inhaling would make it hurt more. I climbed down from the cab of the truck and leaned back against the door.

The French-Canadian's customs' sidekick had wandered over to watch the show. I'd caught him smirking from the door of the border shack.

"Is there a problem here?" he asked. No two solitudes at this remote corner of Quebec. English and French working in concert.

"I'm just explaining to this gentleman that he cannot immigrate here," said Officer French.

"Then what's the problem?" said Officer English.

They appeared entertained. I was in pain and dreading my next question. "Where do I have to go?"

"The closest port of entry for immigration is Saint Stephen," said Officer English.

"Why the hell would I want to go to New Brunswick?" Saint Stephen is where we entered Canada from Calais, Maine, on our trip earlier that summer.

"Where is it that you are going?" asked Officer French.

"Toronto."

"Ah," he said, "then the nearest port of entry would be Rock Island."

"Where the hell is that?"

"Vermont," Officer English said. He was smirking again.

"Vermont!" I walked off, a few paces, back in the direction of the United States. I was breathing heavily and hurting badly. The concept of taking deep breaths to calm down didn't work with pleurisy. I tried to clear my head, not think about how far I was from home, how many more hours I'd be at the wheel of the big mother truck.

I didn't want to talk to these guys anymore. I climbed back into the cab and started to roll. It took four tries, forward and back, to complete a U-turn. I worked my way through the gears, got up some speed and stopped at the first gas station. Bought a map. Plotted a route that would take me to the border at Derby Line, Vermont-Rock Island, Quebec.

It turned out to be a six-hour detour across northern New England, mostly on two-lane roads, in the dark, washing down painkillers with Coke, to the border crossing. I arrived just before 10 p.m.

Unlike the narrow goat track where I met Officer French and Officer English, here were several lanes feeding into booths staffed by border agents.

I got in a lane reserved for big mother trucks, waited my turn, and presented my documents to a young woman in a crisp uniform with a starchy demeanor. "Pull over there," she ordered, pointing to a long, one-story building, "and give your papers to the immigration officer inside."

Déjà vu. Surrey, B.C., 1973. But this time I was prepared. Or so I thought.

The immigration officer stamped my passport. Did the same with the appropriate form to seal my landing. "Are you bringing any goods into Canada?"

I laughed. It hurt. I told him I had a truck filled with stuff. He summoned a customs' officer. I met the guy outside. We walked over to the truck.

"Take everything out for inspection," he instructed.

"You're fucking kidding me."

He glared at me. Tough guy. I glared back. Mexican standoff. Wrong border. Canadian standoff.

I opened the back double-doors of the truck. Extended my arm toward the jumble of furniture and boxes inside.

"Be my guest, but there's no fucking way I'm taking anything out."

I stood my ground. He blinked first, turned on a flashlight and climbed into the truck.

I succumbed to a cigarette. Coughed. Cringed. Coughed. Cringed. I stamped out the smoke and sat on a curb. The bastard took his time.

It was nearly midnight when I was on the road again. More than seven hours later, after dawn, more than twenty-four hours after I awakened in Waterville, I arrived in Toronto.

In October, we received the last post-mortem report on Sean, and a letter from Dr. Dransfield. It concluded:

> *I hope for you both that you can come to some acceptance of this final report with its lingering aspect of uncertainty. I want to emphasize the certain findings. No congenital anomalies were found. The brain injury was extensive as was so evident before death and it was of the hypoxic type (injury due to lack of oxygen). These findings to me suggest no genetic or hereditary reason to suspect that such a tragedy should happen to you if you have other children.*

CHAPTER 23
THE POPE AND THE QUEEN

By the new year, 1983, Linda was pregnant again. We'd settled into the apartment on Watford, hooked up the cable TV, bought a VCR, and ate a lot of takeout Chinese food. We traded Fenway for a nice used car, a brown AMC Eagle.

I was freelancing again. But, after being out of the loop for a while, assignments came tough. One night, in the bathtub, I was reading Russell Baker's memoir of his childhood, *Growing Up*. It was sweet and funny and evocative of his formative years in Virginia during the Depression.

In the steamy bathroom, soaking in the tub, I had an inspiration. I would call my dad and interview him about growing up in New York in the 1920s and '30s, before I came along. I didn't know much. I wanted to know more.

My dad and I did not always get along. When he managed our little league baseball team, he was hardest on his son. Through my teenage years, he became more and more competitive, asserting his status as the alpha male in the house.

My parents were very different people. My mother read books and was a devotee of the Broadway musical theater. Her son would be weaned on show tunes. My first of many Broadway shows was *Bells Are Ringing*, with Judy Holliday. For my twelfth birthday, my parents gave me tickets – to take my sister – to see *West Side Story* at the Winter Garden Theatre.

Dad was a working stiff who liked to play softball during the summer months and poker with his cronies year-round.

After I left home, I tried to improve our relationship. I invited him to Montreal, when I was working there, for a father and son weekend. Took him to an Expos game. Took him out to dinner at a Spanish restaurant down the street from my apartment, where I was a regular and got the VIP treatment. Took him to the press club in the Mount Royal and introduced him to my colleagues. He didn't drink much. Jews aren't boozers. But he seemed to accept his son as the exception.

He seemed especially proud of me when I was on the baseball beat. It would have been his dream job – other than pitching in the majors – when he was a young man. I got him tickets to Yankee games when I was in New York covering the Blue Jays.

Baseball was the strongest bond between us. That's where I took the story after I interviewed him on the phone a couple of times in early 1983.

The piece ran about five-thousand words. I called it *Red and Me* since I flashed back and forth between his baseball career and our baseball relationship. I particularly loved his tales of playing ball in the sandlots of the Bronx, the pictures painted of the borough of my birth in the years before the war.

> *Tall apartment buildings surrounded the field. Middle-aged men and women, mostly immigrants from Eastern Europe, sat and watched the games from rickety fire escapes. Boys in short pants pressed their faces against the chain-link fence. Girls in Sunday dresses perched on wooden benches. A ballgame was an entertainment for the neighborhood and the neighborhood turned out.*

During our interviews, dad was Red again. He may have been in his sixties, yet he was back in the spotlight, on the pitcher's mound. He seemed happy. Then, never one to hide his emotions, sad when he told me about the day his dream died during a mass tryout for the Giants at the Polo Grounds in the summer of '41.

> *The young men were arbitrarily divided into groups of ten or fifteen and assembled at the right field foul pole. Each group was directed to dash to the left field foul pole. When they arrived, most – Red included – were told to go home. "They never even saw me pitch," he'd tell me, more than forty years later. "I was fast, I felt sharp, and they never even saw me pitch."*

I would give the story to my dad for his birthday later that year. But, in the meantime, with Linda about halfway into her pregnancy, I needed a real job.

I touched base with a couple of former colleagues from UPI-Montreal, Bob McConachie and Marie Grebenc. They were now running United Press Canada, based in Toronto. It was no longer only a division of UPI. The *Toronto Sun*, which had sister papers in Edmonton and Calgary, had made a sizable investment in taking over the small Canadian wire-service operation.

UPC covered Canada from bureaus in St. John's, Newfoundland, Halifax, Montreal, Quebec City, Ottawa, Winnipeg, Edmonton, Vancouver and Victoria. The Toronto headquarters was in a converted warehouse loft, just east of downtown, a couple of blocks from the *Sun*.

Bob was the news editor, Marie the second in command. They gave me a job as an editor. I quickly moved into the night slot, the main man – like Lucien Carr – handling copy on deadline for morning papers.

A few months after I started at UPC, on August 17, 1983, at 7:15 p.m., Jodie Caitlin Becker was born in Mount Sinai Hospital in Toronto. She weighed seven pounds, fifteen ounces. She emerged screaming and nursed energetically. This was a relief to Linda, who recalled that Sean barely cried and showed little interest in feeding.

Still, we were seriously paranoid the second time around. We'd interviewed obstetricians and chosen one who worked at Mount Sinai, which had both maternity and a neonatal intensive care unit. We carefully selected a pediatrician associated with the hospital, explained our experience with Sean, and insisted that our baby be monitored around the clock.

Jodie was put in a bassinet equipped with an alarm to signal if she stopped breathing. The problem was the damn thing kept going off, to the point that it repeatedly panicked Linda and me, and drove the nurses nuts. We told them to turn it off. We decided this baby was healthy and strong, which she was.

Linda and Jodie came home from the hospital to our apartment on Watford. Yaz was happy to see Linda, curious and instantly protective of Jodie.

I had Jodie Foster in mind when I suggested the name. Guess I was stuck on naming my kids after actresses. But the name Jodie, unlike Katherine – or Katharine – was sporty, fun, not formal. It would always suit her.

After maternity leave, Linda went back to work at Labatt's. We hired a nanny, an English girl. Everything seemed smoothly on track, maybe for the first time for me.

By 1984, I was Toronto bureau manager for UPC. I had held this title before for UPI, but merely to manage myself – obviously a chore – in a one-man bureau. Now I had to manage a dozen or so reporters and editors in Toronto, which was the editing desk for all copy generated in Canada, as well as the relay point to Canadian clients for all UPI stories from around the world.

I was in management for the first time, which was unnerving after years of looking down at my bosses. It was equally strange to join a management team with Bob and Marie, who had been gung-ho union shit disturbers when I worked with them in Montreal.

Now, they were gung-ho management sharks. Screw the workers. When one employee became a troublemaker, I was told to schedule him on overnights – midnight to 8 a.m. – until he shaped up. When another looked like he wouldn't make the grade, I was ordered to fire him before his probation was up. I wasn't cut out for this part of the job, upsetting people's lives and livelihoods. But I loved being in charge on a big story.

And there were a lot of them to cover in 1984, including visits to Canada by Pope John Paul II and Queen Elizabeth II.

Early in the year, there was also some dramatic news from Ottawa. Pierre Trudeau, who became prime minister in 1968, announced he was quitting politics. No one saw it coming.

The enigmatic and supercilious Trudeau explained that he took a solitary walk in the snow that morning in Ottawa and decided it was time to go. It was February 29, leap year, an anniversary that could only be marked every four years. Typical Trudeau.

Then, in May, a Canadian army corporal, Denis Lortie, walked in a side door of the provincial legislature – pretentiously and prophetically, for some, called the National Assembly – in Quebec City. He was dressed in camouflage fatigues and carried two submachine guns. He said he had a beef with the separatist government of Premier Rene Levesque. He said he was hunting politicians.

He killed three government workers and wounded thirteen others before taking a seat in the speaker's chair in the legislative chamber. The sergeant-at-arms, Rene Jalbert, approached Lortie. Jalbert said he was a veteran of Lortie's unit, the Royal 22nd Regiment, and showed the young soldier identification to prove it. They talked for six hours before Lortie surrendered.

As our reporters at the scene called in every scrap of new information, I cranked out urgent leads. A wire story may start with only a shred of information, a few sentences, but grows as more details emerge and quotes are added.

At UPI, some of the best writers were editors, like Lucien. UPC worked the same way. The other editors and I would rewrite the copy from correspondents across the country, calling the reporters with any unanswered questions before it went on the wire.

I had no qualms about sending a rookie reporter right out of journalism school, Rob Russo, on the federal election campaign trail in his first weeks with UPC. "Just get all the quotes and take lots of notes, and call it in," I told him. "We'll take care of the rest."

Young Russo did the legwork, got the byline and the glory. I, or my best slotman, Allan Golombek, wrote Russo's stories top to bottom.

When Colin Thatcher, a well-known politician in Saskatchewan, went on trial for killing his ex-wife, our reporter in the courtroom, Bob Lee, never wrote a word. He'd phone in all the details of the day's proceedings – notes and quotes – and we'd write the story from scratch in Toronto. This resulted in one of my favorite leads, what I'd come to call the "Hamburger Helper defense."

SASKATOON – Colin Thatcher testified today that he was home eating Hamburger Helper when his ex-wife was being bludgeoned and shot to death in the garage of her Regina home last year.

One story that seemed frightening but turned out to be amusing, at least from where I sat, was the case of the Briley brothers, Linwood and James. The killers from Richmond, Virginia, led an escape of six inmates from death row in the state prison at Mecklenburg on May 31, 1984. While the other four fugitives had been recaptured quickly, the wily Brileys were on the loose for nearly three weeks. It was during this time that Canadian news outlets began broadcasting sightings of the brothers in Quebec's placid and picturesque Eastern Townships.

I figured someone in the area had seen a couple of black guys, a rarity in those parts, assumed they were up to no good, and called the cops. The gendarmes with the Quebec provincial police checked their most-wanted lists and settled on the Brileys.

Next thing you knew, cops armed to the teeth were combing woods and fields, setting up roadblocks and generally scaring the shit out of everyone in the province. We reported what the police said, and the hysteria they had unleashed.

While this went on for nearly a week, I talked daily with one of the editors in UPC's Montreal bureau, Nelson Wyatt. The information was so flimsy, we started joking about the phantom fugitives.

"Where do you think they really are?" he asked.

"Disneyland?"

"Vegas?"

"Probably never left Virginia," I concluded.

I was close. Linwood Briley, 30, and brother James, 28, were cornered and captured in their uncle's garage in Philadelphia on June 19, 1984.

The big challenges for me that year, though, were the Los Angeles Olympics that began in late July, the Pope's twelve-day tour of Canada in September, followed by the Queen's thirteen-day visit at the end of that month.

While UPI sent its usual team to L.A., we sent Canadian sports editor David Tucker and his one full-time sportswriter, Randy Starkman. Their job was to cover the Canadian team and put a Canadian angle on stories. While the UPI lead writer did a story on the opening ceremony for U.S. papers, Tucker did his own version for us – which I screwed up.

With the power of the last edit, I usually made the story better. This time I made it worse, turning Tucker's straightforward lead into an endless *New Yorker* sentence, with too many words and too many commas to count. When Tucker saw it, he phoned, furious. While I tried to argue the artistry of my sentence, he got madder and madder. Finally, I admitted he was right and sent out his original lead to sub for the monstrosity I had created.

By this time, more than ten years removed from UPI-NX, I had caught up with the Computer Age again. Before I left New York in 1973, UPI and AP were among the first to install video-display terminals, VDTs, in their New York headquarters.

Besides making the writing cleaner, if not better, the speed of editing a story and sending it on the wire increased significantly. For a poor typist like me, it was a gift from the gods of journalism.

One of the badges of honor among good wire service people is to recognize a mistake quickly and get a correction out ASAP, so the error is not published by a client newspaper. But since Tucker's messed up lead did not require a correction, only a new version of the story, I wondered whether any newspapers decided mine was better and printed it.

The Los Angeles Olympics garnered a lot of front page news in Canada. With the Russians and the rest of the commies staying home – payback for the West's 1980 boycott of Moscow – Canadians won by far their most medals at a Summer Games.

While UPC sent out the UPI story on many events, inserting how Canadians fared, nearly every medal won by a Canadian required a separate treatment, including quotes from the athletes.

With Canadians winning forty-four medals in L.A., we were busy "Canadianizing" stories every day of the two weeks of the Olympics.

Except for the blunder with Tucker's opening-ceremony story, I was hitting my stride as an editor. A good editor should take the same oath as a doctor – do no harm.

Our reporters and correspondents knew they would get a heavy edit, often a complete rewrite. Some bitched – mainly the political writers in Ottawa, since those working at the seat of power anywhere tend to have an inflated sense of their stature – but most appreciated better stories appearing in papers from coast to coast with their bylines.

I enjoyed the anonymity, the personal satisfaction, of writing under other people's names. During my years as a reporter, I had been like a pitcher trying to throw a perfect game every time out – craft the perfect lead, make every story a gem.

As an editor, I understood that the idea was merely to win the game – put out the best story possible, as quickly as possible, and get editors at the papers to use our story over the one from our rival, the Canadian Press. I was back in the wire-service game of winning logs. We did well.

But we couldn't compete with CP all the time. It had access to every story that appeared in nearly every paper – except the *Suns* – in the country. The best we could do was hit the big stories hard and get it faster. We practiced the UPI tradition of writing better, tighter and brighter than the competition.

Since the *Sun* had dropped CP when it started up UPC, our masters were always on our backs to match every CP story their competitors – the *Star* and *Globe* in Toronto – had.

In early September 1984, a bomb went off in the main railway station in Montreal. People were injured, maybe dead.

Our three reporters in Montreal went to Central Station. In Toronto, we worked the phones, calling Montreal police, hospitals, the railroads. I banged out leads as more information came in. In the middle of all this, I got a call from the *Sun*.

"How we doing on the Montreal story?" asked Paul Godfrey, a career city politician who had just taken over as the paper's new publisher, though he admitted when he took the job that he knew nothing about running a newspaper and less about journalism.

"Good," I said.

"Do we have people there?" he asked.

"Of course we have people at the scene," I said. "Our whole Montreal bureau is there."

"Is there anything we can do to help?" he said.

"Like what?" I said.

"I don't know," he said. "Just thought I'd ask. We're here to help you, you know."

You could help by not wasting my time with small talk, I didn't say. While I felt a certain comfort at UPC, it was creepy to again be under the thumb of the *Sun*.

As the story in Montreal unfolded, we learned that the bomber, Thomas Bingham, was an elderly U.S. Army vet. He managed to kill three people and injure more than thirty in some mad protest against the Pope's upcoming visit to Canada.

The next day was even busier. While still chasing fresh leads on the Montreal story, we had to cover a federal election. There was less drama on that front, as Brian Mulroney's Conservatives routed the Trudeau-less Liberals and his successor, John Turner.

All this was happening as we prepared for the Pope's arrival. Two UPI reporters – religion writer David Anderson and my old friend Peggy Polk from New York, now in the Rome bureau – would be traveling with John Paul. They would report on what he said and did in the context of his papacy. UPC reporters would cover what the visit meant to Canadians, cover the scene from the crowds, the participation of Canadian government and religious leaders.

While Peggy and David tagged along with the Pope's media entourage, we had to have reporters in place before the Pope arrived at every stop: in a small fishing port in Newfoundland and a remote Catholic shrine in rural

Ontario; at sports stadiums in Montreal and Vancouver; in the muddy Halifax Common and a muddier field at an old airfield outside Toronto, a scene reminiscent of Woodstock – up to half-a-million worshippers huddled in the rain for a performance by the rock star pontiff.

The Pope's tour was chronicled in thousands and thousands of words dictated to and transmitted from the UPC office in Toronto. I handled much of the copy, and all of the complaints from reporters who were cold, wet, tired and hungry. I responded with a line I'd heard Lucien bark on the UPI desk in New York. "You want sympathy? Check the dictionary. It's between shit and syphilis."

Personally, I couldn't care less about the Pope coming to Canada. My main concern was making sure I had a reporter nearby if he got shot, as he had three years earlier in St. Peter's Square. My favorite story from the visit was about the guy selling likenesses of John Paul for use in the shower, which he called *Pope-Soap-on-a-Rope*.

Marie Grebenc-Vosniacos, the *grande dame* of the newsroom, threw a big party in her swanky midtown apartment for the troops, with Peggy and David the guests of honor. As long as I knew her, Marie was rolling in dough and very generous. I have no idea where it came from but she was always elegantly attired, draped in mink in the winter. She drank like a whale and smoked like a broken tailpipe.

Three days after the Pope left, the Queen arrived. These royal tours were pretty predictable, though every event had to be covered. Canadians love their Queen. She showed up every so often, mainly when the weather was nice, to wave her way across the country.

Since she never said much worth reporting, that left the stories to be told from the point of view of people in the crowd. "Just make sure you interview every kid and old lady she talks to," I advised our reporters on the tour. "And, for god's sake, don't forget to describe what the Queen is wearing, from the hideous hat down to the sensible shoes."

My favorite Elizabeth story was told to me by a retired Canadian Forces colonel, who had been assigned to a royal tour, which required him to be on the plane on the flight from Britain to Canada.

"We were approaching the coast of Newfoundland," he recalled. "It was a beautiful day, not a cloud in the sky. You could even see the whales and icebergs in the water. The pilot asked me if Prince Philip might want to come up to the cockpit to see the view. So I asked the prince and Philip went up front, stayed there for a while and admired the view. When Philip turned to go back to the cabin, the pilot asked, 'Do you think Her Majesty would be interested in seeing the view?' Philip laughed and said, 'If it doesn't eat oats and fart, she's not interested.'"

While I mainly ran the desk and supervised the editors and reporters, Bob and Marie often spent time in their offices doing whatever administrative stuff had to be done. I only retreated to my office to make up staff schedules.

By late 1984, the *Sun* had appointed a new general manager for UPC, a very tall, very bald, very loud lout, a half-dozen years younger than me, named Ken King. Born and raised in a small town in Saskatchewan, King made his bones on the business side of newspapers in the west. He should have monogrammed his white dress shirts *Hatchet Man*.

I noticed Bob was spending a lot of time behind closed doors with King and that the two of them seemed to be going to a lot of meetings at the *Sun* building. I kept asking Bob what was going on.

First, he replied, "Nothing."

Then, it was, "Can't tell you."

Then, "I'll tell you as soon as I can."

I was feeling betrayed by Bob. I considered him a friend.

Just after the calendar flipped into 1985, Bob finally gave me the word. "The *Sun* is shutting us down."

"Does that mean we're all out of work?"

"I don't know yet," he said. "I hope not."

Before I got the verdict, I had to go to New York – to a funeral.

When I was growing up in Queens, nearly every weekend, it seemed, my parents schlepped us to the Bronx to see the grandparents. More accurately, my mother told my dad we were going to visit *her* family.

Her father, Louis Goldfarb, originally from some *shtetl* in Russia, met his wife Sadie, a Jewish refugee from the Austrian side of the Austro-Hungarian Empire, in New York. They had three children. First my Uncle Sidney, then Fay, then my mother, Dorothy.

I don't remember much about my grandparents. Louis was wiry and stern. Sadie was plump and sweet. He died when I was seven years old, she three years later.

The hallways in their apartment building on Gerard Avenue smelled like chicken soup. Or, perhaps, more like *schmaltz*.

Uncle Sidney and Aunt Ann lived down the street. So, after my grandparents died, we kept going to basically the same place. Same smell too. Aunt Fay lived nearby.

Everybody else in Queens and Long Island must have been making the same weekend pilgrimage because the traffic was always bumper-to-bumper on the Triborough Bridge.

If we went on a Saturday, shopping was usually on my mother's itinerary. She and Fay would hunt bargains at Alexander's on Fordham Road. Dad and I would sit in the car – I have no idea where Janice was – and listen to the radio, a ballgame or *The Lone Ranger*.

At least once a year – and reliably before school started – they'd take me to Sid's Slack Shop – Sid was Uncle Sidney – on 167th Street, just down the hill from the elevated subway tracks on Jerome Avenue. As a kid, I was never allowed to buy a stitch of clothing anywhere else.

Dinner with my aunts and uncle had two bonuses for me. First, my Aunt Ann was a fabulous cook, if you liked chicken soup with *lokshn*, chicken fricassee with meatballs, and other Jewish specialties. Which I did.

But the real treat was spending time with my cousins, Elaine – who changed the spelling of her name to Ylain when she was in college – and Carol. Older sister Ylain was a super-achiever who went to Hunter College at sixteen and graduated phi beta kappa.

Carol was super-cool. She took me to the movies, taught me how to dance to rock 'n' roll before I, and a bunch of kids from my junior high class, appeared on the New York version of *American Bandstand*, with Duane Eddy as the guest star.

Uncle Sidney, who never had much schooling, was a wise and imposing man, taking his place at the head of the table at family dinners, whether it was an ordinary weekend evening or leading the Passover seder.

As the only boy, I would ask him the Four Questions at the seder. He never mocked my performance in the duet, but regularly expressed his disapproval as I grew older and failed to meet his expectations – to be what he considered a serious person, a top student, like Ylain.

In mid-January 1985, I flew to New York to attend Sidney's funeral at Riverside Memorial Chapel on the West Side of Manhattan.

Linda was home with year-and-a-half-old Jodie. I went straight from LaGuardia to the chapel the night before the service. The family was there.

There was no viewing. Jews aren't big on that. But, for some reason, I wanted to see Sidney's body. Maybe it was the reporter who wanted to confirm the fact of death. Maybe it was the writer doing research.

Carol's husband, Steve Feder, took charge of my request. While the family was in an adjacent room, a funeral home minion opened the casket for me. I took a moment. "You can close it again."

I'd seen dead people before, starting with those little kids in Livermore with their heads blown off. I'd been to funerals before, mostly notably the grand show for Jackie Robinson.

But I'd never seen the body of someone I knew so well in life. It was not a profound moment. Just another thing I needed to experience.

The next day, after the cemetery, we went back to Aunt Ann's apartment for the traditional post-burial nosh – platters of deli meat, potato salad, coleslaw, and the like. While wolfing down a genuine New York pastrami sandwich, I also managed to put my foot in my mouth.

Ylain had written an obit that was published in the *Times*. I read it at the dining room table. My only comment: "You spelled judgment wrong." Asshole!

I flew home that night, took a cab to the new house Linda and I had bought five months earlier in Mississauga, about twenty miles from downtown Toronto. The western suburb with the long, funny, unpronounceable Indian name had always been someplace I drove through on the freeway, on my way to someplace else, usually the border.

In any case, I had never ventured into the section of Mississauga between the freeway – the Queen Elizabeth Way, QEW for short – and Lake Ontario before Linda spotted a fuzzy black-and-white picture of a house in the *Globe* real estate pages and wanted to check it out.

It was a small, Cape Cod-style, built in the 1950s by the owner, now being sold by his widow. The inside was dreary and rundown. But the property was seductive for a kid from the Bronx – about a half-acre with a mighty oak and an evergreen in front, apple and pear trees in the back.

I envisioned Yaz running in the backyard, Jodie and I having a catch, tossing a football. Room to play, trees to climb.

The house was at the foot of Clarkson Road South in what was once the village of Clarkson, named for an original settler who, like me, was an expatriate from the state of New York. Within walking distance were a series of parks running down to the Great Lake, and the Rattray Marsh, a conservation area with walking trails, deer, muskrats, foxes and other critters. Plus, lots of birds, both migrants and residents.

We moved in around Jodie's first birthday, in August 1984. Kate was living with us as well.

Anita had called me and said, "I can't control her anymore. She says she's moving to Paris to take a job as an *au pair.*"

"No, she's not," I said, "Send her to me."

In the new old house, Kate occupied a room off the kitchen – she called it "the maid's room" – while Linda and I had one bedroom upstairs, Jodie the other.

We enrolled Kate in Clarkson High School. She was hard to place, since she had not had much of an education in Switzerland. She spoke English with a cute Swiss-German accent. Spelling and grammar were not her strong suits. She studied my Oxford dictionary and filled the margins with notes.

I insisted she start in a class with students her own age – she'd be sixteen in December. I didn't want her feeling alienated in school, as she had been in Bern. Kate would excel at drama and find an ally in her drama teacher.

When Kate was at school, Bridget, from Belfast, looked after Jodie. She showed me a scar on her shoulder from a shrapnel wound, a reminder of The Troubles in her homeland.

For me, life in the suburbs was not all that different than life in the city. I commuted by car, which took about the same amount of time on a rush-hour freeway as it had in crosstown traffic. I still went out for drinks with my colleagues after work.

Linda and I went to ballgames, sat in a row of Labatt's seats behind home plate at Exhibition Stadium. At the end of August, I caught a foul ball hit by Carl Yastrzemski in his last visit with the Sox to Toronto before he retired.

I rejoined the Fireside League with an expansion team I named the Clarkson Expats. Gord "Duke" Shank had taken over the Rivers when I left on our cross-continent trip in 1980. The Quinn brothers and the others were reluctant to mount too many expeditions to the western suburbs, so I played mainly road games in Toronto.

In summer I cut the grass. In fall, I raked mountains of leaves from the oak on our front lawn and the maples that lined the road. In winter, I shoveled our fifty-foot-long driveway.

It doesn't snow all that much in and around Toronto, though the sun seems to disappear in November and not reemerge until late spring. There were times when a winter storm would blow through, leaving high drifts just north of us and barely a dusting in our neighborhood near the lake. Karma dumped most of the snow on Buffalo before it reached us anyway.

I went to Buffalo for the *Sun* after the Blizzard of '77. Photographer Hugh Wesley, often a sidekick on assignments, and I drove down from Toronto, where there was no snow on the ground. No snow along the hundred-mile route, either. Cross the Peace Bridge. Bam! Snow apocalypse.

Following tales of looting, Hugh and I plowed through the streets to Arnold's Arsenal, a gun shop which was doing a brisk business with white folks. Arnold, the proprietor who tossed the N-word without shame, proudly showed off his deadly wares.

We also dropped in on the county executive, and told him Toronto had these giant snow-melting vehicles. "You just drive one of those suckers down the street and it melts the snow beneath it and pours the water into the tank at the back," I explained. "Get all your streets cleared in no time."

On our advice, while we were in his office, he called Metro Toronto chairman Paul Godfrey and arranged to have the super snow melters sent. We found out later that Godfrey had come through, but the Army Corps of Engineers couldn't figure out how to operate the machines.

Now, in January 1985, that same Paul Godfrey, as publisher of the *Sun*, was melting United Press Canada.

I was thirty-eight years old, with a wife, two kids, a dog, an Irish babysitter and a mortgage, just getting on my feet and squared away, and I was out of work. Or so it seemed.

The news proved more shocking than anything I imagined. United Press Canada was being sold – for a buck, I was told – to Canadian Press. Everybody would be offered a job, either at CP or the *Sun*. For most of the young people – the reporters and editors who worked for me and most of the correspondents across the country – this was good news. At least they'd have a job.

For me, it was a choice between going back to a paper I despised, which was turning into more of a tabloid rag every year, or go to a wire service I considered the enemy.

I had spent much of my career loathing AP and CP, trying to beat them in every conceivable way. I felt like Jackie Robinson must have when he was traded from the Dodgers to the hated Giants. Robinson quit.

"I think I'd rather go back to the *Sun*," I told Bob.

"We don't have a choice," he said.

"Where are *you* going?" I asked.

"To the *Sun*," he said. "But they're not offering you anything. As managers, they don't have to offer us anything at all. But that's part of the deal, that we all get offered a job. The *Sun*'s only taking a couple of us, me and Allan, and, of course, Ken King."

"How long have you known about this?" I asked.

"It's been in the works a while," he said.

I called Linda at Labatt's.

"Do you think the *Sun* would take me back?" I asked.

"You hate the *Sun*," she said.

"Yeah, but I hate CP more."

I called Hartley Steward at the *Sun*. He was the managing editor and, like many in Toronto's journalism community, he'd bounced around from one paper to another and back again. I'd known him for years.

He said I could come over for a talk. I did most of the talking. I begged. I pleaded. I almost choked up a couple of times. He said "sorry," and that was that.

Over the next few weeks, managers from CP came to the UPC office and interviewed all of us individually. I kept the reporters and editors busy, trying to beat CP with some good stories before we closed up shop. I didn't say much in my interview, after being handed a letter that began: *I'm pleased to offer you a position in Toronto as a reporter-editor on the Universal Desk. It is possible you may be reassigned within the bureau if circumstances change.* It was signed by Andre Prefontaine, General Executive.

I arranged a meeting with Prefontaine in his office. He was a well-groomed, well-tailored fop, more business-man than journalist.

I asked about severance pay. It wasn't much, ten grand. I asked what my duties would be if I accepted his offer. He explained that the Universal Desk was an editing operation, mainly for smaller papers across the country, that I would be editing stories already on the CP wire, making them shorter.

I suggested this didn't sound very challenging and reminded him I was the Toronto bureau manager at UPC. He said I was being offered twenty-five bucks merit pay in deference to my management position at UPC, adding, "You can't expect just to walk into a manager's position here."

Haughty bastard! Typical AP/CP. Thought themselves superior, when I knew they turned out crap compared to UPI/UPC. I asked Prefontaine for more time to think about it. He said I could take three weeks – without pay.

I went back to the UPC office, thoroughly depressed and uncertain what I would do next. It didn't help that my final days with UPC would be spent arguing with Ken King, who was trying to pick the pockets of the corpse of the wire service. It got especially nasty when he accused one of the young reporters of trying to cheat the company with an overtime bill that I knew was legit.

One of the benefits of working at UPC was that the office was above a bar called the Montreal Bistro. It was a stylish joint run by a Swiss-Canadian couple with a taste for jazz and good food and treated its regulars well, even delivering burgers and fries and glasses of beer to the UPC desk for those working late.

On the evening of January 31, 1985, the UPC staff gathered for the last time in the office before retiring to the Bistro. The farewell was full of laughter and tears, the way these things usually go, I guess. At midnight, the UPC wire would be switched over to the CP wire, supposedly a seamless continuation of service for all clients. A couple of us went back to the office to witness the event. The first item on the wire after midnight was a CP correction.

CHAPTER 24
WHO'S JACK KENNEDY?

I would spend the next ten years with Canadian Press. To no one's surprise, least of all mine, it was a rough ride. I believe I shocked the CP brass when, after taking the three weeks to think about their offer, I decided to accept it. From the conversations I had with Prefontaine and the personnel manager, Norm Graham, it seemed they were hoping I'd take the ten grand and disappear.

In the years before a baby, a teenager and a mortgage, I would probably have talked Linda into another adventure. Instead, I decided to tough it out, to fight. Our little band of Unipressers would show the bastards how to run a real wire service and would eventually take over. (Our ranks would eventually produce an Ottawa bureau chief, foreign editor, sports editor and some of CP's best writers.)

Besides, with Bob gone to the *Sun* and Marie, in her early fifties, taking severance and retiring, I was the most senior UPC manager at CP, which made me feel responsible for the younger draftees.

My days on the Universal Desk were drudgery. But I made the best of it, turning some dull CP copy into bright UPI-like stories. Tighter, written with flair.

I showed my new colleagues how to write a quirky yarn with an eye on a surefire front-page box, instead of the CP or AP norm of turning a man-bites-dog story into a 500-word thesis, including the history of the breed of dog. "Four paragraphs, maximum," I instructed, "and you'll get front pages across the country."

I tolerated the scut work for months, getting to know the CP people while keeping an eye out for my UPC colleagues. Rob Russo, the kid I had sent out on the federal election campaign the previous fall, was among the most discouraged working beside me on the Universal Desk. "This work is for cretins," he said one day.

"Don't worry," I told him, "we'll get you out of here." He would soon move on to CP's Montreal bureau and quickly up the ladder.

My plan, if there was one, was to keep my head down, my nose clean and establish relationships with the men – they were all men – who could advance my career and do the same for the others from UPC.

In my first performance appraisal – I had never before experienced such bureaucracy – Universal Desk supervisor Mike Brown wrote: *I can't say enough about the professional way Ken handled his arrival at CP. He won himself a million friends with his co-operative approach when he came to CP… Younger colleagues from UPC looked to him for guidance, especially in the early days.*

After nine months on the Universal Desk, with stints on the Foreign Desk – rewriting crappy AP and Reuters copy – I made my move. There was a posting for foreign editor. I applied for the job.

In response, in November 1985, I got a note from Peter Buckley, the top editor in the newsroom: *Your bid was a good move. And your positive attitude, in the face of discouraging circumstances is certainly to your credit.*

The same day, I also got a note from the executive suite, from Jim Poling, the managing editor who would have the final say on the foreign editor's job. *While there are a variety of factors at work in this posting which don't allow me to be encouraging at this time, I think we should have a talk about how we can make the best use of your skills. I hear encouraging things about your work and attitude.*

When Mike Brown moved across the newsroom to become Ontario bureau chief, he invited me along, to run the desk at night as slotman. The work was more interesting, taking stories from the *Toronto Star* and the *Globe and Mail* – the *Sun*, now back in the CP fold, had little to offer – and turning them into readable wire service copy for placement in papers across the country.

The Toronto papers would send them to us at night, when they were supposedly ready for publication in the next day's editions. They'd be available to all CP members, except in the city where they originated.

I supervised the staff on the rim, getting them to stop simply cutting stories from the bottom, as had been their practice, and rewrite them into tighter, better copy. It was always an eye-opener for new CP employees, especially those who aspired to work at the *Star* or the *Globe*, to see just how awful the copy was when you picked it apart.

CP member papers didn't exactly appreciate it when I called their editors to ask about holes in stories or to check facts. To which I politely responded, "If the copy wasn't so damn confusing to begin with, I wouldn't have to call you all the time."

One night, handling a story from one of the *Star*'s star reporters, I smelled something fishy. It was trumpeted an "exclusive" on the meltdown of the nuclear power plant on a Soviet submarine in Arctic waters.

It sounded familiar. I did some checking in CP's electronic morgue, a rudimentary computer system that contained a couple of years' worth of archived stories. I called the *Star*.

"This story," I said, "was reported months ago by *60 Minutes*, and also by *Jane's Weekly*."

"I'll check into that," the *Star* editor said.

"Let me know," I said, "because, as is, there's no way I'm putting this story on the wire."

I never heard back from the *Star*. I didn't put it on the wire. The next day, the submarine story – possibly cribbed from other sources and clearly old news – was presented as an exclusive on the front page of the *Star*.

About twenty months after I started at CP, I had a new job and Linda and I had another baby. Lacey Megan Becker arrived on August 19, 1986. I plucked her name from my memory of a *New York Times* reporter I admired, Lacey Fosburgh. I swore it was coincidence that my last two children were born nine months after my birthday.

Soon after Lacey joined the family, I was sent to the hospital to get fixed. Yaz, who was never neutered, was now eight years old. Jodie was three – Sean would have been four – and Kate was seventeen.

We all lived in our little house in Clarkson, with the enormous backyard, the apple and pear trees that bloomed in the spring and bore fruit in the summer. I hung a swing on one of the apple trees. We had a big deck built to better enjoy the great outdoors in the Great White North, weather permitting.

I was promoted to "general night editor" of the Canadian Press. I was forty years old and had climbed back to a position of some authority. As the title suggested, I worked nights, 4 p.m. to midnight. My duties were to check every story on the CP wire, determine whether there were any problems that needed fixing and ensure that they were fixed.

Since most of the major stories of the day moved between four and seven for the next day's papers, I needed to be quick off the mark. Peter Buckley, the general news editor, my immediate supervisor, usually left at about six, which left me running the news service from my post, which was called Main Desk.

The frustration, of course, was that I was dealing with stories already on the wire. That didn't allow me to improve the writing, though I often ordered new versions of a story when I found the lead buried or the copy incomprehensible. I spent a lot of time on the phone talking with CP news editors across the country, ordering fixes.

Not surprisingly, the Ottawa bureau was the biggest pain in the ass. Since I was the new guy on Main Desk, I was tested at every turn, to the point I had to order "just fucking do it" and move on to the next task.

Buckley, not one to ruffle feathers and always eager to avoid confrontations, arranged for me to go on a goodwill tour of the bureaus, starting with Ottawa and Montreal in April 1987.

I pretty much got the cold shoulder in Ottawa and it wasn't much warmer when I arrived in Montreal. The most welcoming were the refugees from UPC, including Russo.

Another, a photographer, gave me a tour of the bureau's darkroom. The walls were decorated with photos not intended for publication, candid closeups of couples having sex in the backseat of cars, women flashing their breasts and the like.

When it was time for evening aperitifs, the bosses punched out and left me alone with a couple of grunts on the night shift. I was sitting at an editor's desk when all hell broke loose.

A TV station had gotten hold of the Quebec budget before it was scheduled to be released in the legislature and was broadcasting details. Government budget documents are closely held secrets, since new tax and spending policies can tilt stocks and other money markets.

I took over the story, directing the grunts – not a derogatory word in my book – to work the phones and feed me whatever they got. I pounded out lead after lead for the wire. The Montreal news editor returned, pitched in, but left me in control of the story.

In the middle of all this, the Ottawa bureau was breaking news on Prime Minister Mulroney and the provincial premiers reaching an agreement on what became known as the Meech Lake Accord. It was a constitutional bribe to tamp down separatist sentiment in Quebec, recognizing the province as a "distinct society" within Canada.

The most prominent opponent of granting Quebec special status was Pierre Trudeau. As a French-Canadian, he considered it patronizing. And, if there was one thing the Liberal Trudeau couldn't abide, it was being patronized, especially by the likes of the Conservative Brian Mulroney. Fellow Quebecers, they were the Bette Davis and Joan Crawford of Canadian politics.

"Somebody call Trudeau, get his reaction," I hollered across the newsroom.

"I'll do it," said Rob Bull, a drinking buddy from the press club during my time in Montreal with UPI.

A few minutes later, Bull came over to me and said, "He's not home."

"You know where he lives?"

"Everybody knows where he lives."

"Good," I said, "go to his house and bang on his door."

Bull looked at me like I'd told him to go to the Vatican and wake up the pope. But he got his coat and left.

The bureau took up the third floor of the *Gazette* newspaper building, in Old Montreal, with its cafes and cobblestones, majestic Notre-Dame Basilica nearby. Trudeau lived a couple of miles away, in an art deco house on a flank of Mount Royal, behind McGill University.

I figured Bull would go to a bar and call an hour later to say Trudeau wasn't home. Around midnight, he returned to the office. "He wasn't there," he said.

Our work done, Bull and I and a few others walked over to Au Cepage, their local watering hole, a crowded, cozy little bistro. Taking our drink orders, the bartender said, "You just missed Trudeau." He pointed to a corner of the restaurant. "He was right over there, having dinner."

I slapped Bull on the shoulder and laughed. "If you would have done what I thought you'd do, you would have got him."

My position on Main Desk put me in management, back among the schemers. One day, the top honcho, Jim Poling, asked me about an employee, an Ottawa desker who was approaching retirement age. Poling wanted to push him out the door ahead of schedule.

"How do we get rid of this guy?" he asked.

"Well, Jim, we could tell him he's been incompetent for the past thirty years but we hadn't noticed it until now. Or we could find out who hired him, and if that guy is still around, fire him instead."

"You're kidding, right?" he said.

"Not really," I said, showing my disgust with bosses screwing around with people's lives.

Poling was a smart guy and probably a good journalist. But when reporters and editors are Peter Principled to an office outside the newsroom, they seem to spend a lot of time daydreaming and scheming.

Poling did not confide in me again about personnel matters. The Ottawa desker later accepted an early-retirement package.

There was no question that CP, in the late 1980s, was on a youth kick. The top brass, all men older than me, had nothing to lose. They had reached their career goals.

They could appear magnanimous – and in tune with the times – by promoting young staff, especially young women, who would not challenge their power or authority.

One new appointment to Main Desk – there were three of us working around the clock – was a young woman who one day turned to me with a puzzled look on her face. "I'm trying to get all these Kennedys straight," she began hesitantly. "There was John Kennedy, the president, right? Then there was Bobby Kennedy, who also got shot. Teddy Kennedy is the one who went off the bridge with that girl, right? But who the hell is this Jack Kennedy I keep hearing about?"

Another young woman who had a meteoric rise to Ottawa bureau chief was last seen sitting on a curb outside the bureau, bawling uncontrollably. Others fared better. But the push for younger managers obviously didn't include me. It also didn't help that I didn't mind embarrassing and showing up the bosses.

When the news flashed that Canadian sprinter Ben Johnson had tested positive for steroids after winning the gold medal in the 100-metre dash at the 1988 Seoul Olympics, I gathered key staff and marched into Buckley's office for a quick meeting to plan coverage.

Buckley rose from his chair, went to his coat rack, put on his jacket and excused himself. "I'm going to get a haircut," he said. While I banged out leads through the night, Buckley, freshly groomed, occasionally stood over my shoulder and pointed out typos.

The Canadian media quickly shifted from writing about "Canadian" sprinter Ben Johnson winning gold to "Jamaican-born" sprinter Ben Johnson being stripped of his medal. Soon, Johnson had a new first name, *Disgraced*, as in "Disgraced sprinter Ben Johnson ..."

By the late '80s, in addition to an influx of women in key positions, there was a much more earth shattering change in the newsroom – smoking was banned.

When I worked at UPI in New York, there were brass spittoons on the floor and ashtrays on every desk, though we routinely stomped out butts on the carpeting, which had to be periodically replaced.

I'd smoked in newsrooms from Gotham to Livermore, Zurich to Waterville, Montreal to Toronto. I laughed in recognition when Dustin Hoffman, as Carl Bernstein, lit up in an elevator and Redford/Woodward asked, "Is there anywhere you don't smoke?"

At CP, the woman who took over Main Desk after me always arrived with a bottle of disinfectant and a scowl directed at my overflowing ashtray.

I once heard John Updike say in a TV interview that he lit a smoke every time he was stuck in his writing. It was my habit as well. Going outside to smoke was a routine that took some getting used to. It was also a bitch in winter in Toronto, and once nearly put me in handcuffs.

During the 1988 summit of G7 leaders, Margaret Thatcher and Ronald Reagan were bunking, separately I presume, at the King Edward Hotel across the street from the CP office. I was outside having a smoke when I was suddenly surrounded by cops in suits.

They put me up against a wall. One patted down me down, going straight for my waistband, and extracted the box of du Maurier from the small of my back.

The four Secret Service men – I spotted their telltale triangular lapel pins – relaxed. Handed back the pack of cigarettes. Didn't say a word and retreated across the street. "Nice talking to you guys," I called out after them.

Later that year, I moved from Main Desk to become Ontario news editor – filling in for a woman on maternity leave – back in a position to have my hands on copy before it went on the wire. One of my duties was to go to morning news meetings – the model from *All the President's Men* had become a ritual at every news operation.

Poling sat at the head of the conference table and the rest of us were supposed to show how brilliant we were in planning the day's coverage. This was also a time to discuss story ideas to be developed.

One day, Buckley, a smart and sophisticated Montrealer who had been an award-winning journalist in his day, offered in his slow, ponderous way, "Did you ever notice that all these right-wing politicians out west are Dutch?"

Bill Vander Zalm was the premier of British Columbia. I couldn't think of any others. "Are you suggesting," I asked Peter, "that we write a story with a lead that says 'most of the right-wing politicians in the west are of Dutch origin'? What's the second sentence?"

This drew muffled chuckles around the table but failed to ingratiate me with the powers that were. The daily dog-and-pony shows were designed to emphasize who were the dogs and ponies, and who was the ringmaster. Besides, we weren't putting out a newspaper, deciding what would be on the front page, what prominence we'd give certain stories. We were running a wire service, churning out copy as fast as we could.

Poling also had a habit of arriving at these meetings with clippings from his local paper, the *Mississauga News*, and tossing them down the table to me, the Ontario news editor. One was about a post office being torn down in his neighborhood. "I think we should look into it," he said.

"Why?" I asked. "Do you think tearing down a post office in Mississauga rates the CP wire?"

"It might," he said. "You never know until you look into it."

"Yeah," I said, "maybe Jimmy Hoffa's buried in the basement."

I really didn't care if I pissed off the bosses. I preferred to suck down, not up. I'd taken a group of young journalists under my wing. I convinced bureau chief Mike Brown to allow our best reporter, Steve Thorne, to cover only big stories and not have to work any editing shifts, as the others did. "A newsroom is not a democracy," I told Mike. He agreed.

I ran the Ontario bureau as a meritocracy, which made the good ones work harder. I didn't give a damn about weak sisters and malcontents. I championed the work of the best reporters, inviting them into my small office as I edited – rewrote – their leads, structured and tightened their stories.

I took them out for drinks after work, at a tacky bar called Cyrano's – owned by a tacky Greek – with shiny black tables and red Naugahyde cushions on the high backrests of the booths. We talked about writing until closing time. Some appeared as devoted to me as I had been to Lucien Carr. But while they showed great loyalty and gratitude, they had their own careers to worry about and were in no position to promote me. I'd alienated all the people who were.

In 1990, my days as Ontario news editor were over. The woman I had been filling in for had returned from maternity leave.

The reporters and editors, the kids who had worked for me, threw me a going away blowout at Cyrano's. They gave me a giant bottle of Dewar's for the road.

I woke up in a taxi in my driveway in Clarkson. When I got into the house, I realized the cabdriver was on his way home wearing my Omega, the watch I'd bought in Switzerland more than twenty years earlier, and drinking my Dewar's.

I still have the other gifts from that night, the notes and cards from the kids on the Ontario Desk. One read: *Thanks for your help, time, patience ... You have an endless stream of energy that is infectious. I have learned from watching and listening.*

From the bosses, I got a take-it-or-leave-it offer of my old job on Main Desk. The people who offered it knew I wouldn't take it. They were right. I'd spent too much time working on breaking news and polishing reporters' copy to go back to obsessing over stories already on the wire.

I elected to tread water on the rim of the Ontario desk, working the night shift alongside the people I had been supervising, rewriting stories from the newspapers. At least I was working with words.

I was called to action one last time, the night the bombs started falling on Baghdad. I wrote the main leads on the story for weeks, while coordinating CP's coverage of Canada's participation in the Gulf War. But once the war was over, I was cast aside, back on the rim.

Sliding down the ladder at work, my wanderlust returned and Linda agreed to move if the opportunity was right. I applied for one of the plum positions at CP – London correspondent. I knew I wouldn't get it. I didn't. There was some talk of a position in Ottawa as a feature writer but that fizzled.

In May 1991, I applied for the job of Vancouver news editor, in a five-page, single-spaced screed to the personnel manager, Norm Graham, suggesting CP had discriminated against me because I was over forty, had been passed over in favor of younger, less qualified applicants. It said in part:

> *I know you have told me that news editor jobs are designed for younger staff, that they are training grounds for higher management. But the fact is, CP is now populated from coast to coast with bureau chiefs and news editors in their 30s and younger.*
>
> *Is there not room for one polished, proven professional wire service editor over 40 to do what he does better than most – coordinate coverage, rally staff to chase news, offer story ideas, exhibit judgment and improve writing skills. Is there not a place for someone who has spent the past six years improving the CP report?*

Graham replied in a two-page single-spaced letter. It emphasized that I lacked interest in anything other than writing and editing news, that positions such as news editor included paperwork and administrative duties.

I felt I had been fighting forever to steer clear of the bullshit, to be left alone to practice journalism. Let others, less skilled, do the chores. My mind, in such times, always returned to the legend of Homer Bigart, the *New York Times* reporter paid more than the managing editor. Amen. Why was I stuck in a dead-end job in a company I never wanted to join in the first place?

Norm Graham concluded his letter with a kiss off. *I recognize you are frustrated and, by the tone of your letter, angry with the company ... Frankly, I doubt we can provide you the job you really want. It does not exist and we won't be creating it.*

I wanted to punch back. I'd get a shot in before I walked out the door. But, by then, there were also significant family issues to deal with.

Kate, at twenty, had eloped with a Swiss guy who would not have been my ninety-ninth choice for my first son-in-law. Stefan Beyeler, five years older than Kate, spoke little English. He had a questionable past – drugs and such – and not much of a future.

Still, Linda and I threw them a proper wedding in our backyard, in May 1989, with family and close friends and Anita flying in from Switzerland. The young couple would wander aimlessly from Bern to Honduras to New York, a constant worry.

Later that year, we visited my parents in Florida. My dad had retired, and they'd bought a house in a new development of lookalike red-tile-roofed bungalows in Lake Worth, near West Palm Beach.

The previous two winters, Linda and I and the kids had vacationed in the same cottage on the other side of the state, on Sanibel Island. We'd loved our spot on the beach, on San Carlos Bay. But we couldn't turn down the invitation to stay with my parents, to see their new digs.

They'd told me about their house on a lake. I pictured *On Golden Pond*, not the little manmade tank we started calling "the puddle."

The back lawn down to the puddle was spiky Bermuda grass, dotted with fire-ant hills. Jodie, at six a responsible and devoted big sister, took charge of steering three-year-old Lacey clear of danger.

The puddle was swampy, not fit for swimming. But the girls, both competent swimmers, enjoyed the pool for residents and guests of the Egret Isle gated community.

As long as they were outside, things were fine. But grandma and grandpa were fanatical about maintaining the pristine state of their first brand new home and all their brand new furniture. Playing in the house was frowned upon. It wasn't long before my parents made it clear we were no longer welcome. We'd been there less than a week. Linda and I had spent one of those days assembling a gas barbecue we'd bought them as a housewarming gift.

I told my parents we were leaving. They didn't protest. I found an envelope with five-hundred dollars in cash among my things when we were packing. I left it behind.

With more than a week remaining in our vacation, we drove to Sanibel without a place to stay. The tourist bureau found us one large room with a kitchen in a rundown house right off Sanibel-Captiva Road, across from the Ding Darling National Wildlife Refuge.

We spent much of our time in the refuge – we had become enthusiastic birders, and Ding was bird heaven – and at the beach. We made an unscheduled stop in Disney World on the way home.

The drama with my parents would change my relationship with them forever. I would keep in touch, never considered shutting them out entirely, but maintained an emotional distance.

We'd stop at their house for a couple of days each year – when we went to Sanibel, back to the cottage on the bay – but Linda and I would book a hotel for us. By then, my parents wanted their grandchildren to stay with them.

These winter vacations necessitated us getting a dog-sitter to look after Yaz. By 1991, he was thirteen years old and ailing badly. He could barely walk. I had to carry him up the stairs in our house. He fell down them a couple of times. The anti-inflammatories and the painkillers weren't doing much good.

He had been a wonderful companion. I thought about our walks in the Moore Park ravine. And Travels with Yaz on our 1980 road trip. The bears he treed in Riding Mountain. The porcupine that got the better of him in the Rockies. Running on beaches from Vancouver Island to California, from Maine to Newfoundland. Walking the trails in the Rattray Marsh. Always running ahead, then looking back, waiting for me to catch up.

Playing catch in the backyard. Playing hide-and-seek with the girls in the house. "Yaz, go find Jodie." He did. "Yaz, go find, Lacey." No problem.

Snuggling in bed. On the couch. In Fenway. Face licks. I never minded.

I didn't have the heart to take him to be put down. Linda did it for us that July of 1991.

In August, around the time of the girls' birthdays, we got a puppy. Black, male, standard poodle. We named him Jasper after my favorite park in the Canadian Rockies – yes, I seemed to be in charge of naming kids and dogs.

At Canadian Press, I was languishing on the editing desk when the president of the company, Keith Kincaid, announced that he was creating an annual award for extraordinary contributions by employees. He was nearing retirement and this would be his legacy. The President's Awards would be in two categories: one for journalism, and the other on the administrative side.

Late one night, during a break from my duties on the rim of the Ontario Desk, I composed a long letter nominating myself for a President's Award, lauding all my extraordinary contributions to CP. I gave it to one of my most trusted colleagues, asked her to sign it and to collect signatures from other reporters and editors. The letter went across the country and back. I pretended to know nothing about it. Left no fingerprints.

In March 1992, the first President's awards were announced, the winners each receiving $1,000 and a plaque. I didn't win, but I was told the number of nomination signatures was so high that Kincaid could not ignore it. In a circular distributed to staff, Kincaid wrote:

Ken Becker, reporter-editor in Toronto ... receives an honorable mention for his ongoing contribution to CP's editorial report. His work helps CP shine. It is multi-dimensional in that he guides others, edits, rewrites, and writes features and spot news equally well. Younger staff who nominated Becker cited the high journalistic standards he sets for them.

After making the announcement, I was told Kincaid went ballistic. "What the hell is Becker doing working nights on the rim of the Ontario Desk?" he asked his senior managers. "Can't we find him something better to do?"

I was transferred – banished? – to the features department as a fulltime writer.

CHAPTER 25
AUTHOR! AUTHOR!

In middle-age, I wrestled with the conflict between being a news hound and a writer. As a writer, I preferred the softer, quirkier stories. But I never lost the desire to be at the center of the action, if not necessarily on the scene.

During my time in the Canadian Press features department, the sports editor reeled me in to write the main leads on the 1992 Albertville and Barcelona Olympics, and to write sidebars on the 1992 and '93 World Series games in Toronto.

But, while I still had the itch to go back to the newsroom and take charge when a big story was happening, I never again had my hands on the controls at CP. I'd sit out the L.A. riots, the bombing at the World Trade Center, the election of Bill Clinton, the conflagration in Waco, O.J. Simpson – American stories that interested me deeply and were front page news in Canada.

I was interviewing a little known Canadian author in a restaurant in Toronto when I heard about the bombing in

Oklahoma City. I had nowhere to go, except to carry on the conversation about his novel.

Our little group in the features department was called Arts-Life. The Life side covered food and fashion, as well as health issues. The Arts side did movies, TV, music and books, which became my beat.

The first author I interviewed for CP was Tony Hillerman, whose mysteries set on the Navajo reservation were among my favorites. I met him in his room at the Sutton Place hotel in Toronto and discovered that he had worked for UPI, in Oklahoma City and Santa Fe, in the 1950s.

A half-hour later we were still telling UPI stories, mainly about its legendary cheapness. My contribution included a lengthy retelling of my failed effort to get to North Vietnam in 1972.

He chuckled all the way through my tale. "Sure sounds like the UPI I knew," he said, "get the news but hold down expenses."

We finally got to the interview, about his new book, *Sacred Clowns*. Before saying goodbye, I congratulated him on getting out of the news racket when he was still young and offered that I planned to soon make my escape and do some real writing. In my copy of Sacred Clowns he wrote: *To Ken, Another of us Hold Down Club refugees. Good luck.*

I enjoyed chatting with writers whose work I admired – Joseph Heller, Pat Conroy, Tim O'Brien, Nelson DeMille, Carl Hiaasen. But I was starting to yearn to be on the other side of the interview, the author not the reporter. In my mid-forties, I believed journalism was something I would outgrow, that I was destined for something more.

If meeting with good writers proved disorienting, meeting with "authors" who couldn't write a lick was infuriating. My job was to give the newspapers stories they wanted. Which meant I had an obligation to score interviews with every well-known name stamped on a book jacket.

Since Toronto was a must-stop on most book tours, the publishing houses were constantly calling, knowing my stories on the CP wire would be printed in papers across Canada. That meant I would sit down with the likes of Wolfman Jack, Dan Quayle and the rudest person I ever interviewed, a Nobel Peace Prize laureate.

In the fall of 1994, Archbishop Desmond Tutu was in Toronto promoting a book called *The Rainbow People of God: The Making of a Peaceful Revolution*. It wasn't really a book, just a collection of his sermons, speeches and letters between hard covers being sold for thirty bucks apiece.

His publisher arranged for me to join Tutu for lunch at the Four Seasons hotel. All eyes followed the great man, wearing a dark suit-jacket over his trademark red cleric's shirt, as he strode into the restaurant, trailed by a personal assistant and a Doubleday publicist. The other diners were probably thinking what I was – he's a lot shorter than he looks on TV.

I rose from my seat at the table to shake his hand but he didn't take it and sat without introduction. I moved to put my small tape recorder in front of him. But this time he extended his hand, palm out, a stop sign. "Not until I have had my drink," he said.

He ordered a Jack Daniels mixed with ginger ale and sipped it without making eye contact with anyone else at the table. When he finished, he turned to me and said, "Now, ask me your questions." I got in about three before the waiter returned with lunch.

"That's enough," Tutu told me, motioning for me to turn off the tape recorder and shut up. He ate a bowl of squash soup, rose and left the restaurant without saying goodbye. I turned to the publicist. "What a jerk." She rolled her eyes. I finished my club sandwich before catching a cab to the CP office.

I wrote what was basically a news story, on Tutu's reaction to the announcement that day of the latest members of the Nobel Peace club, Yasser Arafat, Yitzhak Rabin and Shimon Peres.

Going into these interviews I rarely had an agenda. There were obvious hooks to a story when the person was in the news. But most of these "authors" were just flogging their books.

An exception to my no-agenda approach was an interview with the former vice president of the United States, Dan Quayle. The only question I wanted Quayle to answer was, "Are you as dumb as I think you are?"

Getting to the question, I knew, could be tricky. I'd first have to gain his confidence. For the occasion, I wore my best – only – suit, navy blue, with a blue oxford shirt and dark blue tie. I usually wore Wrangler jeans, the blue Bean oxford, Nocona cowboy boots and an Akubra Australian cowboy hat. The only time I felt uncomfortable in my work clothes was when I interviewed a real cowboy, singer Ian Tyson, and realized he might think I "dressed up" just for him.

I met Quayle in his suite at the downtown Crown Plaza hotel. He greeted me with a handshake and a practiced smile. We sat down and I asked him about his golf game – he was a good golfer and making some appearances on the celebrity circuit – to get him warmed up. I moved on to his plans for running for president in 1996, which gave me an opening.

"In your book," I said, "you write about spelling potato with an 'e', the misquoting of the United Negro College Fund slogan, and your feud with Murphy Brown, a fictional TV character, for having a baby out of wedlock. Do you think those incidents will come back to haunt you in the campaign?"

It wasn't exactly "how dumb are you?" but it allowed me to pose the question in my story, and quote his response. "If I decide to run, in a weird way, this could be quite helpful," he told me. "There will be a natural tendency to say, 'here's an underdog, here's somebody who's getting off the mat, here's somebody who's been treated grossly unfairly. Let's give him a break.'"

Arranging interviews with visiting authors, whether they were political has-beens who couldn't spell or real writers, was pretty much the same routine. Every day, my desk at CP would be piled high with boxes of new books from all the major and minor publishing houses. Inside each book was a press release hyping the book, but also announcing where the author would be stopping on his or her publicity tour.

If I noticed an author would be in Toronto, there were two things I considered before arranging an interview: whether it was someone whose work I read and enjoyed, or someone whose name was known well enough to grab the attention of editors across Canada. Celebrity stories usually got better play than the ones about real writers.

Since I chose mainly to write about Americans, I'd often make clear that I was one of them, which made us both visitors in a foreign country. I also had a habit of mimicking the accent of the person I was interviewing – I could put on a southern drawl, western twang or New York crude – and decide quickly on what vocabulary to employ.

I wouldn't say "fuck" with Tutu or Quayle, but dropped it in every other sentence when I sat down with Wolfman Jack in a hotel bar, talking about the life he had chronicled in his book, *Have Mercy! Confessions of the Original Rock 'n' Roll Animal*.

"Just call me Wolf, man," he said when we were introduced, before the conversation got going, him chain-smoking unfiltered Camels and slurping espresso.

At the end of the interview, he wrote in my copy of his book: *To Ken Baby, A man who knows. Yes, you're the best. Your friend always, Wolfman.* Our friendship didn't last long. A couple of days later, the fifty-seven-year-old disc jockey, born Robert Smith in Brooklyn, dropped dead of a heart attack at his North Carolina home.

I was writing news features, with the accent on news. But that didn't stop me from putting a personal stamp on a story, conveying my takeaway on the experience of the interview. Some of the people I met along the way presented more of a challenge than others. One was crime novelist Patricia Cornwell, who seemed utterly delightful and completely nuts.

We met in her suite at the Four Seasons. The publicist left – they always returned exactly when your time was up, generally after an hour or less – and another woman, who looked like a cross between Janet Reno and Arnold Schwarzenegger, retired to the next room and closed the door. "She's my bodyguard," Cornwell confided.

This led the interview down a path I hadn't expected. Cornwell was promoting her latest book, *The Body Farm*, which I had read and liked. But now I wanted to know why a novelist needed a bodyguard. Cornwell was happy to oblige – in great detail.

I came away thinking this woman had morphed into her crime-fighting character and was seriously paranoid. I didn't offer a psychiatric diagnosis but got the point across.

> **TORONTO (CP) – Patricia Cornwell travels with a bodyguard, stays in hotels under false names, demands police protection at public events and always has a handgun handy when at home in the United States.**
>
> **"When you become wealthy and well-known, you draw a lot more attention to yourself in a bad way," she told me. "I can't even have a book-signing in the United States without police there because there are problems with obsessed fans – we've had some menacing people ... Every single fan letter is looked at to make sure this isn't someone we should worry about."**
>
> **Sounds a lot like the on-the-edge exploits of Dr. Kay Scarpetta, the fictional chief medical**

examiner of Virginia, who has hunted and been stalked by serial killers and other psychos in Cornwell's five novels.

Some interviews with authors were a lot more fun. I had a great time cracking wise with Dave Barry, trying to prove to myself that I was funnier than he was and equally deserving of a syndicated humor column. Having established that we were both forty-eight years old and from New York suburbs, after swapping life stories for half-an-hour, we got down to business. I needed a story and he wanted me to promote his latest book, *The Complete Guide to Guys*.

"You gotta help me out," I told him. "I'm in journalism, you know. I need a peg."

"You want me to ..."

"No, I got the peg. You're just going to have to accommodate me."

"Okay, I'll come up with quotes around it."

"That's the idea. Father's Day is coming up, so you gotta tell me: What is the guy's perfect Father's Day, from beginning to end?"

With little prodding and an understanding of where this needed to go, he filled my tape recorder with the stuff I asked for.

TORONTO (CP) – The perfect Father's Day gift for the average guy is to let him sleep around the clock while his family rotates the tires on his car, cleans the gutters on the house, pours beer down his throat and tells him on Monday that he had sex with Heather Locklear.

Though I always tried to lighten the mood, some encounters with authors didn't allow it. I spent nearly two hours over lunch with Joyce Maynard as she told me about the pain and betrayal she felt more than twenty years after her teenaged affair with fifty-plus J.D. Salinger and what compelled her to write a book, *At Home in the World*, enraging the guardians of the reclusive author. As the father of three daughters, I didn't hesitate to take her side in my lead.

TORONTO (CP) – Whether it's Bill Clinton or J. D. Salinger, the solution is simple. If you don't want to get caught with your pants down, keep them zipped up.

"If you really want a private life you can have it," I quoted Maynard. "Of course, one way to ensure no one is ever going to write about your affair with an eighteen-year-old girl is not to have an affair with an eighteen-year-old girl."

I also felt great sympathy and admiration for Tim O'Brien, whose torment from experiences as a young soldier in Vietnam drove his account of the war in *If I Die in a Combat Zone* and such novels as *Going After Cacciato*, *The Things They Carried*, and the one we were talking about, *In the Lake of the Woods*. He didn't pull any punches, his anger building, as he explained why he eviscerated the perpetrators of the My Lai massacre in the book.

"I didn't see any reason not to name names. They were putting their guns up against babies heads and admitting it on television and admitting it in court and nothing happened to them," O'Brien told me between gulps of coffee and cigarette smoke in his Toronto hotel room. "These people are trying to erase their culpability and their guilt through being quiet, living their lives. There are some things I think ought not be erased – murder is one of them, mass murder is certainly one of them."

I met with O'Brien on November 18, 1994, the day before my forty-eighth birthday. Here was a guy of my age who was making a living writing novels, who had won the National Book Award for *Cacciato*. And here I was, the doting stenographer. Did I need to feel O'Brien's pain to produce his prose? I didn't know. All I knew was I wanted to get out of my business and get into his. I was convinced I had a novel in me.

Around the time I met O'Brien, I talked to Joseph Heller on the phone. He was at his home in East Hampton, still recovering from his bout with a rare nerve disease called Guillain-Barre, and promoting *Closing Time: The Sequel to Catch-22*. I opened the conversation by saying, "Hey, we met about ten years ago when I was with United Press and you were touring with *God Knows*. We sat in the Harbour Castle here in Toronto and talked about the old days in New York. And to answer your question that you wrote in my book – No, I haven't started my novel yet."

Before calling Heller, I had looked at the inscription in *God Knows*. It read: *To Ken, With good wishes to a fellow New Yorker. Good luck with your own novel – if you ever start another one. Joseph Heller. 11-27-84. Toronto.* That novel I started was four pages written in longhand in San Francisco in 1968, when Anita was working and I was unemployed and pretending to be doing something.

Ken Becker

I realized I had told just about every serious writer I met that I intended to join their ranks soon, that this journalism thing was merely a warm-up.

As my dad would say, *Shit or get off the pot.* He died before I followed his advice.

CHAPTER 26
NOVEL INSPIRATION

In March of 1995, we loaded up the minivan in Clarkson and headed for Florida. We'd made the same trip every winter for the past eight years. Sometimes we flew. Most times, I drove.

Leaving home at dawn, we crossed the border at Buffalo, picked up the Interstates, bypassed Erie, Pennsylvania and Pittsburgh, down through West Virginia and Virginia. After twelve hours, I needed a scotch, a meal and a bed. Then it was twelve more hours through the Carolinas, Georgia and down the Florida peninsula.

We went first to my parents' house to spend a couple of days before crossing the state to Sanibel and the same rental cottage on San Carlos Bay that had become our winter retreat.

Linda and I dropped off the kids – Jodie was now eleven and Lacey was eight – and checked into a hotel on the ocean, on Singer Island.

The next day, we went to the Loxahatchee National Wildlife Refuge, where my mother enjoyed walking the trails. She had adopted my hobby of nature photography.

My dad wasn't up to the walk. He had been deteriorating with Parkinson's. The previous June, he had turned seventy-five and my parents had also celebrated their fiftieth wedding anniversary.

We'd all gathered for a birthday party at my sister's apartment in Washington Heights. By this time, Janice had divorced Steven, my sidekick on the kidnap caper in Bern, and married Alan Lighty, a musician from Pennsylvania. They had a son, Mathew, who was four.

Kate was living nearby. She was twenty-six, had left her husband, Stefan, and was working the reception desk at the Dorset Hotel in Midtown.

The day after dad's birthday dinner, there was a bigger anniversary party in a ballroom at the Dorset. My cousin Brian Mayer, now Rabbi Brian, performed a remarriage ceremony. Jodie and Lacey sang a song I had written for them, more of a cheer:

> *Grandpa! Grandpa!*
> *You're our leader.*
> *You're the king of Flor-i-di-da.*

Dad looked happy, if frail. It was a nice party. A good time. I was still keeping my emotional distance from my parents. If the conversation got too deep, too personal, I changed the subject or clammed up.

During our last day visiting with them in Florida this March, we all went to play miniature golf. Again, dad wasn't up to it. He walked along, shaking badly, sat on a bench while we putted.

On one hole, I backhanded a short putt and it spun out of the cup. I laughed and picked up the ball. Jodie, keeping score, asked, "How many, dad?"

"Three," I said.

My dad, sitting nearby, barked, "He didn't putt out. That's cheating."

Golf was the only sport I'd always been better at than him. Much better. He'd come to the game later in life. I'd tried to teach him golf the way he'd taught me to pitch a baseball and swing a bat. But he never accepted my instruction. He was a lousy golfer. He said he didn't care. "It's not a real sport," he'd say.

We left, as planned, after mini-golf, headed west, leaving behind the ugly side of the Sunshine State. We passed the prison at Belle Glade and the southern tip of Lake Okeechobee at Clewiston. Drove through all the nondescript tiny towns – LaBelle, Alva, Olga, Tice. Skirted Fort Myers, to the causeway linking the mainland to Sanibel.

Time to exhale. Turn off the air conditioning. Open the windows. Breathe in the salty air.

Pelicans floated alongside our vehicle as we crossed San Carlos Bay. Terns took turns diving for fish. We looked for dolphins in the bay.

We turned right at the stop sign onto Periwinkle Way, passed the familiar Dairy Queen, the only fast-food joint on the island, the Bait Box, where we bought shrimp for bait, She Sells Sea Shells, which we shunned because we could find shells on our own, and the place where we rented bikes.

Right turn on Dixie Beach Boulevard. Almost there. Down to the dead end at the bay, with the tall pole supporting an osprey nest. Left on Woodring Road, into a tunnel of mangroves, shells crunching beneath the tires. Passed the Woodring homestead, where chickens, and sometimes peacocks, ran loose.

Esperanza Woodring, the matriarch of the clan, had died three years earlier at the age of ninety-one. Also gone was her toothless, longtime boarder Earl, who had washed ashore in a hurricane and never left. Her sons owned the Bait Box, stocked daily by their shrimp boat, which left the dock at the ramshackle house and trawled the bay every evening.

I drove about a hundred more yards down the crushed-shell road and pulled into the driveway of the small yellow cottage. Home.

The kids ran around the house to our dock. Linda went inside to air out the cottage. I, as usual, like Jimmy Stewart in *Mr. Hobbs Takes a Vacation*, was left to unpack the minivan.

Our days were always full on Sanibel. I'd wake with the dawn and drive to Ding Darling, mosey along the road, stopping to photograph the masses of birds that wintered here – herons, egrets, anhingas, ibises, roseate spoonbills, wood storks, pelicans, and many more.

With the telephoto of my Nikon, the big birds filled the lens. But my camera looked like a toy compared to the gear of the legion of khaki-clad pros and hobbyists who lined the shores of the shallow ponds where the birds were thickest.

When I got back to the cottage, I made a big breakfast of eggs with salsa, hot Jimmy Dean sausage – couldn't get it in Canada – and Thomas' English muffins.

There was much to do for all of us every day. We'd hunt for live shells – whelks, conches, cockles, arks, angel wings and more – or fish off the dock. Cast a line with a piece of shrimp on the hook, never with an inkling of what might emerge from the saltwater. We hoped for snook, a grouper, or snapper for supper. But pulled up sheepshead, puffer fish, and, once, a stingray. Threw them back.

The kids would swim. We'd all bike around the island. Walk the trails of the Bailey Tract of Ding Darling. Rent canoes to explore the channels among the mangroves at Tarpon Bay.

Before dark, we'd go shopping at Jerry's or Bailey's store. I liked food shopping in the States. Everything was cheaper, there was a greater selection, and you could buy beer, wine and booze in the same market as groceries.

This trip, my old pal Joey and his wife, Nora McCabe, arrived from Toronto to join us. Joey and I sat on the dock at night, drinking and smoking, talking and laughing.

At around 5 a.m., the phone woke us all. My dad had had a massive stroke.

Linda and I and the kids left before dawn. I retraced our route across the state. Just after the sun came up, I spotted a caracara picking at some road kill. I'd never seen one before. I'd have to make a note of it – *Near Clewiston, Fla.* – beside its drawing in my National Geographic field guide.

We went straight to my parents' house and got the story. My mother – by then, I called her Dot – and dad had been out with friends the previous evening. They'd stopped at a frozen yogurt shop. Dad bit into his cone and immediately remarked that the chill went straight to his head. An ice cream headache.

But it wasn't that. A few seconds later, he collapsed. An ambulance came. Took him to JFK hospital in West Palm Beach. Dot had been there all night. She'd waited until the prognosis was clear before calling us. Aunt Fay, who had retired and moved nearby from New York, had taken her home.

Now, I took Dot back to the hospital. Dad was in the intensive care unit, hooked up to machines. The sight reminded me of Sean in Portland. Dad too was basically brain dead, a ventilator keeping him breathing.

Dot and I talked to his doctors. We decided to keep dad breathing for mainly logistical reasons. Janice, Alan and Mathew were in the Bahamas, coincidentally close, as we had been. We'd buy some time until they – as well as Kate, from New York – arrived. When the family was all there, we agreed to have dad taken off the ventilator. He was moved from the ICU to a private room on the same floor.

Dot and Jan and I were sitting around his bed talking, telling funny dad stories. Laughing. A nurse came in. "He can hear you, you know," she scolded. When she left, we laughed some more. A while later, Jan took Dot back to the house. Kate would join me on the next shift of the vigil.

I was standing next to the bed when suddenly his eyes shot open. He stopped breathing. With the index and middle fingers of my right hand, I closed his eyes, as I'd seen done in movies.

I summoned a nurse who confirmed my pronouncement. I phoned Jan at our parents' house, and gave her the news. "He looks different," I warned her.

Soon enough, the family – Linda stayed at the house with the kids – arrived at the hospital. Jan and Kate walked into the wrong room, where a Hispanic man was in bed.

When they caught up with me outside the right room, Jan said, "You weren't kidding. He did look different."

Soon after, Kate and I went for a walk around the hospital grounds. When we got back, my dad's older brother, Hal, and his wife, Millie, were standing at the foot of the bed. Dad was still in it. They were staring at him.

"He's dead, you know," I said.

"Oh," said Aunt Millie.

Dot and dad had bought space – not exactly a plot – in a cemetery about twenty miles from their house. Dot and Jan and I went there to complete the arrangements.

Dad died on March 15, the Ides of March. The funeral would be two days later, on St. Patrick's Day, to allow people time to arrive from out of town.

As a child, I had been shielded from the funerals of grandparents. But there was never a question whether Jodie and Lacey would attend their grandpa's funeral.

The chapel at Menorah cemetery looked like everything else in the endless suburban sprawl of South Florida – modern and soulless. The room would require no alteration to host a seminar on time-share condos after we and the casket cleared out.

There was a nice turnout, as is said, for the early afternoon service. Most of my mother's side of the family flew in from New York. My father's siblings – the aforementioned Hal, sister Emma and kid brother Jack, who had been my boss at *Changes* – were there. So were a handful of my parents lifelong friends from Queens and newfound friends from their neighborhood at Egret Isle.

Before the service began, before the casket came out, I folded a baseball into his left – pitching – hand. I considered adding a videotape I had sent him – of his Mets beating my Red Sox in the 1986 World Series – but there was no room in the box for a VCR.

I'd been to funerals where a rent-a-rabbi or rent-a-minister pretended to know the deceased after cribbing notes from the family. There was none of that. I read an excerpt from *Red and Me*, my story of his baseball career.

I got through it, overcame my dread of speaking in public. Jodie and Lacey stood with me at the podium for support. Having not packed for a funeral, I wore a ratty denim shirt and jeans to address the properly attired crowd.

Others spoke, including one of my dad's childhood friends, a fellow named Mac who would later become my mother's boyfriend, a complicated affair that apparently upset his wife.

Kate gave her best shot at a eulogy but broke down crying. I rescued her from the podium. I didn't cry. I never cry.

Afterwards, we moved outside where a forklift raised my dad's casket to his vault in a wall, joining all the other Jews who retired to Florida and wound up in an enormous filing cabinet.

We all went back to what was now Dot's house. The traditional post-funeral feast was catered by one of the Jewish delis that sprung up throughout southeastern Florida to capitalize on the great migration from the cities of the Northeast.

Lacey and Mathew channelled their own entrepreneurial spirit, standing outside their grandma's door and charging each visitor a two-dollar admission fee. Cute kids. Made a bundle.

Driving back to Sanibel the next day, I replayed my dad's death and funeral in my mind and tucked it away in my memory. Research.

Drinking with Joey on the dock seemed a sensible way to recover from the hangover of operating a minivan shuttle across the state of Florida. A few days later we drove home.

The previous month, I had passed my tenth anniversary at Canadian Press. It was longer than I'd worked anywhere and, adding the couple of years at United Press Canada, by far my longest stretch of uninterrupted employment.

Linda and I had lived in the house in Clarkson for twelve years. Again, for me, an adult record for staying put.

Life in the CP features department had become tiresome and my relationship with my bosses remained strained. I'd done good work. My writing kept getting smoother, more conversational.

It was appreciated by many. And recognized too, with a fistful of CP Story of the Month prizes – $150 added to my paycheck – and the 1992 Story of the Year ($400) for a piece on what first basemen talk about with visiting baserunners.

But I was nearing my forty-ninth birthday and convinced I had coughed up my last bits of journalism. It was time to move on. The questions were: Where to? And how do I extract a nest egg from my years at CP/UPC?

My former bureau chief Mike Brown and I had once talked about how much money would be needed to retire at fifty. "A couple of hundred thousand," I ventured.

He laughed. "A couple of million is more like it."

Linda and I considered our options. She was tired of secretarial work after twenty-five years of doing chores for middle-aged men. She too wanted a change and needed to get the most out of her years at Labatt.

We came up with a plan. First, we would put our house up for sale. We had bought it in 1983 for just under $100,000 and figured we could double that. I initiated discreet talks with the company to determine what kind of buyout they'd offer me.

Linda checked her pension position to see how much she'd walk away with. I didn't plan to accept any offer from CP until the house was sold. Even if the company made a good offer, I would dicker until both aspects of my escape plan dovetailed.

We told the kids we might be moving and spread out a map of North America on the dining room table. "We can go anywhere," I said, hoping to make it sound like a great adventure.

I was still an American citizen and a landed immigrant in Canada. As the children of an American, Jodie and Lacey had U.S. citizenship. By birth and through Linda, they were, of course, also Canadian. Linda still had her green card.

For weeks, Linda and I began eliminating places we didn't want to live. We knew we wanted a house in the country, with a view of water – an ocean, a big lake – or mountains. Or both.

We decided to stay in Canada, hoping any culture shock would not be as jarring for the kids. We crossed out all of Atlantic Canada because, after our trip there, it reminded of us Maine, where people were less welcoming of outsiders. Quebec was also out. Language. So was southern Ontario, since we wanted a change from the flatland that had long been our home. The Prairies were never considered for the same reason.

British Columbia was eliminated because it was just too groovy. We never looked north to the territories, since none of us had the palate for seal blubber or musk ox stew.

In the end, we focused on Canmore, Alberta, and Thunder Bay, Ontario.

Canmore was a fast-growing community on the eastern edge of the Rockies. But, though we truly loved those mountains, it was just too far from Linda's mom in Toronto, mine in Florida and Kate in New York.

So, the winner was Thunder Bay. It seemed to be a big enough city – with more than a hundred-thousand people

— to provide the creature comforts we would need. And we could live on Lake Superior, just outside the city.

By late August, we had sold the house, I agreed on a buyout package and gave notice at CP. Linda flew to Thunder Bay and found us a fabulous house on the greatest of the Great Lakes.

While she was gone, I read the entries in my journal from our 1980 trip, the only time we'd been in the place what would be our new home.

April 12
Stopped for propane at an RV dealer just outside Thunder Bay. The idiot girl behind the counter told me to pull up to the tank. Then she told Linda the guy who pumps the propane had gone to lunch and we couldn't get a fill for half an hour. After half an hour, she told me it would be five minutes. Twenty minutes later, we left without propane and a long cold night ahead.

April 13
Been gobbling Halls and Tylenol. Feel rotten. Checked into a motel. Best Western near the airport, $28 a night.

April 14
Woke up with a mean, raspy cough. Worst throat since I was a kid. Feel like we'll never get out of Thunder Bay.

April 15
Went to the emergency room. Waited around with an Indian named Frank, who wanted a bed. At least two

nurses and a doctor told Frank the hospital was booked. Frank said he couldn't go back to detox, they wouldn't take him anymore. Doctor, while cleaning dirt out of Frank's ears, suggested he get to the Salvation Army shelter early. Frank told me he was impressed with the amount of dirt he was carrying around in his ears. He asked Linda if she wanted to see the dirt but she declined. Poor sport, I thought. It was obvious Frank was a regular visitor at the hospital. The nurses scolded him, treated him like a child in front of a waiting room full of people. Frank didn't seem embarrassed. You get the sense Frank hasn't been embarrassed in many years.

Me? I got a 30-second checkup and a prescription for tetracycline. Between the antibiotics and all the store-bought remedies – cough medicine, cough drops, aspirin, vitamin C, and hot tea with honey – I ought to shake this monster cough.

Went for dinner at the Lotus Inn, Chinese restaurant and motel. (What's a Chinese motel? Fortune cookies for breakfast?) Food was okay but damn expensive. Everything around here is expensive.

My last week at CP, I sat down to breakfast with Pat Conroy in an outdoor café at the Intercontinental hotel in Toronto. I had not been a Conroy fan. I knew he had written *The Prince of Tides* and *The Great Santini* only because I'd seen the movies. Dysfunctional-family melodrama. Psycho-babble. Chick flicks. I figured he'd be one of those sensitive guys, comfortable with his feminine side, whatever the hell that was.

When I'd talked to Dave Barry we'd traded stories that reinforced our macho indifference to such things as analyzing relationships. "Did you ever notice," I said, "that women talking about their ex-husbands or ex-lovers always say 'he wasn't nurturing, he wasn't caring, he wasn't sensitive enough to my needs.' But when men talk about their ex-wives or ex-girlfriends they just say 'she's fucking nuts.'"

Dave laughed. "The other night in Miami," he told me, "I went out with a group of six women, and they were talking about other women, some of whom they like and some of whom they don't like. In each case, every woman at the table would discuss that woman in detail – maybe she's thinking this, maybe she's thinking that. When the end of the evening came – and I've been very quiet the whole evening – they turned to me and said, 'How would a group of guys have talked about this?' And I said, 'in discussing anybody we didn't like, we would have said 'he's a fucking asshole' and there would be no need to figure out why he was a fucking asshole. He just is.'"

I didn't expect the conversation to drift in a similar direction with Pat Conroy. But a lot of things about Conroy surprised me. Starting with the fact I really liked his new book, *Beach Music*.

Conroy, a big man in a T-shirt and battered Atlanta Braves cap, offered a warm handshake and spoke with a slightly high-pitched southern drawl.

He was about a year older than me and had been born in Atlanta, had been there when the Braves first came to town. We started out talking baseball, the names and stories tripping along easily. From Hank Aaron breaking Ruth's record to Cal Ripken embracing the fans in Baltimore after he broke Gehrig's record.

Conroy told me about meeting Ted Williams. I told him about Rick Bosetti and the 1978 Toronto Blue Jays.

Finally, I said, "I better get something on tape."

"Sorry," he said, "I guess I'm not doing you any favors here. But I get off on this stuff."

"So do I. I'd rather have a conversation than do an interview."

"I have to apologize," he said.

"I don't know if your publicist told you," I said, "but I've already quit my job. This is my last interview."

"Good for you," he said. "What are you going to do?"

"I'm going to try to do what you do. I won't do it the same or as well …"

"What are you going to write?"

"I'm going to write a novel," I said.

"Are you really?"

"Yeah, after thirty years in journalism I've just had it. We've sold our house and …"

"Have you really?"

"And we're renting a house on the north shore of Lake Superior, out in the country.'

"Where?"

"Near a place called Thunder Bay," I said.

"I know it well," Conroy said with a smile. "It's beautiful. Are you going to write your novel there?"

"Yeah."

"You know what it's going to be about yet?"

"Sort of," I said. "I've got two characters and a vague idea of where I'm going. I haven't written a word yet, though."

"Don't worry, it's alright," he said. "Let me give you a little un-asked-for advice. Try not to be afraid ..."

"I'm not."

"Especially after a life in journalism. Journalists are driven crazy by editors who say 'cut it down, cut it down, cut it down.' And have fun with the language."

"That's what I've been doing for the last several years, anyway," I said. "I've been playing around with the language, within the confines of journalism, anyway. I know what those confines are, and I've stuck to it, but I've been fishing around, trying to present stories in a narrative form, with a different tone than you usually read in newspapers. Because I can't read this shit any more and I don't want to write it any more."

"It excites me, what you're doing," Conroy said.

"It excites me – and scares me. I haven't given myself a deadline for the writing, but we'll go up there, hope to survive the winter and go from there."

"What about your kids?" I had mentioned Jodie and Lacey.

"They think we're fucking nuts. We've sold the only home they've ever known, and we're packing up. The other day, I took down the swing in the apple tree and they were crying. They think we're crazy."

"Well," he said, "you're changing their lives."

Conroy asked for my new address, which I wrote on the back of one of my CP business cards. He wrote his address and phone number on the back of another card.

"My wife flew up there a couple of weeks ago and rented us this house right on Lake Superior, on a point, where you can't see your neighbors. I've seen pictures. It's a big modern chalet-style A-frame, all cedar, with one side facing the lake, all floor-to-ceiling windows. Same with the master bedroom. My office looks out on the lake too. It's the whole writer's cliché."

"It's not a cliché," he said. "It should feed you. And feed what you're doing."

"But what I'm going to be writing about will be set in other places."

"That's okay," he said. "That's why you have an imagination."

"I tend to write with my ear," I said.

"That's a great way to write," he said.

"If it sounds right, it's usually right."

"To me," he said, "the story is the thing. It is the beginning and the end for me. To me, storytelling is a prehistoric need – it's like air, it's like food."

"That's the thing I've been preaching in journalism for the past ten years – that the only thing that's going to save newspapers is getting back to storytelling."

"I totally agree," Conroy said. "And I think they are in trouble because they're not doing this."

"They're giving us this crap that nobody wants to read and people already know about because they saw it on CNN. So why bother reading it. It's so fucking boring that I sure don't want to read it."

I caught myself in mid-rant, thinking I didn't have to worry about this stuff any more.

Conroy looked me straight in the eye to insert a pause. "When you said you had two characters, I thought, 'ah, a writer.'"

How could I fail? Pat Fucking Conroy thinks I'm a writer.

Linda and I finished packing up the house. The movers would be coming in a few days.

My CP colleagues gave me a sendoff at our regular after-work hangout, Cyrano's. None of the bosses came. Or maybe they didn't know about it. Or weren't invited.

George the Greek, who owned the bar, poured me a double Dewar's on the house. There would be more shots poured before we closed the joint.

I was given the gift of a black Akubra hat to go with the brown one I used to wear. I'd switched to baseball caps to cover my inherited Becker baldness. "We prefer the Crocodile Dundee look," said one of my protégés from the Ontario Desk.

There was a nice card – naturally from a woman, since men don't buy greeting cards or write gooey inscriptions. It read, in part:

> *You've taught me how to write and how to think. You've been a mentor and a friend over the last five years and without your guidance I wouldn't have the desire and satisfaction for the craft I do now.*
> *A quick 'nice job' from you has always meant more than anything.*

Linda and I were taken out for a bon voyage dinner. It was the usual gang of couples who had come to our house every August for lobster steamed in a big pot over an open fire, fresh corn from the local market, Linda's famous Caesar salad.

I'd miss the laughs and smart talk. There was no telling what we'd find in Thunder Bay.

CHAPTER 27
A NOVEL RETREAT

We arrived at our new home in late September. It was even more spectacular than Linda had described it. The pictures she'd taken had not shown much of the interior, the great open space that included the living room, dining room and kitchen, with a view of the lake, tree-covered islands and a peninsula called the Sleeping Giant, because, from afar, it looked like a giant lying on his back, with his arms folded across his chest.

Jodie had her own bedroom and bathroom upstairs, in the loft. Lacey had a bedroom on the main level. Our bedroom was a separate wing.

I set up my office in the family room, bought a new computer and put it on my desk, facing the lake. I filled shelves with books, hung my framed red, white and blue poster of a smiling JFK – *Kennedy for President, Leadership for the 60's* – and put a stack of paper next to the printer.

I planned to write in the morning, when the kids were at school – the bus picked them up at the top of our long driveway and took them to a rural schoolhouse that included kindergarten through eighth grade – and Linda was doing whatever Linda wanted to do.

Jasper was delighted with the new digs, since he was set free whenever he asked, to wander in the woods or trot down to the lake for a drink. As far as I could tell, he never left the property – three-hundred-and-fifty feet of lakefront, with dense bush on the other three sides – except once, to chase a moose away.

Remarkably, Jasper avoided confrontations with the foxes, wolves and other critters that outnumbered people in our neighborhood, though he did bark an alarm in the house one night when a huge black bear uncovered the tub of sunflower seeds I'd left on the deck, near the birdfeeder. Another time, he treed a small bear for his – and our – amusement.

I welcomed any diversion from writing – trips to town to go food shopping or to the library to do research, long walks to think about writing, drives to the mailbox off the highway, drives through Sleeping Giant Provincial Park to photograph wildlife, volunteer work at the kids' school to do my civic duty, hours spent splitting wood to heat our home. Anything but typing.

The two characters I'd mentioned to Conroy were a fifty-year-old expat American living in Canada, with a wife and kids, who takes off with a teenage stripper, a former Olympic gymnast from Romania, on the run from the mob in Canada and the secret police in her homeland. I couldn't decide whether to tell his story in the first-person or the third, whether he lived in Toronto or in the country outside Thunder Bay.

I knew Richard Nixon would play a part in the plot, but I wasn't sure how. I didn't know what tone I wanted to take, whether it was Conroy's southern lilt, Tim O'Brien's manic edge, or Carl Hiaasen's off-the-wall craziness. Would I find my own voice? I didn't know where to look.

Conroy had advised me to take five great books with me to Thunder Bay. "I'd reread *Anna Karenina* while writing *Beach Music*," he told me. "I studied it. I tried to figure it out, How did Tolstoy do that?"

I'd brought all my books. Boxes of them were stacked in the loft. But I knew I wasn't going to find Tolstoy among them. I didn't read foreigners. I read Americans, mainly men, mainly mysteries and thrillers.

I tried rereading Mailer but concluded his best work was journalism. The sun had set on my ardor for Hemingway. I revisited Philip Roth and Updike, favorites in my twenties, but they no longer spoke to me. I cracked open *Catch-22*. It no longer made me laugh.

I got a call from a radio station in Thunder Bay, asking if I would agree to an interview. It seemed they didn't have many big-time journalists living hereabouts. On the air, I chatted with the host, confessed I had moved to the country from Toronto to work on a book and talked about my "friends" – Joe Heller, Tim O'Brien and Pat Conroy.

A librarian phoned me, said she'd heard me on the radio, and asked if I would talk to a book club that was meeting the next evening. "Of course," I said, "I love to talk about writing." Anything to avoid doing it. I brought along a tape of my interview with O'Brien and played it for the group. I listened closely too.

I heard myself ask him, "Are you at times almost grateful that you went to war, so you have these stories?"

"Not really," he replied. "I'm grateful I survived that war. But it's like if you had cancer and survived it. You don't want to go through cancer again. But having gone through it, you make use of what life gives you. And life gave me Vietnam in a way that, for other writers, life gives you a broken family. Or, if you're black, like Toni Morrison, it gives you the black life and the degradations that go with it – the anger, the bitterness. And, as a novelist, you really have no choice but to make use of the materials that life gives you ... I think you need a kind of driving, obsessive passion to write, and the war gave it to me."

But I didn't have a war. I wasn't black. I wasn't from a broken family. I grew up in a boring middle-class family in one boring middle-class neighborhood after another. I had a wife, an ex-wife, three kids and a poodle.

Like Hemingway, I drank too much. Like O'Brien, I smoked too much. Like Kerouac and that bunch, including my friend Lucien, I fucked around too much, at least when I was younger.

But what story did I have to tell? I wanted to write fiction. But I didn't know how to do it. Did I lack a novelist's imagination? Could I not free myself from the yoke of journalism?

A couple of wire service guys had turned to fiction with great success. Frederick Forsyth said he wrote *The Day of the Jackal* in thirty-five days while working for Reuters in the 1960s. I'd been told that Thomas Harris hatched the plot for *Black Sunday* in a bar in New York with a couple of his AP colleagues in the 1970s.

But they were in their thirties at the time. Was I too old to start fresh? Too set in my writing ways? Were too many doubts spinning in my head, paralyzing my thoughts, killing the flow?

I started and stopped. Started and stopped. Started again and stopped again.

I gave up writing in the morning as the empty bottles of Dewar's, Absolut and Finlandia – a toast to Thunder Bay's large Finnish community – piled up in the bin for the recycling depot.

Winter arrived on Halloween. One snowstorm left us stranded for days, until the guy we hired to plow the driveway showed up.

We took a break, drove to Minneapolis, and caught a flight to Florida. It would be our second last vacation at the cottage in Sanibel.

Once back in the northland, I drew no inspiration from the frozen landscape outside my windows. Conroy had told me "never start a novel with the weather, you can get a weather report on CNN." So, what's the opening line that will remain forever in the memory of an old Swiss lady in an English bookshop in Bern?

Winter lasted until June, when the ice on the lake broke up in a storm one night, throwing boxcar-sized chunks onto the shore. The kids got through their first year at Mackenzie Public School. They, at least, seemed to be thriving.

Jodie would be going into the eighth grade – Grade Eight, in Canadian – in the fall. Lacey into Grade Five. They both excelled in academics and sports. They both had nice friends. One of Jodie's was the daughter of a fisherman whose whitefish found its way to the Fulton Fish Market and Jewish delis in New York.

But Jodie hung out mainly with a group of boys. She was their equal in every way, on the basketball court, jumping off cliffs into Lake Superior. She was the jock in the family, the son I never had. In Thunder Bay, she beat me for the first time in a game of one-on-one basketball.

Lacey was one of the two girls in a Cub Scout troop. They hiked and camped and did all that woodsy stuff.

Both girls learned to ski and loved the wilderness. I was less up to the challenge of surviving in the sticks.

Linda and I were in Thunder Bay when a beaver pond overflowed and washed out the Trans-Canada Highway. We couldn't get home, where the kids were, until the next day.

Truckers and other cross-country travelers had to stay put, as we did, or turn back to Michigan or Minnesota on a detour of hundreds of miles to get around Superior on the U.S. side. What was I doing in a burg – or a country, for that matter – where there was one transcontinental highway at the mercy of beavers?

After midnight, on November 19, 1996, my fiftieth birthday, I sat alone in the dark, in a place I had grown to despise, with a bottle of scotch. More than a year had gone by since we moved to northwestern Ontario. I tried writing late at night, tried writing drunk since sober wasn't working. Nothing was working. I started and stopped. Started and stopped. Started again and stopped again.

We got internet service and I was plugged back into the world through email. I began doing freelance assignments, some for CP, for a hundred bucks a story.

I got an assignment from a birding magazine in California for a piece I pitched on an outfit called Blue Loon Adventures, based in Thunder Bay, run by a trio of Canadian biologists.

Starting at 5:30 a.m., I spent a morning in the bush with one of them, John Woodcock – yes, that was his real name – capturing and tagging a smorgasbord of birds: warblers, thrushes, flycatchers, vireos, grosbeaks, and many more of the visiting migrants.

While the birds fed on bugs, the bugs fed on us. "That's part of roughing it," John said with a chuckle. The kid from the Bronx was not amused.

By the end of our second year in the country, Linda had gotten a real estate license and was working all the time, though the payoff was usually chickenfeed. Our nest egg was nearly gone, the profit from the house sale and severance check from CP nearly spent. Another dream was fast becoming another nightmare.

One way to forestall the crash was to collect unemployment insurance. I may be a rugged individualist, but I'd been paying into the fund for more than twenty years and wanted some of my money back.

In January 1997, I went to the appropriate federal government office in Thunder Bay and filled out a stack of forms. About a month later, I received a letter that my claim had been denied but I had the right to appeal.

I went back to the office one morning in early February. The place was crowded. My fellow clients looked like they really needed money.

I took a number. Two civil servants were on duty. The other three stations behind the counter were unoccupied. More than an hour went by before it was my turn.

The short young woman behind the counter was wearing a tank top. It was minus-a-thousand degrees outside. I guess she just wanted to show off her tattoo. Big sucker. Looked like a cartoon of a bird, maybe a crow or a raven.

I showed her my rejection letter and began my spiel on the obvious miscarriage of justice. She looked bored. I don't think she listened. She handed me a pink slip – Was she firing me? – and told me to take it to a room upstairs. The room was empty. There was a bell. I rang it. No reply.

If the government of Canada wanted me to go away it succeeded. For the moment.

I went home and into full reporter mode. I worked the phones. Called people from Thunder Bay to Ottawa until I got my day in court, a hearing before a three-person appeal board.

I went back to the same government office building. But this time I was ushered into a cozy boardroom. My judges were middle-aged, like me. They all looked like Chamber of Commerce types, unlike me.

My argument was this: When I'd received a buyout from CP I wasn't aware I was eligible for unemployment insurance. I didn't need it, anyway. But now I needed it and wanted it.

Their judgment was this: I'd waited too long to apply. Tough luck. Next case.

It soon became apparent I would not write The Great Canadian-American Novel. Not at this time, anyway. I'd had four false starts on the manuscript. On the fifth, I caught a wave and rode it through about forty pages, twenty-thousand words.

I had settled on the title *The Obituary Writer* and told the story in the first-person through Charlie White, who was a lot like me, an expat New Yorker living in Toronto, a lapsed Jew living in a Gentile world, a lifelong news reporter of fifty with a Canadian wife. The teenaged Romanian stripper, once my idea for a second major character, was relegated to a minor role. The story began:

> On the day Richard Nixon died, I went to synagogue for the first time since my bar mitzvah. It was a Friday, April 22, 1994. I'd buried my father in Florida that morning, left my mother alone, in her empty house, and boarded an early evening flight back to Toronto.

I was not dissatisfied with some of the writing. The words flowed nicely when Charlie was going gonzo with my experiences, like the deaths of my dad and Nixon. I thought the best parts were long stretches of dialogue, some of which made me laugh aloud, including one which borrowed heavily on research I had done in phone calls and emails with my cousin Brian, the rabbi, in Los Angeles. The writing seemed to take flight when Charlie arrived at the synagogue.

> "I'm Rabbi Black. I understand you want to see me." So sincere. So sweet. A kid. A mark.

"Are you Jewish?" I asked.
"Of course, I'm Jewish," he said. A hint of a smile. A good sign, as he led me into his office after Friday night services at Temple Aleph Gelt.
"I don't mean to be a wiseass," I said, taking a seat. "It's just that I didn't know Jews were called Black. Jews of color are usually Greene. Like Shecky Greene."
"Well," he said, "my family name is Black. My father was Black. My grandfather was Black."
"You mean they were Negroes?"
"No, they were white." He was smiling now, fully engaged.
"I'm White," I said.
"I can see that."
"No, I mean my name is White. Charlie White."
"White doesn't sound like a Jewish name," he said. "Are you sure you're Jewish?"
"My father was. He was White too. He's dead."
"I'm sorry to hear that – z ikrono l'bracha."

The scene went for a few more pages. I'd smiled when I wrote it. Smiled when I read it. As my fellow reporter on the *Sun*, Jerry Gladman, had said twenty years earlier, "You must really love the sound of your own words."

I also remembered Tim O'Brien telling me he never knew where his story was going, that his novels simply poured out as he wrote them. I had no idea where my story was going. And I couldn't afford to see where my fiction would take me next. I was stuck in the real life of being broke and desperate in Thunder Bay. I needed a job.

I'd left journalism at the top of my game, a deft and cool editor in the mold of Lucien Carr, as talented and smooth a writer as anyone in the business. Why wasn't that enough? Why did I keep searching for something else, something more?

As I flew to Toronto in January of 1998, leaving Linda and the kids behind in the house on the lake, I thought maybe I should have tried writing a screenplay. Sent it to Mel Brooks.

No time to worry about that now, though. I'd screwed up again, let down my family. I was going home and back to journalism. Were there any bridges left to cross, or had I burned them all?

CHAPTER 28
TV OR NOT TV?

My friends Joey and Nora invited me to bunk in their house just south of Danforth Avenue in the Riverdale section of Toronto. I immediately put the word out that I was looking for a job. By then, I not only knew most of the older editors in the business, but some of the younger ones who had worked with me at CP or UPC.

In the meantime, I got some freelance assignments. I wrote about the time Trudeau told me to fuck off for the op-ed page of the *Toronto Star*. I wrote a biweekly CP travel column, which I had started when I was on staff and picked up again when I was in Thunder Bay. I wrote a lot about golf, which was all the rage in the late '90s, thanks to Tiger Woods.

I had a bedroom on the top floor of Chez Slinger-McCabe. They set me up with a laptop on the dining room table to work.

Joey had been writing for the *Star* since the late 1970s. His columns had earned him a National Newspaper

Award. A collection, compiled in a book, *No Axe Too Small to Grind*, won the Stephen Leacock Medal for Humour – Humor, in American – in 1986.

Joey wrote his column in his home office, taking a break for lunch. We'd often go to a greasy spoon down the street. He'd have a Western omelet on brown toast. I'd have a Denver omelet on whole wheat. Same sandwich. Different place names.

At night, despite the sub-freezing temperature – on both the Fahrenheit and Celsius scales – we'd go outside on his deck to smoke, drink beer, shiver and crack wise. There was something special about that Guelph-New York humor.

In February, Joey arranged for me to do a "tryout" at the *Star*. The idea of auditioning for a spot on the copy desk was humiliating. But crow was now my meal of choice.

At the same time, another old friend, Michael Enright, told me the cable-TV news operation of the Canadian Broadcasting Corporation was looking for writers. I had no idea what it took to write for television. But Michael, who was a star on CBC Radio, assured me I could do it and told me to contact Jay Mowat, executive producer at CBC Newsworld.

Since I was working nights at the *Star*, I went to see Mowat one morning. I liked what I saw in the CBC-TV newsroom right away. It was a huge open space, filled with attractive people, young and older, who dressed casually and seemed to be happy to be there. The *Star* newsroom looked more like the headquarters of a large insurance company, populated with glum gnomes hiding in their cubicles.

I met Mowat in his office at the CBC Broadcasting Centre, an ultra-modern building that occupied a square block in downtown Toronto, near the SkyDome and CN Tower. Mowat appeared to be a throwback hippie, about my age, with a full gray beard and long gray hair pulled back into a ponytail.

I started by dropping Enright's name, saying he had told me about the job posting, which led to more talk about mutual friends in the business. Finally, he said. "I hear you're a great writer."

"If I were a great writer, I probably wouldn't be working nights on the copy desk at the *Star*," I said. He laughed. A good sign.

"Well," he said, "I'm looking for seasoned writers for our weekend operation. We have a lot of young kids, and I think they could learn from an old pro like you."

"I doubt it," I said. "I know nothing about writing for television."

"I'm not worried about that," he said.

"I need a real job," I said. "Weekends won't be enough to feed my family."

"Don't worry," he said. "If it works out, I'll get you enough shifts during the week to make it fulltime."

We talked some more, seemed to click. I told him I was going to Thunder Bay that weekend to see my wife and kids. He said he'd email me a writing test – "It's more of an editing test, which I'm sure you'll have no trouble with," he said – and asked me to call him when I got back.

Since I didn't have a car – Linda had the family minivan – and couldn't afford to rent one or buy a plane ticket, I had arranged to write a travel piece for the *Financial*

Post on taking the bus to Thunder Bay. Since it was an assignment, the general manager of Greyhound – was it Grayhound in the USA? – gave me a free pass for the twenty-two hour trip north, and the twenty-two hour trip back.

I'd made the drive several times – in fourteen hours. But I discovered Greyhound's primary business was as a courier service, taking a detour at every town to pick up and deliver packages.

I figured something was up when the driver stopped at Lola's Confectionery on the way out of Sudbury, Ontario, the soot-stained nickel capital of Canada.

I had already been on the bus for more than seven hours since wheeling out of Toronto at 12:30 a.m. In that time, I could have flown from Toronto to London, taken a cab to the Cadogan, checked into the room where Oscar Wilde was busted, ordered up a Scotch and a sandwich, taken a shower, phoned the palace, and planned a night of club-hopping with the Queen Mother.

Instead, I was folded into a third-row seat on a Greyhound, sleep deprived and fighting nausea, surrounded by fellow sad sacks with one-way tickets to oblivion, still fifteen hours from my destination, and parked on the dusty tarmac of Lola's Confectionery.

I wrote the story for the *Post* during my brief stay with Linda and the kids. I also did the test for the CBC.

During my years at UPI-New York, I sometimes wrote for the broadcast wire. I'd simply take the print version of the story, change the verbs from past to present tense, and make the sentences shorter.

I did the same when I wrote my scripts for radio reports I voiced on the trial in Zurich. The broadcast editor on the other end of the phone in London had to stop me several times when I lapsed into a David Brinkley imitation, taking five seconds to spit out a couple of words.

As a lifelong consumer of TV news, I knew there was no place for five-dollar words, no showing off by dropping a ten-syllable speed-bump into the script. The main thing was to communicate, which was always my objective anyway. I also thought I might be able to write broadcast copy because, as I've said, I wrote with my ear, heard the words in my head.

The first part of the CBC writing test was to take a thousand word AP story and turn it into a two-minute TV script. I attacked this as I would rewriting a newspaper story for wire service, cutting it down to its essential ingredients. No problem.

The second part was titled "Where's Waldo?" a short story in which I had to find ten mistakes, spelling and factual errors. I found thirteen.

The third part was to take a CP bulletin – one sentence – signaling a major development on an ongoing story, put it in context with the appropriate background and write a few sentences that could be put on the air as breaking news. With my wire service training, this was a snap.

Part four tested knowledge of world events. In this case, understanding the barriers to Middle East peace. Piece of baklava.

The final part read: *You've just died. But you're not very important, so all you deserve is a 30-second copy story. Write your own obituary.*

I had some fun with this, playing with the recent news that CBC had "lost" ten million dollars.

It would have been nice if Ken Becker could have written this story.
But he can't ... because he's dead.
He was one of the many writers who put words in the mouths of people like me. And he did it well ... made us sound more intelligent than this.
He worked for Newsworld in its formative years in television. Then he disappeared suddenly ... and mysteriously ... at about the same time the CBC reported a 10-million-dollar shortfall it could not account for.
Ken Becker died today of boredom at his private island in the South Pacific.
He was 95.

After I returned from Thunder Bay on the Greyhound, I phoned Mowat. He said I'd done well on my test and that we should talk again soon.

"Listen, Jay," I said, "I'm not playing games, but the *Star* has offered me a fulltime job. I haven't said yes yet – I've been stalling – but I need to know right now if I have a future at the CBC."

"I can't promise you a fulltime job," he said. "I can't offer you a staff position. You'd be what we call a 'casual employee,' which means you can fill shifts on the schedule but you're not guaranteed steady work."

"I realize that," I said, "but if you can give me some assurance that I'll work every weekend, and get a couple of shifts during the week as well, I'd much rather work for you than the *Star*, which is a nightmare."

"I'm sorry, I'm not sure I can do that," he said.

The conversation ended. I was devastated, doomed to the copy desk at the Toronto Fucking Star. Two minutes later, the phone rang.

"Listen," said Mowat, "I want you here. We'll make it work. You want to start this weekend? I'll make sure you get some weekday shifts as well."

"You got a deal," I said.

I was elated. But I had some explaining to do, to Joey and to Linda. Joey understood how awful it was for me at the *Star* and said it wouldn't matter to him if I walked away from a job there. Linda was seriously concerned. She was still enduring the hard life in Thunder Bay.

The *Star* was offering me the security of a fulltime job, at a much higher pay-rate than the CBC. But Linda also knew how degrading it was for me at the *Star*, exiled to the copy desk, with the rest of the washouts. Some of the kids who had worked for me at CP were now reporters and editors at the *Star*. And I was stuck with a bitchy copy chief who tried to slap me down at every turn.

"You can't be substantially changing a reporter's copy without his or her permission," she scolded me when I did the kind of rewrite that was routine at the wire services.

"Why would I call some kid who can't write for shit to ask permission to make his copy better," I countered.

"That's not the point, that's not the way we do things around here."

The *Star* seemed to think a story that could be told well in three-hundred words should be bloated into a thousand-word monster that nobody could, or would, read. I kept trimming the stories and the crazy lady kept dressing me down.

"You don't understand," she said once, "we have a big paper to fill." I laughed aloud and went for a smoke.

At the end of my shift on the Friday before my first Saturday at CBC in March 1998, I went into the office of assistant managing editor Paul Warnick, who had hired me at the *Sun* and now, twenty years later, was my boss again at the *Star*.

"I don't think I can do this, Paul," I said.

"Do what?"

"Work here," I said.

"What's the problem?"

"It's just not working out," I said.

"I thought you needed this job," he said.

"I do," I said. "But I've also been offered a job at the CBC and I've accepted it."

"I see."

"It's just that television, for me, is something new, something I can learn in my old age. This is just too far a step back. I really appreciate you taking me on, and offering me a job. But I just can't take it."

We parted on good terms, I thought. But, if I didn't make it in TV, I knew there was certainly no chance I'd ever again be offered a job at the *Toronto Star*.

CHAPTER 29
SOUND-UP BAGPIPES

In the early summer of 1998, three years after we moved nearly a thousand miles from home, we were back in the old neighbourhood, about a mile from the old house in Clarkson. Linda joined a real estate brokerage nearby. I was back to commuting to Toronto.

The kids eased into old friendships and didn't seem spooked about going to new schools. They had done well in their time in the country. Jodie had won an award as the outstanding student in her graduating class at Mackenzie Public School. She had just finished a year of high school at Port Arthur Collegiate in Thunder Bay, where she was a star on the freshman basketball team.

Their grades were solid and they'd both won medals at a citywide track and field competition. Lacey had also completed a mini-triathlon, while her sister pushed herself too hard, as usual, and staggered to a halt before the finish line.

Jodie would soon be fifteen, Lacey twelve. They were smart and pretty, like their mom, and healthy and athletic. I braced for life with two teenaged girls. Wondered how it all would be different if Sean had lived.

Jasper and I, both fixed, were the men of the house we rented in Lorne Park – four bedrooms, three bathrooms, and a decent-sized, fenced-in backyard for Jasper. No moose to chase. No bears to tree. But raccoons often wandered into our garage when we left the door open at night, and foxes occasionally patrolled the streets at dusk before returning to their home in the Rattray Marsh down the street.

That summer, we went to New York for Kate's second wedding. The groom was Jorg Mauelshagen, originally from Wuppertal, Germany, near Dusseldorf.

Kate had met him on one of her jaunts to Honduras, where he had adopted the Spanish name Jorge. I'd met him once before when he and Kate visited us north of Superior. I liked him right off. For one thing, it would be nice to have a son-in-law who spoke English. For another, he was smart and funny, with only a trace of the stereotypical Germanic know-it-all.

Kate, still my red-haired beauty, was twenty-nine. Jorge, tall, dark and handsome, was thirty-one.

The wedding was in a Swiss restaurant called Roettele in the East Village, where Kate had worked as a waitress. The guests included Anita and her boyfriend; Dot, Fay and Aunt Ann; Janice and Alan and Mathew, as well as cousins Ylain and Carol and their husbands and their adult children.

After dad died, we lost touch with his side of the family. Dot had never cared for them much, in any case.

So, we all gathered in the restaurant for a nice ceremony and a nice meal. I was not imbibing, having finally kicked the habit of drinking and driving. But that didn't stop me from dropping a turd on the proceedings.

As the father of the bride, I accepted my responsibility to give a speech. And, as I had with the vows at my wedding with Linda, I wrote a love-conquers-all tribute to their differences.

There were a lot of German jokes. I didn't use the N-word – Nazi – or the H-word – Hitler – but the war and the Holocaust were definitely lurking. My cousin Carol couldn't stop laughing. The rest of the crowd looked like the theater audience during *Springtime for Hitler* in *The Producers*. Frozen in horror. Mouths agape.

Jorge's mother had flown in from Germany for the occasion. I don't know whether my words got through to her, but the bride and groom were not amused.

Kate didn't talk to me for two years. I'd learn that girls/women do that – hold grudges. Men, of my generation, anyway, just tell you to fuck off, smack the back of your head, and go for a beer.

When I applied for the job at CBC Newsworld, I told Jay Mowat in a fax: *As you can see from my resume, I have moved effortlessly through the various angles of newspapering and am sure the strength of my writing will adapt quickly to TV.* I was wrong.

I thought I knew something about TV news since I had come of age watching it. But I'd mostly looked down on TV news, endorsed the sentiment that it was superficial, incapable of telling a thousand-word story in a minute or two. Not serious journalism.

When I was in Vancouver, I had friends in TV, including an anchor and a couple of reporters. We talked about news and storytelling, what we liked and didn't like – we all loved Charles Kuralt's road stories on CBS.

But I was never interested in *how* they did what they did.

By the time I arrived in a TV newsroom in March 1998, I understood the tables had turned. Sure, newspapers dug deeper. But on big stories, they could not compete with TV, which showed them live, as they happened, with non-stop reporting and commentary – on the bombing of Baghdad, the L.A. riots, O.J. in the Bronco.

The televised rape trial of William Kennedy Smith in Florida was better theater than any episode of *Perry Mason*. The O.J. trial was a flop only because the judge had too big a part and was a terrible actor. CBC Newsworld, created in 1989, carried many of these events.

My tasks suited my ability. Initially, I was given a full hour to produce a thirty-second voiceover for the newscast at the top of the clock. At a wire service, the slogan is "a deadline every minute." In cable-TV news, you count the seconds.

I now understood and appreciated the scene in the movie *Broadcast News*, where Joan Cusack sprints with a tape to the control room to get it into the playback machine on time to make its slot.

One of my biggest problems in my early days at CBC was I kept getting lost. The Broadcasting Center is a maze of corridors zigging and zagging around a central core, an atrium that rises ten stories to the roof. I would head from the newsroom to the rooms where editors cut tape, make a wrong turn, and wind up in Albuquerque. Or I would be running a tape to the control room, which was two floors above the newsroom, and find myself staring into the abyss of the atrium.

I also had to learn a new language: VO for voiceover; SOT for sound on tape; BG for background audio – the natural sound of traffic, the wind, a helicopter in flight. I discovered those who make TV news in Canada are particularly fond of starting an item with the sound of bagpipes, which whine through every occasion in this country, from the opening of a hockey game to the closing of a funeral.

My first VO was a story about a tomb unearthed in Egypt. My first line, when the pictures rolled, began: *This smiling sarcophagus ...*

It was a good start. But it took me a full year to get the hang of TV writing. Maybe it was my ego, thinking my words could carry every story. Maybe I was just too old a mutt to learn new tricks. But there were many trials and many errors in that first year before it finally clicked – that the pictures carried the story, that without pictures there was no TV news.

Once I conquered the concept, I fell in love with using moving pictures to tell a story. For me, it was in many ways easier than writing for print. I'd always had trouble describing a scene and now I could simply roll the pictures. Every story, even that thirty-second voiceover, was like making a movie.

I kept plugging away at the craft of combining words with pictures. Creating an entire story, up to three minutes of sound and visuals, became my ambition.

When JFK Jr.'s plane went down in July 1999, we had a lot of pictures and clips from his life, but no obit. So I sat with a tape editor, went through all the available material, produced a long profile piece – we couldn't say he was dead yet, just missing – and had our anchor, Ben Chin, voice my script.

This seemed to give Jay Mowat a wild idea. "How would you like to do some reporting?" he asked.

"Me?"

"I think you'd be good," he said. "You could do some features, the off-beat stuff nobody else does?"

"Me? On TV?"

"Your voice is great – unique, gravelly – with that tough American accent," he said.

"I don't have an accent," I said.

"Trust me, you do," he said.

"Me? On TV?"

"I'd like you to come to me with an idea and I'll assign you a field producer and a camera," he said.

In September 2000, when Tiger Woods unexpectedly showed up for the Canadian Open down the road in Oakville, I went to Mowat with an idea.

"Why don't I do a story on Tiger?" I asked.

"What could you do that everyone else isn't doing?" he asked, reminding me that even *The National*, the main network's evening news show, was sending a reporter to Oakville.

"Yeah," I said, "but I want to do a story on all the other players who are getting sick of playing second-fiddle to Tiger, sick of going to the media room and being asked about Tiger. There's a great clip from Ernie Els at the U.S.

Open, practically crying, begging the media to stop asking him questions about Tiger."

"Okay, go for it."

He assigned me an experienced field producer, Carrie Schipper. I had no idea what a field producer did. But it seemed Carrie was there to get me whatever I wanted. I asked her to find some archival footage of Ernie Els and other top golfers imploring reporters to stop asking them questions about Tiger.

She picked up our media credentials and parking pass, arranged for a cameraman to go with us to the course, Glen Abbey, about twenty-five miles west of downtown.

Early Thursday morning, the opening round of the tournament, we drove in a white CBC News van to Oakville. And Murphy's Law took over.

I told our cameraman to follow Tiger for a while, get shots of him playing, and the crowds following him. "And," I said, "try to get some shots of the guys playing with him, reacting to him, especially if they look intimidated or pissed off."

While he and Carrie went off to the first tee, I went to the media room. I knew most of the writers and some of the players. Since covering my first Canadian Open for UPI in 1975, I had bounced in and out of the sport as a reporter and magazine writer.

Now, I was back in 2000 as a TV reporter, with a field producer and cameramen. When I next met up with Carrie, she didn't look happy. "I've got some bad news," she said. "The camera's broken."

"Did you get anything?"

"Nothing," she said. "The cameraman's gone back to Toronto to get another camera."

Making TV news is always a team effort, dependent on others – and gizmos that sometimes break. I sat under a tree with a reliable pen and notebook, trying to figure out what pictures we had in the bank and what we'd need to get the piece done. There was no hard deadline, though I wanted it ready for play on Newsworld the next morning.

By the time the cameraman returned, Tiger had finished his round and left. It was late afternoon. I directed the cameraman to the seventeenth tee to catch a group of better-known players –competing in Tiger's shadow – teeing off.

Carrie said we also had to get some streeters.

"Why?" I asked.

"You always need streeters," she said.

"Okay," I said. She was the pro. But I'd never understand why every TV story needs a clip from some bozo in the street. Anyone who's ever sat at a bar next to a stranger knows everyone has a stupid opinion on everything.

I approached fans at random, talked to a few guys who looked like semi-knowledgeable golf fans. Carrie wasn't satisfied. "They're all middle-aged white men," Carrie told me. "We need some women and people of color." Typical CBC, I thought.

I interviewed the requisite rainbow of colors and sexes. I stifled a sarcastic impulse to ask people their age, religion and sexual orientation. As we headed back to the clubhouse, Carrie said, "We need to do your standup."

"I don't want to be on camera," I said.

"We'll shoot it anyway," she said. "We can decide later whether we want to use it."

My on-camera experience had been limited to sitting in the Peanut Gallery on *The Howdy Doody Show* when I was six, dancing with a junior-high classmate on *American Bandstand*, and stammering like Ralph Kramden – *hummana-hummana-humna-hummana* – when interviewed on the CTV network morning show *Canada AM*.

Standing at Glen Abbey in the September sunset, I scribbled a few useless lines in my notebook and recited them with microphone in hand. It took three takes to record something I had no intention of using.

By the time we got downtown to CBC, it was well after dark. Carrie had called ahead and told the tape editor we would probably start cutting my piece around nine o'clock. That gave me about an hour and a half to write a script, based on the pictures and clips we had.

Carrie ordered a pizza and organized the archival tapes I'd asked for. We looked at my awful standup, laughed, and discarded it.

The editor was getting impatient. "Remember," Carrie told me, "every minute of the piece takes an hour to cut. If we don't start soon, we'll be here all night."

I banged out a script based on my vision of the story. I printed it and handed Carrie a copy. "I'm happy with it," I said.

She read it. "It's good," she said, which I translated to mean, *Who gives a shit, it's getting late.*

I went into a little soundproof booth with my script and rehearsed it a couple of times. I put on a pair of big earphones which made me feel like a radio announcer from the 1930s, maybe Orson Welles broadcasting *The War of the Worlds*. I stumbled over my own words a couple of times and started again. Carrie kept instructing me to make it "bigger."

So I stood up, leaned into the mike and gave it some body English. It seemed to help. Finally, Carrie and Brian, the tape editor, had a take they liked – or considered the best an old rookie could do.

When Carrie had said "bigger" it made me think of all the short guys, like me, on TV, who probably gravitated to a profession where a camera could make them appear to be average height.

We finished around two in the morning, seventeen hours after we arrived at the golf course. Carrie left the tape on the desk of the morning show producer with a note attached. I assumed it said something like, *This really sucks but give the old man a break.*

Newsworld played the piece a few times throughout the next day. The reviews were mixed, though most colleagues never mentioned it. Mowat said he loved the writing, but added, "We should work on your performance."

"You mean you want me to do this again?" I asked.

"Sure," he said, "if you come up with more good ideas."

I did two more features for Newsworld. By then, I was working only weekends at the CBC and had two other part-time jobs: teaching college journalism and writing free-lance features for a variety of newspapers and magazines.

I turned one of my TV scripts nearly word-for-word – lengthening the sentences – into a freelance piece for the *Star*'s automotive section. I'd done the reporting at the annual Auto Show, exploring the way car companies come up with names for their models – *Did a focus group name the Ford Focus after itself?* – and mocked the brands that have utterly no meaning in English, such as Altima, Bravada, Camray and Corolla.

The TV version was better. Not because my performance skills had improved. But because when I wrote "two young women in skintight silver body suits, accompanied by the usual pyrotechnics," there were pictures and sound.

That item was the last I did for CBC. Mowat was soon replaced as executive producer in a management power play. The new regime had no interest in putting an old white guy on TV.

Meanwhile, I moved on – and up – to producing, which meant I was a boss again. In military terms, I was more like a squad leader, a sergeant with a small bunch of grunts under my supervision. Many others of much higher rank commanded the various battalions, the corps of The Corp.

Having final approval on scripts, I often rewrote them from top to bottom, bruising the egos of the more fragile writers. I was told that others, behind my back, were calling me "The Bulldozer," a comparison to Ariel Sharon. But, unlike the Israeli, I was making the work better, not leaving a trail of debris and dead Palestinians.

I was yet to do battle with my bosses, as I had everywhere else. That would come. And the world, and my place in it, would change after September 11, 2001.

CHAPTER 30
'I HATE THOSE BASTARDS'

Linda woke me with a call from her office just before 9 a.m. "There's something going on in New York," she said. "A plane has hit the World Trade Center."

My first thought was that a small plane had wandered off course, and that I would turn on the TV to see the tail of a Cessna sticking out the window of some stockbroker's office.

I was reminded of a late-night call I made to Linda in 1978, when I was in New York covering baseball, waking her after seeing a news flash on the TV in my hotel room. "The pope's dead," I told her.

"I know," she said, and hung up. It took me a moment to realize she was thinking about Paul VI, who died a few weeks earlier, not John Paul I, who died that night.

On this Tuesday morning, I switched on the TV in the bedroom, seconds before the second plane hit the South Tower. "Holy shit," I shouted in the empty house, startling Jasper from a snooze in the hallway.

I rushed downstairs, turned on the TV in the living room, stared thunderstruck as CNN showed the replays. I went into the kitchen and put the kettle on for tea. A mug in hand, a cordless phone on the coffee table, I sat on the couch – and stayed there for the rest of the day and into the night.

I kept switching from CNN to CBS to NBC to ABC to CBC. They were all replaying the same scenes. There seemed to be no doubt that two commercial airliners had deliberately crashed into the towers. But, beyond that, the anchors – and the rest of us – had no idea what was going on. They, unlike us, had to keep talking, telling us what they knew. Which was next to nothing.

When the picture switched to Washington, the story became even more confusing. "The State Department seems to be on fire," one anchor said. The problem was that the camera was pointed toward Virginia. From that angle, the smoke rising from the Pentagon looked like it was coming from the State Department.

I watched as one tower collapsed, and then the other, the clouds of dust and debris coming straight at my TV screen, the full horror of the day cascading into my living room.

"We have a report that another plane has crashed in Colorado," the CBC anchor intoned at one point. "The target may have been the North American Air Defense Command, known as NORAD."

"We are just getting word that a plane has crashed in western Pennsylvania," another anchor said later.

That made it five planes: Two in New York, one into the Pentagon, the fourth in Colorado and a fifth in Pennsylvania.

In early afternoon, I called CBC and talked to a friend, anchor Ben Chin. The network's lead anchor, Peter Mansbridge, had taken over the coverage – as had all the big boys at the U.S. networks – but Ben was standing by and trying to help out.

"What are we missing?" he asked.

"Hard to tell," I said. "Just make sure you keep counting the dead. It's about people. You have to keep telling the viewer, as often as possible, how many are confirmed dead and injured. And remind us that fifty-thousand people work in those towers every day."

"Yeah," he said, "I'll pass that on."

"What about that plane in Colorado?"

"What plane in Colorado?"

"Peter said a couple of hours ago that a plane went down in Colorado," I said. "It must have been the one that crashed in Pennsylvania. Might be a good idea if someone is keeping track of any mistakes and that they get corrected fast. We've got to watch what goes on the air. There are going to be a lot of bogus stories that need checking before putting them on."

"Yeah," he said, "it's pretty crazy."

"You going to get on the air?" I asked.

"Maybe at midnight," he said. "Peter's not giving up the chair anytime soon."

"Right," I said, "but people are going to start crashing and they'll need fresh bodies at some point. Pass the word that I'm ready to come in when they need me."

A big story in Canada that day was all the planes landing from coast to coast, planes headed for the United

States but diverted north of the border when the U.S. closed its airspace.

One of the visitors to Canada was a Korean Air 747, which was escorted by fighter jets into the airport at Whitehorse, the capital of the Yukon Territory. CBC carried the landing live, with Mansbridge's ominous suggestion there might be hijackers aboard. There weren't.

On this day I had personal concerns as well. Much of my extended family was in New York. I spent most of the day and night trying to get calls through to Kate, sister Janice, Aunt Ann, cousins Ylain and Carol. By the end of the day, all were accounted for, though everyone seemed to know someone missing and presumed dead in the towers.

Two days later, I was called in to run the Newsworld desk through the night. There was obviously still a lot to report, but I wound up spending much of my time fighting to keep half-baked stories *off* the air.

"There were eight people arrested at LaGuardia," I was told that Thursday night. "Don't you think we should get that on the air."

"Not until we know what it's about," I said. "It could have nothing to do with the attacks, like what happened in Boston yesterday." The TV cameras had spent hours the previous day focused on a Westin hotel in Boston, speculating that accomplices of the hijackers were cornered. They weren't. There was no story at LaGuardia either.

Later in my shift, there was a report that five firefighters had been found alive in an SUV under the rubble at Ground Zero. "We've got to get this on," a higher-ranking producer told me.

"You kidding me?" I said.

"It's on the wire," he said.

"Yeah, I saw it. It's a local ABC report quoting unnamed sources. When the cops confirm it, or the fire department, or the mayor, I'll put it on."

But he wasn't giving up. "Attribute it to AP."

"I can't," I said, "because they're not reporting it, only saying that ABC is reporting it."

"Then attribute it to ABC," he said.

"I can't," I said, "without saying that they're attributing it to unidentified sources. Do you really want to go on the air with a script that says: 'The Associated Press is distributing a story, attributed to the local ABC News station in New York, which is quoting unidentified sources as saying five firefighters have been found alive in the rubble of the World Trade Center?'"

"Can't we just say 'there is a report that five firefighters have been found alive in the rubble of the World Trade Center'?"

"No," I said.

"Why not?" he said.

"Because we have no credible, attributable source for the story – and know it's probably bullshit."

"But that's not our job," he said.

"What's not our job? To report only credible news from reliable sources?"

The argument ended when the wires moved a bulletin saying the story was a hoax.

The problem with CBC Newsworld – later renamed CBC News Network – and the other news channels is that they do very little reporting. They mostly rely on wire

The Expat Files

services. And since the wires often do little original reporting, the news gets washed several times before it goes on the air. It's like one great game of telephone, where a tidbit of truth or nonsense is whispered from one ear to another and inevitably comes out all wrong.

After September 11th, the prevailing attitude in TV news became throw any shit on the wall – on the air – and see if it sticks. Get it fast and hope it's right.

The words "rumor" and "speculation" started creeping into news stories. The word "report" became a catchall for a medium that was notoriously sloppy with attribution.

> *Osama bin Laden is rumored to have fled to Pakistan.*
> *Speculation is that Osama escaped a cave at Tora Bora before the fighting started in Afghanistan.*
> *There is a report that Osama is hiding in a falafel stand in Jersey City.*

This approach was compounded at CBC by top managers who seemed to prefer to *manage* the news, not merely report it.

Soon after 9/11, an edict came down that we would no longer show the pictures of the planes hitting the towers. Why? No explanations accompanied such pronouncements. Maybe the bosses were bored. TV people have short attention spans.

Yet, a few days later, when CBC bought the rights to previously unseen video taken by a French camera crew – capturing a low-angle of one of the planes, with deafening audio of the jet's engines moments before it struck the World Trade Center – CBC ran these pictures at least once an hour for days.

The patriotism inspired by 9/11 in the United States also began to make the people at the CBC uncomfortable, if not hostile. Outbursts of Americans singing *God Bless America* on the U.S. networks were met in the CBC newsroom with derision, shouts of "turn that crap off."

Canadians tend to define themselves in regional terms: Newfoundlanders, Maritimers, Quebecers, Ontarians, westerners. If there is any national identity it is what they are not – Americans. Many Canadians suffer high anxiety when they find themselves siding with the United States, as they did in the days and weeks after 9/11. In the halls of the CBC, the angst became most acute.

Besides not broadcasting scenes of Americans being patriotic, the CBC brass decided in 2002 to ban the words "terrorist" and "terrorism," except in direct quotes. It was considered American jingoism or, as some argued, "one person's terrorist is another person's freedom fighter." Similarly, at CBC, the War on Terror became "Washington's so-called War on Terror," or was avoided altogether.

When more than seven-hundred Canadian troops joined coalition forces in Afghanistan in February 2002, Canadians seemed to support the mission. But, as the shock of 9/11 wore off, anti-Americanism seemed to be the rule rather than the exception in the Liberal government of Jean Chretien – and at CBC News. On the first anniversary of 9/11, Chretien expressed what I was hearing more and more from the Canadian intelligentsia – that

American foreign policy was responsible for the attacks on New York and the Pentagon.

"You know, you cannot exercise your powers to the point of humiliation for others," Prime Minister Chretien said in an interview with CBC. "Because they are human beings too." He went on: "We're looked upon as being arrogant, self-satisfied, greedy and with no limits, and September 11th is an occasion for me to realize it even more."

As the Bush administration began beating its drums to go to war in Iraq, Chretien proudly announced Canada would not be signing up for that campaign, while quietly making a side deal with Washington to beef up the Canadian force in Afghanistan.

To my mind, George Bush, Dick Cheney and the rest of the gang who couldn't talk straight were playing dangerous games in the Middle East. But that didn't mean I was going to keep my mouth shut in the face of reflex anti-Americanism.

In the run-up to the invasion of Iraq, whenever someone in the newsroom applauded France's opposition, I borrowed Bart Simpson's line, calling the French "cheese-eating surrender monkeys."

When Carolyn Parrish, a Liberal member of Parliament from my city of Mississauga, was caught by a microphone saying, "Damn Americans, I hate those bastards" – and some of my colleagues seconded the sentiment – I went around the newsroom grumbling, "Damn Canadians, I hate those bastards."

Being an American is a big part of who I am. It is not my nature to conform or keep quiet, two qualities I mock in Canadians. And if my American edge rubbed people at the CBC the wrong way, tough shit.

But I was angry and frustrated when the coverage suffered because CBC refused to allow its reporters to be imbedded with coalition troops in Iraq. CBC announced it would cover the war independently, which turned out to be from the sidelines, with reporters making brief forays into Iraq from Kuwait before being turned back by coalition forces. Much of the CBC reporting, if you can call it that, came from its correspondents in a studio in Washington or London.

At Newsworld, which was trying to cover the invasion of Iraq around the clock, we used a lot of BBC material but were not allowed to use any from U.S. reporters. I guess CBC didn't know the British were fighting the same war, or that Jane Arraf, an NBC reporter in Iraq, was Canadian.

CBC, and the rest of the news media, would never recover from the madness that began on 9/11.

CHAPTER 31
UP IN THE AIR

I was scheduled to go to San Francisco the first week in October 2001 for a bunch of travel-writing assignments. Flights and hotel reservations had been made.

Fairmont Hotels had arranged a complimentary suite at the original Fairmont, on Nob Hill, and Air Canada had booked me a complimentary business-class seat on a non-stop flight from Toronto.

Ford would be providing me a new Mustang GT introduced that year to replicate the green fastback Steve McQueen drove in the movie *Bullitt* more than thirty years earlier. I'd write a piece for the *Toronto Star*'s automotive section on steering the Mustang through the same San Francisco streets McQueen did in the movie. I had researched the film's locations I would visit, and would work in some of my recollections from my time living in the city when the movie was being made in the late '60s, including my encounter with McQueen at the airport.

I had an assignment from the *National Post,* launched in 1998 to rival the *Globe and Mail* – Canada seemed to be adding newspapers when their number was shrinking in the United States – to write a travel piece on what had become of Haight-Ashbury and all the other hippie hangouts.

On most of my trips, I also would discover something interesting to turn into the CP travel column I wrote every other week. I'd also arranged to play a round of golf at the Olympic Club, hoping to get a column out of it for *Ontario Golf* magazine.

Juggling three jobs, I spent Thursdays and Fridays at my newest career, teaching journalism at Humber College in Toronto; Saturdays and Sundays producing the news at the CBC, and the other three days traveling or writing. In my first crack at freelancing, in the late '70s, the most onerous task was pitching stories, schmoozing with editors.

This time around, there were editors who courted me, valued my work and accepted nearly every idea I pitched in a brief email. They included Adam Gutteridge at the *Star,* who solicited me to write road trip stories for his *Wheels* section, arranged for me to pick up a nice car, and paid me $400 per story; Deborah Stokes, travel editor at the *Post,* who encouraged my often critical and crazed view of the places I visited and sent me $350 checks for each; Ted McIntyre, who gave me a column in his golf magazine, at $500 apiece. Former colleague Anne Tobin, CP's arts-life editor, also gave praise to the travel columns I wrote for my old wire service at a cut-rate of $150 per.

As I planned my three days in San Francisco, the planes hit the towers and al-Qaeda sent a message: "The

Americans must know that the storm of airplanes will not stop." I canceled my trip. Not because of the threat, but because nobody wanted stories on *Bullitt* or hippies right after September 11th, and I didn't have the heart to write them at this time anyway. In the ensuing months, most of my travel pieces would be pegged to 9/11.

I went to Shanksville, Pennsylvania, where United Flight 93 went down; to Washington, a capital turned into an armed encampment, and wrote a very personal essay on a Thanksgiving pilgrimage to my hometown.

As we approached New York City that November on the Palisades Parkway, I phoned Kate's apartment in Washington Heights. We were talking again by then, her silent treatment having run its course.

Jorge answered. "They've lit up the George Washington Bridge for you," he said. And, as if reborn, there it was, as I'd never seen it before, the bridge's twin towers and cables outlined in glaring white light. "Makes a better target," I said.

Crossing the bridge, looking south, the spire of the Empire State Building was aglow in red, white and blue. I strained to see the black hole of Lower Manhattan.

We checked into The Plaza. The small, shabby suite was as depressing as the wounded city. For supper, we ate takeout sandwiches from the Carnegie Deli. Kate and Jorge joined us, then took Jodie and Lacey uptown to stay the night at their apartment.

Linda and I went to the Macy's Thanksgiving Day parade, watched it from my cousin Ylain's window on Central Park West.

"You planning to go to Ground Zero?" Ylain asked.

"No," I said, "and I don't slow down for car wrecks, either."

Thanksgiving Day was spent in Tarrytown, up the Hudson, where Jan, Alan and Mathew lived in a nice old white-framed house on a hill. Dot and Aunt Fay had flown in from Florida. Kate and Jorge, Jodie and Lacey completed the Norman Rockwell tableau around the table.

On Friday, Linda and I strolled Midtown. I love walking in New York, with all its historic buildings, familiar landmarks at every turn. We stopped at Bloomingdale's to shop. We lunched on spicy-meatball heros – subs elsewhere – on a bench in Central Park.

We passed dozens of sidewalk vendors selling hats and shirts stenciled with either FDNY, NYPD or USA, and/or the American flag. We bought a stars-and-stripes scarf as a gift for the young woman who was dog-sitting Jasper.

Early Saturday, in foggy gloom, we walked to the East River. We stood for a while at the water's edge, under the 59th Street Bridge – title of a Paul Simon song, backdrop for Woody Allen's *Manhattan*. That afternoon, our last in New York, I succumbed to Linda's entreaty to go to Ground Zero. We filed past the jumbled ruins with the silent and solemn queues, a cop keeping up a steady chant, "Please keep moving. Take your pictures, and please keep moving." People did as they were told. Maybe they were all Canadians.

"What do you think?" asked Linda.

"About what?" I replied.

"About being here?"

"I'm not sure," I said, "except everything's changed."

We walked through the financial district to a restaurant at the South Street Seaport. I could see the Statue of Liberty in silhouette in the hazy harbor. A jetliner flew overhead. What's next?

I wrote the story of this trip for the *Star*. The narrative was sprinkled with lyrics from Paul Simon's *American Tune*. Every stanza of the song worked with the post-9/11 mood.

Linda and my kids were often characters – played themselves – in my stories. My roles in these first-person pieces ranged from curmudgeon to happy jester.

My reporter's knack for recreating scenes and conversations served me well as a travel writer, as when Linda and I returned from a three-day spring getaway in Paris.

We sat in the afternoon sunshine, in the front row of the Cafe Select on the Boulevard Montparnasse, sipping cold beer after a long walk from our hotel on the Right Bank, giggling at the menu's twisted-English homage to its literary and artistic heritage ...

"Listen to this," I said to Linda, reading from the first page of the menu: "Picasso, Cocteau, Max Jacob all sat at the Select's terrace, as well as Derain, Matisse and Foujita, Henri Miller" – I think they mean Henry – Ernest Hemingway and Scott Fitzgerald, author of Happy and Cursed, and Tender is the Night."

"Who's Foujita?" Linda said.

"The Japanese inventor of the fajita?" I said, laughing at my lame joke, still sputtering when I asked, "And what's with this Fitzgerald book called Happy and Cursed?"

"Must be some weird French translation of The Beautiful and the Damned."

> "That's us," I said.
> "You're not beautiful," she said.
> "Yeah," I said, "but I'm very happy. And, good Canadians should feel cursed for that."

Another story I got out of that trip to Paris was a take on Art Buchwald's madcap column called *The Six-Minute Louvre*, where he tells the tale of fictional tourists clocking the time it takes to view "the Big Three," the only things worth seeing: *Winged Victory of Samothrace*, the *Venus de Milo* and the *Mona Lisa*.

Armed with a stopwatch, I raced through the museum, Linda in my wake. I checked off the first two and made a beeline for da Vinci's smiling Renaissance minx.

> *The corridors were crowded, people stopping unexpectedly to glance at one masterpiece or another. I started to pick up signs for Mona, but the obstacles kept getting bigger, and traveling in packs.*
> *I snaked through, seconds ticking down to the finish line, my wife snapping pictures of her idiot husband. Suddenly, I hit the wall. There was a roped-in lineup for Mona, moving slowly. I skirted the line, ignoring curses in six or seven languages.*
> *An agitated security guard reached me just as I stood in front of Mona. I smiled back at the painting and clicked my stopwatch – 5:52.*
> *"It's okay," I told the security guard. "I'm leaving, seen all there is to see."*

When Jodie was living in Whistler, and later in Vancouver, I flew to the West Coast at least once a year to combine work with the pleasure of seeing my daughter. Most times, I included in my itinerary an adventurous assignment to share.

> When I signed up for a three-hour Seafun Safari – "Victoria's wildest whale watching ride!" – I missed the exclamation point in the brochure and imagined myself The Old Man and the Sea, in his initial stage of futility, drifting in calm waters, spotting an occasional flying fish, not Ishmael helplessly lashed to a hurtling ship in the hands of a crazed captain, chasing monstrous mammals ...
> Once clear of the harbor, with Jodie at my side in the front row of the Zodiac, and nine survival-suited strangers behind us, the exclamation point stabbed me in the chest, as Jeff gunned the twin 175-horsepower engines, knocking me back in my seat and taking my breath away. Literally.
> "What a rush," said Jodie. What's the rush? I thought.

Jodie and I had been a traveling twosome since she was five, when I took her on a business trip to Alberta and tacked on several days for us to go camping in the Rockies.

Lacey was less adventurous and less enthused about spending time on the road with dad. But, when she was thirteen, I took her on a three-day trip to Fort Worth, Texas. I opened my story with an admission I'd conned Lacey from the start.

Before we left home, I read Lacey the riot act: "Keep to my schedule, don't interrupt when I'm talking to people – don't talk at all when I'm in a meeting – in fact, speak only when spoken to."
"Are we going to have any fun, Dad?"
"Sure," I said.

She did have some fun. Riding one of the Texas longhorns paraded through the streets in the Stockyards District; feeding a giraffe at a drive-through game park; feeding tokens into slot machines at Billy Bob's honkytonk.

Whenever I am in Texas, or anywhere south of the Mason-Dixon Line or west of the Mississippi, I keep my eyes peeled for pistol packin' mamas and papas, while never taking the bait on a Second Amendment debate with the local yokels.

My daughter, however, had the Columbine school shooting on her mind when she disobeyed my admonition only to speak when spoken to. Over lunch with one of our hosts, we learned her last PR job was with the NRA.

"Why does anybody need a gun?" Lacey asked.

"To protect yourself."

"But if nobody had guns ..."

"But they do."

"But, what if they destroyed them all? Then nobody would have one."

"Except the criminals."

"Anybody want ice cream?" I said, ending the debate.

The headline on my story in the *National Post*: *Travelling with Dad: Not so bad.*

Guns were also an element of the story when I went to see Kate and Jorge late in 2002, the year they moved from New York to Tucson. They were the navigators in my rental SUV on a day trip to Mexico. The first stop was a café off a dirt road in Arivaca.

As Kate went in to order, a tall, grizzled cowboy with a handlebar moustache came out, a sizable revolver in a holster on his hip, a gunbelt filled with extra ammo. I stared at the gun. He stared at me staring at the gun. I kept a hooded eye on the aged gunslinger until he drove off in his pickup.
A younger cowboy with a wispy moustache, also packing, was sitting at a table on the patio, being berated by a haggard young woman. As the conversation became more heated – she did nearly all the talking, complaining that they needed a new truck but couldn't afford one – I gulped down my tea and urged Kate and Jorge back on the road before we wound up catching a stray bullet.

We parked in Nogales, Arizona, and walked across the border into its namesake town in Mexico, where we were immediately accosted by merchants standing outside their shops in the narrow streets.

"You need prescription drugs?" one hustler said, getting in my face. "You look like you need Viagra."

We moved on. "How about a nice sombrero? Make you look like a mariachi."

"No thanks."

One persistent seller chased me down the street. "Hey, mister, don't be a cheapskate. Buy some nice jewelry for the lady."

"The lady is my daughter," I huffed.

"Okay, I give you two blankets and a bottle of tequila for your daughter."

In these stories, I was mindful of never writing anything that could offend Linda or my daughters. They usually read and signed off on a piece before I filed it.

Such personal narratives took a lot more care than the average slab of journalism. They underlined the Red Smith line that "writing is easy – you just open up a vein and bleed."

Travel writing also reminded me of the quote from Smith's sportswriter friend, Bill Corum – "I don't want to be a millionaire, I just want to live like one." Corum was talking about traveling the wide world of sports, covering events. I was chasing my whims and desires – first-class, all expenses paid – writing features, not news.

As a freelance travel writer, I had to adjust my attitude as a journalist. For one thing, I needed to get to the destination and wasn't about to bunk in some fleabag when I got there. For another, who can afford to shell out thousands of dollars for airfare and hotels for a story that netted a couple of hundred bucks?

Most travel writers go on organized trips called FAMs, the three capital letters short for familiarization tours. A tourism board, for example, invites a gaggle of writers to follow a strict itinerary to see everything the sponsor wants them to see and write about.

This was why in a place like Toronto, where there were four daily newspapers, their travel sections some weekends would all feature stories on the same destination, describing the same spectacular scenery, the same fabulous food, and the same posh accommodations in the same hotel.

In more than ten years of freelance travel writing, I went on three FAM trips – to Quebec, the Canadian Rockies and Bordeaux – and they were mostly awful. I simply did not work and play well with others, dismissing most of my fellow travelers as hobbyists, not journalists, mooching free trips and then writing some version of the press release supplied by their benefactor.

One of these amateurs, who wrote part time for Canadian Press, as I did, filed a press release word for word, which ran on the CP wire under his byline.

I considered myself a journalist first, looking for offbeat angles and presenting an interesting take on the places I visited. After the Bordeaux trip, I wrote a piece for the *Post* bitching about being force-fed frightful French delicacies of undercooked fowl when all I wanted was an omelet for lunch and steak frites for supper.

I also poked fun at French food served on my long weekend in Paris with Linda, in a piece for the *Post* on visiting the locations of three of my favorite movies – *The Day of the Jackal, Frantic, and Charade* – set in the city.

> *Like Cary Grant and Audrey Hepburn, we set sail on a romantic dinner cruise on the Seine.*
> *"I could eat a horse," a ravenous Hepburn told Grant in Charade.*
> *"That's what you ordered," he replied.*
> *"What do you think of the coquille St. Jacques?" Linda asked me.*
> *"The scallops taste like forty-year-old props from the movie," I replied.*

I was equally blunt in print when I finally ended my love affair with The Plaza, after a sleazy real estate hustler named Donald Trump ran it into the ground. *In recent years, it can be best described by the famous line from Edward Albee's play Who's Afraid of Virginia Woolf: "What a dump!" The last time I was there, a wall in my room fell down.*

Because I could guarantee space in the *Star* or the *Post* and the CP wire, my hosts tended to subscribe to the line that all publicity was good publicity.

In turn, I learned I could order up a trip to practically anywhere, write my own itinerary and often bring a family member along. I expected only the very best and got it, never having to reach into my wallet for anything except a tip.

When I drove to Washington with Jodie, we spent a couple of nights in separate suites at the Watergate hotel and a couple more in adjoining rooms at the Ritz Carlton. We dined at Sam and Harry's, on the restaurant's trademark steaks, accompanied by a fabulous bottle of Napa Valley merlot, delivered by the maitre 'd, who stopped at our table to welcome us.

But since this was soon after 9/11, the D.C. tourism board didn't exactly get what it was hoping for in a piece that began:

> **WASHINGTON – At night, through the open window of my room at the Watergate hotel, I heard the choppers. Flying low. Up and down the Potomac River. Sounded like a scene from Apocalypse Now. I was hoping not to awaken to the smell of napalm in the morning ...**

After 9/11, the last traces of glamour associated with air travel died. I dreaded going to the airport, the apprehension of my fellow passengers, the frustration of being herded through long lines, the anxiety in the eyes of airline personnel, the paranoia of the security agents.

I began to restrict my travel plans to seeing Jodie in Vancouver, Kate and Jorge in Tucson, my mother and Aunt Fay in Florida, sister Jan and other family in New York.

I always stayed in an upscale hotel, usually with a spa, feeding my addiction to massages. If I wrote about them, I'd play the rube.

> *"You want your glutes done?" the masseuse asked.*
> *"What's that – or them?" I replied.*
> *"Your butt," she said.*
> *I blushed. "Oh, what the hell, I spend most of my time sitting on it – or them."*

I didn't mind being a self-indulgent slut. But I was damned if I was going to be branded a whore. That's what would end my travel-writing career.

After nearly ten years of writing a column for Canadian Press, I got a call from editor Anne Tobin. "Have you noticed what the *Toronto Star* is doing in its travel section," she said.

"What do you mean?" I replied.

"At the end of every story there's a line that says who paid for the writer's trip," she said. "We'd like to do the same."

"Why?" I said. "Do you plan to say at the end of every sports story that the writer got a free pass to the game? Or at the end of every book story that the writer got a free book? Or at the end of every record review that the writer got a free CD? Or at the end of every movie review that the writer got a free ticket to a private screening?"

"It's not the same," she said. "Travel costs a lot more."

"I don't know what it costs," I said. "I never asked anybody. All I know is that to write about travel you have to travel, the same way to write about baseball you have to go to the ballpark. When I was on staff at CP and covered the Blue Jays in the playoffs and World Series, there were no disclaimers that I got a free seat in the press box while the fans in the stands were paying hundreds of dollars."

"Well," she said, "this isn't my idea. It comes from higher up."

"Maybe they should rethink it," I said. "I don't know what the *Star* is doing or why it's doing it, but none of the other papers – CP members – do this."

"I'll get back to you," Anne said.

I checked the *Star* and, sure enough, there was a tagline after some stories that read something like: *The writer's trip to Timbuktu was subsidized by Timbuktu Tourism.* But I noticed these tags were only attached to freelance stories, not the ones by the *Star*'s travel editor or other staff.

I phoned a friend who ran a big Toronto PR firm that specialized in travel. I told her about my conversation with Anne and mentioned the *Star*'s policy.

"Don't believe a word of it," she said. "There wouldn't be any stories in any travel pages if the writers – staff or freelancers – had to pay for their trips. At least some portion of every trip by the *Star* – and even the *New York Times*, which has a stated policy against it – is subsidized in some way."

I thought of calling Anne back to relay what I'd learned from my PR friend but decided to let it slide. Anne didn't raise the issue again for a while. Then, in the spring of 2005, while in Ottawa, Fairmont booked me a suite at the Chateau Laurier. I stayed in Room 358, which was called the Karsh Suite, because it had been the home of the great Canadian portrait photographer Yousuf Karsh and his wife Estrellita for eighteen years.

I wrote a CP column about the couple's time in the hotel – before they moved to Boston, where he died at the age of ninety-three – about the framed Karsh portrait of George Bernard Shaw over the fireplace in the suite. And mentioned the signed Karsh prints – of Churchill, Einstein, Pablo Casals, Georgia O'Keeffe – in the Reading Lounge off the main lobby.

After I filed the story to CP, I got an email from a copy editor, asking if I could include the price of the suite in the story. I refiled the story to include the rate: $1,800. Moments later, I got a call from Anne.

"Did you pay for the room?" she asked.

"Yeah, right," I said with a laugh, "I shelled out $1,800 so I can make $150 on a CP column."

"Don't you think we should say that the hotel paid for your room?"

"No, that's not correct," I said, "since the hotel told me I could only have the suite when it wasn't booked. And it wasn't booked those two days. So the only thing they paid for was the housekeeping service to clean up after me, and I left a nice tip for the maid."

"Okay," she said. But this wasn't the last of it.

In July 2005, I was on the West Coast to do some travel assignments, but mainly to see Jodie. On a Saturday morning, I picked up a copy of the *Post*. In the travel section, there was a story I had written about a trip Linda and I had taken to St. John's.

I usually read my stories after they are published, just to check if an editor did something stupid. My eyes went straight to the line added at the end: *Ken Becker visited Newfoundland as a guest of Destination St. John's.*

I was shaking with rage. If I'd known the *Post* was going to do that, I would have pulled the story.

When I got home, I discovered an email from the *Post*'s travel editor, Deborah Stokes, advising me of a new policy and asking my approval to put the tagline on my Newfoundland story. Too late, I replied with an angry email and angrier voicemails. She didn't call back.

I kept checking the *Post* and didn't see another tagline like the one she had attached to my St. John's story. A month later, the other shoe dropped.

I worked out a story idea with the Four Seasons hotel. The Toronto Film Festival was coming up, which drew a lot of big-name Hollywood stars to the city. Many of them stayed at the Four Seasons.

I thought it would be fun to write about the star treatment. The hotel arranged for Linda and me to spend one night and pretend I was a star. I checked in under the name Rick Blaine, Bogie's character in *Casablanca*, and wrote my next Canadian Press column about the experience.

I filed the story to CP on August 8, 2005. Soon after, I got a message from Anne, advising me that one of her bosses had seen the tagline on my Newfoundland story in the *Post* and wanted the same on every CP travel story.

My Four Seasons story was already on the wire, with the line suggesting I was on the take from the hotel chain. I demanded Anne kill my story in an email which I signed with my wire initials – kmb, in lowercase as always – for the last time.

I still had some unfinished business elsewhere, though. I finally got through to Deborah Stokes at the *Post* and told her how her little stunt had doomed my association with CP. She said she was mortified and terribly sorry. She asked what she could do to make it up for me.

For one thing, I said, she could run my story on the Four Seasons and not put any bullshit tagline at the bottom. For another, she could soon run a couple of pieces I had written on assignment for her that she had yet to publish.

She agreed. But wound up only printing the Four Seasons story. After that, she never returned my calls or answered my emails. It took me more than a year to get the check I was owed, only after complaining to the *Post*'s editor-in-chief.

I had a similar blow-up with the new *Wheels* editor at the *Star*, who had replaced Adam Gutteridge. He was obviously not a fan, as Adam had been.

The new guy ran my last road-trip story assigned by Adam – about driving on the left in Barbados – but sent me nasty email saying he had taken out every reference to the resort where I had stayed because he didn't "run ads for hotels that gave writers free rooms."

After checking *his* column in the latest edition of the *Star*, about driving a Porsche for a week, I fired back in kind: *Was that Porsche your aunt's car?*

I'd had it with these hypocrites, who had one rule for freelancers and no rules for themselves.

Now I had only two jobs.

CHAPTER 32
SCHOOL DAYS

The early 2000s were filled with more downs than ups for me, both personally and professionally. Besides giving up my travel-writing business, working at the CBC was dragging me down. Then, there was the double whammy of Jasper dying and nearly losing my mother.

At the dawn of the decade, we took the kids to Sanibel for Christmas and New Year's, the Millennium, for what would be our eleventh – and last – stay at the cottage on the bay. I still enjoyed their company more than I did most people. But they didn't want to be there, didn't want to spend their vacation, particularly New Year's Eve, with their parents, wanted to be home whooping it up with their friends. Really couldn't blame them. When I was thirteen, like Lacey, and especially sixteen, like Jodie, I was long past partying with the old folks.

We'd brought them up to be independent. That was our job, to prepare them to go out on their own. They always had part-time jobs. As a young teenager, Jodie was a hostess in a Tex-Mex restaurant. Lacey would work as a server at Tim Horton's, where she learned the ways of the world, instructed to give free coffee and donuts to the local cops.

In high school in Lorne Park, their old K-car – handed down from cousins, then from Jodie to Lacey – sat in the student parking lot alongside their classmates' BMWs and Mercedes.

I wondered what son Sean would have been up to at the Millennium. Preparing to go off to college? Fielding academic scholarship offers from Harvard and Stanford? Considering a baseball scholarship from Southern Cal?

The first years of the new century were especially cruel to my mother. After my dad died, Dot tried to get along on her own. She learned to drive, for the first time, in her seventies. She took care of all the chores and errands that had always been dad's jobs.

But then, she had a heart attack that necessitated the installation of a pacemaker, and a vascular breakdown that cost her two toes. This was on top of the crippling psoriatic arthritis, with its accompanying nasty psoriasis, that had plagued her her entire adult life.

She was in and out of hospitals. Pronounced at death's door more than once. Janice was constantly flying to Florida from New York to look after her. I did my duty a couple of times. So did Kate.

But, after her sister Fay died in 2003, and a succession of hurricanes the next year, we finally persuaded Dot to move north. Linda and I went down to oversee the sale of her house on Egret Isle and escorted her on a flight to New York, where we handed her over to Janice.

Dot moved into a ritzy seniors' home in Yonkers, just on the border of the Bronx where she grew up. But the key to the location was that it was only about twenty minutes on the Saw Mill River Parkway from Janice's house in Tarrytown.

In her eighties, Dot had been sick her whole life – I forgot to mention the spherocytosis that had led to the removal of her spleen, as it had mine – and already outlived my father by nearly ten years. She wasn't done yet.

In June of 2004, Jasper had just turned thirteen. We'd chosen him from among his brothers and sisters at the breeder's lovely property in Terra Cotta, in the Caledon hills, about forty minutes north of our home in Clarkson. He was eight weeks old in August 1991 when he'd come bounding up to us, as if to say, *Take me!*

The following spring, we found an orphaned baby raccoon in our backyard. It was evening. We didn't know what to do with it. I put it in the shed and decided to deal with it the next day.

In the morning, I found it frozen stiff. I dug a grave next to the shed. Picked up the rigid raccoon and tossed it in. Shoveled dirt atop the cadaver. It flinched. Then moved. "It's alive!" I shouted.

Linda and the kids came to assist the rescue. We wrapped the raccoon in a blanket. Carried it down to the basement and put it in a basket, next to the furnace.

The day warmed up. So did the raccoon. We took it out on the deck. It mistook Jasper for its mother. Kept climbing on his back. Still a puppy, he was tolerant, gentle and understanding.

Linda shot video of the show. I got on the phone and found a woman who adopted orphaned raccoons. She picked it up later that day.

Jasper's behavior illustrated the kind of dog he was and would always be. We were inseparable during the years north of Superior and again back in the old neighborhood. He and I would walk down the street to the Rattray Marsh. He was never on a leash. Never bothered anyone.

In his later years, he would lie on the front porch or under a tree in the front yard, not anxious or able to move much. It got to the point where he could no longer rise up. Too painful. I would have to carry him from one place to another, as I had Yaz.

Jasper stopped eating. He was the sweetest, gentlest, best dog ever. But it was time.

Linda and I took him to the vet. I got down on the floor in the treatment room with Jasper. Hugged him. Held on. Said goodbye.

Didn't stay for the execution.

I was trembling when we got outside. Gasping. Feeling a thousand times more emotional than when I watched my dad die. But I didn't cry. I never cry. No time to fall into a funk, either. Too busy with work.

I'd started the new millennium with the best writing trip of my life – eight days in Australia, from Sydney to the Sunshine Coast to Kangaroo Island – which produced my favorite opening line of a travel piece:

I was dining on kangaroo fillets when the dingo strolled into the restaurant.

As soon as I returned from Oz, I began a new career, transferring my credentials as a journalist to the classroom. I had been recruited into the teaching in much the same fashion as I had into TV news – being assured this old dog could learn new tricks.

When I started as a writer at CBC, my lineup editor was Judy Charles. She was a few years younger. And Jewish. We shared a sense of humor and a lot of friends in the business. I liked her right away.

Judy worked weekends, as I did. But her day job was as coordinator of the journalism program at Humber College. "You ever think about teaching?" she asked me in the CBC newsroom one day.

"Not really," I replied. "I don't know anything about it."

"A year ago you didn't know anything about TV either," she said.

In January 2000, I began teaching at Humber, very much a city school in a distant section of Toronto, near the airport. My students were in their teens, fresh out of high school. Most of the girls – and there were always more girls in all my classes – wanted to be on TV. Most of the boys wanted to be in sports. They didn't consider that specific skills were required to meet their goals.

I needed some skills as well – to get over my unease with public speaking. My first day in a classroom, before thirty or so blank stares, about all I could muster was introducing myself.

A girl in the front row bailed me out. "Tell us about yourself, Mr. Becker."

"Please call me Ken, or Becker," I said – they preferred Becker, as did all the students that followed – before reciting my resume, recounting some war stories and listing some famous people I had interviewed. The kids looked at me uncomprehendingly when I mentioned such names as Desmond Tutu and Dan Quayle.

I hadn't prepared any lessons because I didn't know how to do that. I got through the first few weeks by telling the students to read the newspapers and be prepared to talk about the stories they'd read. "I don't want to talk about Madonna or hockey," I said. "Read the news section."

Their paper of choice was the *Toronto Star*, probably because it was distributed free on campus. They had questions, most of which were prefaced with, "I read this whole story and didn't understand a word of it."

This proved to be a good starting point. "If the writer isn't communicating, then he or she isn't doing his or her job," I said. "The lead is the most important sentence in the story. If you can't grab the reader with the lead, you've failed. The reader will simply go on to the next story or turn the page. After the lead, every sentence has to flow into the next. Again, if you confuse the reader at any point, the reader will just give up."

My education as a teacher got a big boost when one of the kids told me they had watched *All the President's Men* in another class. I had a large collection of newspaper-themed movies at home and found that I could get through a class by popping a tape in a VCR.

I played the students some of my favorites, including *Teacher's Pet* (1958), with Clark Gable as a tough city editor and Doris Day as a night school journalism teacher.

"We don't like black-and-white movies," one of the boys finally confided. They probably would not have objected to black-and-white episodes of *Leave It to Beaver*.

I read to them some of Rick Bragg's Pulitzer-winning columns from the *New York Times*. I loved the writing. The kids didn't seem impressed.

They also knew next to nothing about current events, history or geography, all the nuts and bolts that journalists should carry around in their heads. Most of them couldn't name the ten Canadian provinces and their capitals, or one member of the federal cabinet.

I knew from my own kids that they learned nothing in high school. I made it my mission to at least give them some knowledge of their country.

I gave them a midterm exam that required them to memorize – and spell correctly – the provinces and territories and their capitals, as well as the names of important Canadian politicians.

In 2004, I was so disgusted with the test results that I wrote an op-ed piece for the *Globe and Mail*, poking fun at their ignorance and giving examples of their dumbest answers.

By this time, I had lived in Canada for thirty years. I had traveled to every province and the Northwest Territories. I knew Canada's history, from colonial times to the present. An American was teaching Canadian kids about their country.

But I had run out of patience teaching children. I had survived my own kids' teenage years and didn't care to relive them with my students, like *Groundhog Day*.

My pal Judy understood my frustration. She assigned me only postgrad classes. All these students had university degrees. Most were in their mid-twenties. They arrived at Humber with a sober attitude and a determination to succeed. They were scared too, knowing they'd bet their futures on becoming journalists.

I taught them the fundamentals of reporting and newswriting in the first semester of their first year. "I will be teaching you a new language, the language of journalism," I said the first day. "Some of you may think you know how to write. You don't. Some of you may have been honor students in English in university, which means you know how to write essays which are basically incomprehensible to anyone except some English professor who is rereading *Ulysses* for the twelfth time and still trying to figure out what it's about. Just because you got an 'A' on some fucking essay, and your mother thinks you're a great writer, doesn't mean you have a fucking clue about writing news."

The cursing got their attention. To keep it, I used the f-word a lot in class.

I paused at this point, took a slug of water, and drank in the faces. Some appeared stunned, others terrified. At least one guy – it was always a guy – snickered. I knew he'd have trouble.

"But," I went on, "within a few months, if you work really hard – writing is hard – most of you will *get it*. You'll go through a lot of frustration, thinking 'I'm never going to get this,' then suddenly something will click. So, if you're serious about this, hang in there. Tomorrow, we get to work."

The next day, I had them rewrite a press release. It was always a straight-forward story, such as a police report on a fatal traffic accident.

The next week, I took them on a field trip, across the campus to a pond in the Humber Arboretum. I stood at the edge of a pond and had them huddle around.

"It's 5 a.m.," I said. "The sun is just coming up. You were home sleeping when you got a call from the city desk and were told to get out to Humber College, that something was going on – it was all over the police scanner. You arrived and saw a couple of cop cars with lights flashing. You asked one of the cops what was going on and he told you to talk to the sergeant. That's me. Now ask your questions."

"What happened here?"

"That's not your first question," I replied.

They tried a few more. I shook my head, refused to answer. Finally, one student came up with the right question: "May I have your name, please."

"Yes," I said, "it's Staff Sergeant Andrew Pepper."

That got them going – Sergeant Pepper.

I created a scene in which a stolen convertible, with a young couple inside, crashed through a row of bushes and landed in the pond. It took about an hour to coax all the right questions out of them.

I told them some "hanky-panky" may have distracted the male driver and his female companion. "There is some evidence that the driver may have been otherwise occupied at the time of the crash," said Sergeant Pepper.

I kept the Beatles theme going to amuse them, identifying the suspects as James Paul McCartney and Lucy Skye Diamond.

We went back to the classroom. They had about an hour to write a maximum 150-word story. I helped them with the lead. They always wrote in class, with me standing over their shoulders, poking them in the right direction.

Over the years, I discovered what worked and didn't work. The car in the pond worked.

So did another field trip – just outside our classroom, hopefully in the rain – when I pretended to be the police chief at a crime scene in downtown Toronto. This time, the story was that Marilyn Lastman, the wife of the former mayor, had plunged ten stories to her death from the couple's penthouse apartment. I left doubt whether she jumped or was pushed, so they had to be careful writing it.

The following week they wrote an obit of Marilyn Lastman, whose husband Mel was mayor from 1998 until 2003. Mrs. Lastman, who was in her early seventies when I began giving this assignment, died every year in my class.

The reason I chose her was because she was well known in the city – for throwing lavish parties, faking her own kidnapping, and being arrested for shoplifting – but not important enough to rate a thousand-word obit. I didn't want these kids writing long stories, partly to teach them discipline, but also because I didn't want to be marking endless pages of double-spaced crapola.

"You should be able to write a great story in fewer than five-hundred words," I told them. "You could write the Crucifixion in five-hundred words. For the Second Coming, I'll give you seven-fifty."

I ran my classroom like the newsroom I broke in with at UPI in New York and the ones I ran at United Press and Canadian Press. I was the dictatorial editor, they were all cub reporters. I made at least one student cry in the first few months of the first semester. I didn't do it deliberately, but it never failed. The tears usually flowed from a failing grade on an assignment.

It didn't matter that I continually told them to "forget about grades. Grades don't matter. Learning how to write is what matters."

They got what they deserved on their stories, mostly sixties and seventies. A misspelled proper name, a wrong fact, or a bungled quote was an automatic fail.

Then, I gave them a midterm exam, much the same as the geography and politics test the younger ones consistently failed. The postgrads knew how to study. Most of them aced it, boosted their midterm grade and began to relax.

I discovered I needed to break these kids of their hoity-toity university writing habits and then build them up again as they learned the craft. "And it is a craft," I told them. "Art class is down the hall."

When their opinions slipped into copy, I said, "I don't care what you think. The reader doesn't care what you think."

I gave them my practiced rant on plagiarism. "If you copy and paste one sentence of somebody else's work, it's plagiarism. I will spot it. I'll know it's not your writing. I'll Google it and find it. Then I will hunt you down and kill you. I know where you live."

By the time the first semester was over, I had a rapport with most students. They were able to write a decent lead and a clean story. They *got it*.

Their second semester, I edited their assignments for the weekly school newspaper.

One of my classes created a Facebook page they called *We (Heart) Chief Becker*. Facebook was a new thing the kids were into. As far as I knew, it was a place they posted photos of themselves and their friends getting drunk, the girls looking slutty and the boys looking wasted.

Their Facebook page was not exactly a tribute to me. It was more of a place to gossip about me.

Chief Becker's Famous Five Ws:

Who THE FUCK SAYS?
What THE FUCK IS THIS?
Where THE HELL DID YOU GET THIS FROM?
When THE FUCK DID THIS HAPPEN?
How THE HELL DO YOU KNOW?

When Becker was editing my story one day, his reaction to the 500-word piece was, "what the fuck is this? a million words?!" After editing it he sang praises for it being over and these are the exact words that came out of his mouth: "God I need a cigarette after editing that! Fuck the cigarette, I need some heroin or something!"
And then he walked out of class to have a smoke. I saw him outside later that day and he told me that it was not the worst thing he's ever had to mark. Which I guess was kind of an apology. Maybe not.

Had a really lovely quote from a very nice lady in my last story. He actually put brackets around it and wrote PUKE and then laughed! I think that means cut-it-out in Becker.

Becker, today, regarding my sappy lead: "No, I won't write PUKE on it, I will actually puke all over it if you put that lead in"

Me: "Hey chief! what's your favourite colour?"
Chief: "Black"
Me (being a smart ass): "You know, black technically isn't a colour."
Chief: "Tell that to Huey P. Newton and Eldridge Cleaver."
I think this was the point when Becker just blew away the competition and took top spot as BEST TEACHER EVER. I seriously got TOLD!

I miss my class with Becker last year! I'll never forget when one of my stories caused him to bust out singing a jazzy rendition of "Summertime." I also remember the first time he told me that my story did not absolutely suck ... I was in shock for days! Becker is the best!

I'm swooning. Becks told me today my work was in between "o.k" and "crap." It must be love between us.

I didn't know what to make of my students' generation. So many seemed to be superficial *and* serious. Superficially serious? Seriously superficial? They tossed around the words love and hate like so much confetti. After getting a bad mark or criticism on an assignment, a kid would say, "Why do you hate me?"

My standard response was, "I don't hate you. I don't have such strong feelings about you one way or another."

In fact, I liked these kids. A lot. Before long, I'd host groups of students at my house to drink, talk about writing and the news biz. I kept in touch with many long after they graduated.

I didn't teach them in the final year of the two-year program, when they chose a path, either concentrating on print or broadcast journalism.

The best and the brightest gravitated to TV, a sound career choice considering the uncertainty in the newspaper business. But the journalism was going downhill on both paths.

Working weekends at the CBC News, I would be surrounded by former students who had gotten a crack at the big time. But the big time was not what it was cracked up to be.

CHAPTER 33
DEATH FAR FROM HOME

In 2006, I turned sixty, Linda and I bought a townhouse – not to be mistaken for a New York brownstone – back in Clarkson. Lacey had pretty much moved in with her boyfriend. Jodie, the only university graduate in the family, was well-settled in Vancouver.

It was forty years since I walked into the *New York Times* as a nineteen-year-old know-nothing. I'd bounced across borders, from city to city, town to town, newspaper to newspaper, one wire service to another, and into TV news. I'd learned a craft – to report, write and edit news – and developed the skill to take command of coverage. But the business had changed.

Every story was presented as the biggest news in history. Many were hyped to scare the crap out of people: SARS, bird flu, West Nile virus, mad cow disease, bombs in shoes on airplanes, audio tape from al Qaeda, video of masked terrorists holding a sword over the head of a hostage.

An obit – Pierre Trudeau, Ronald Reagan, Yasser Arafat, Pope John Paul – turned into a round-the-clock passion play. On CBC, Reagan was given less of a sendoff than Arafat, while the CBC's pope-a-thon contained commentary from so many priests it seemed we turned the network over to the Roman Catholic Church.

But the headline story in Canada post-9/11 was the country's participation in the war in Afghanistan. The military mission had moved from the relative safety of Kabul to the wild south of Kandahar. Soldiers would die fighting the Taliban, military leaders warned. They were right.

The casualties were reported appropriately by the Canadian media. Death in the war zone topped the news agenda, from the time it happened on the battlefield, to the coffins coming home, to the funerals in cities and towns across the country.

Inevitably, it became a numbers game. Four killed in a firefight was bigger news than one killed by a roadside bomb. The natural ebb and flow of news took over.

On Saturday, August 6, 2006, one Canadian soldier was killed when his vehicle crashed into a truck on a highway outside Kandahar. I directed the story be dropped from the top of the lineup late in the day. I got a call from my executive producer.

"We always lead with Canadian casualties," I was told.

"Yeah," I said, "usually, but this was just one dead, in a traffic accident."

"We always lead with Canadian casualties," she said.

"Is that a rule?"

"Yes."

At CBC, it was easier to have rules than exercise news judgment. Especially if you let some higher up make the rules and the decisions, insulating you from any fallout. The most appalling and personally upsetting example of this occurred that same summer, and also involved Canadians in Afghanistan.

The CBC reporter and those from other news outlets in Kandahar were embedded with the two-thousand or so Canadian troops at the base there. Under the terms of an agreement between media and the military, news blackouts would be imposed whenever a Canadian soldier was killed, primarily to allow time for next-of-kin to be notified.

But a blackout would also be put in place if there was a rocket attack near the base – there were many, most harmless – or if publicity could compromise operations, tip the enemy to the location of Canadian and other NATO soldiers.

So, for those of us back in the newsroom in Toronto, word of a news blackout in Kandahar – the jargon was "Kandahar is in lockdown" – did not necessarily spell big news at home. Reading the tea leaves was trickier when NATO commanders in Afghanistan announced the deaths of coalition soldiers, as they often did, without specifying nationality.

On Sunday, September 3, 2006, we got word of a news blackout in Kandahar. Soon after, there was a wire story saying three NATO troops had been killed in an offensive against the Taliban in southern Afghanistan, the territory where Canadians operated.

We were trying to reach our reporter in Kandahar when Reuters moved a story saying three Canadians had been killed in the battle. Just as I was about to put this on the air, I was told that our reporter in Kandahar had called to say *four* Canadians had been killed, but that we couldn't report it until the news blackout was lifted.

I prepared a story that began: *At least three Canadians have been killed in a battle against the Taliban outside Kandahar.*

"We can't say 'at least'," said my executive producer, Nancy Kelly, who was reading my work-in-progress on her computer.

"Why not?" I asked.

"Because Cynthia says so," she replied. Cynthia Kinch was one of the big cheeses at CBC News, and was trying to direct our coverage, via telephone with Kelly, from home.

"What does she want us to say?"

"That three were killed, and to attribute it to Reuters."

"But we know that's wrong," I said. "That's why I wrote 'at least three.'"

"That's what I told her, but those are her orders."

"Well," I said, "I'm not going to put something on the air that I know is wrong. If that's what you want to do, *you* do it."

I left the newsroom, left the building and took a walk around the block. It was either get in my Chevy Blazer and go home – and never return to CBC – or go back and get to work correcting the story when the all-clear came from Kandahar. I went back.

That night, I wrote Cynthia Kinch a long email saying that in forty years of journalism I had never been ordered to put out a story I knew was wrong. She never replied.

Later that month, I left the building again when we got word of another Canadian killed in Afghanistan. But this time it was to call Jodie in Vancouver.

She and Josh Klukie had been classmates in the seventh and eighth grades at Mackenzie Public School. They'd been good friends.

Josh, at twenty-three, the same age as Jodie, was a private in the army when he was on foot patrol outside Kandahar and stepped on a bomb buried in the road.

Jodie and I reminisced. The Josh we remembered was smart and handsome, a good student, a good athlete, quietly self-confident, a sweet guy. He and Jodie shared a love of sports. They competed on the basketball court and jumped off cliffs together, into Lake Superior.

I wondered why he had chosen to join the army, while reminded that most of the Canadian casualties in that war were from small towns – three from Thunder Bay that year – with few opportunities for young people.

The death of a friend of mine, originally from Thunder Bay, hit me much harder that year. Lorne Saxberg was the weekend anchor when I started at CBC. He was a good guy and a good journalist.

When I arrived in the newsroom at five o'clock on a weekend morning in May, one of the bosses, who I didn't know very well, was there. He told me he had been informed that Lorne had died while on vacation in the Indian Ocean resort island of Phuket, Thailand.

A couple of CBC supervisors pushed me to get the news of Lorne's death on the air. "I'm not putting it on until we get confirmation from a reputable source," I argued.

Eventually, the Canadian embassy in Bangkok confirmed the death – a snorkeling accident – and that the RCMP had notified Lorne's parents in Thunder Bay. I talked to them before I aired the story.

It was a nice mix of words, pictures of Lorne, and a clip of his deep anchorman's voice. I also gave a quote to the CBC News website editor to include in the online story about Lorne.

> *"He was the consummate pro and an exceptional journalist," said Ken Becker, a Newsworld producer who worked with Saxberg for many years. "When he was in the anchor chair, you knew you could throw Lorne any story – from the outbreak of war to the birth of a panda at the zoo – and he'd deliver it to the viewer with exactly the right tone. He brought to every story a vast knowledge on nearly every subject, a reporter's curiosity, and an appreciation of fine writing."*

Lorne Saxberg was forty-eight years old.

During most of my time at CBC I worked only weekends. This was my preference, since it made my commute easier and the newsroom on weekends was not full of bosses playing political games and making everybody miserable.

But as Newsworld evolved, our happy little band of weekend warriors grew into a large uptight "unit," with more producers talking than workers working. The joke going around the newsroom was:

> *Q: How many producers does it take to screw in a lightbulb?*
> *A: Thirteen: One to hold the bulb, and twelve to say, "I don't know. What do YOU think?"*

I was in charge of the news portion of the lineup. Another producer handled the rest of the show – the features and interviews.

I was obliged to attend morning meetings to plan the day and post-mortem meetings to congratulate ourselves or rehash screwups. These circle jerks reinforced my belief that there are two types of people in a TV news operation – the "TV people," who put the "show" in the show and could just as easily switch to producing a children's program, and the journalists. The problem was, the TV people seemed to be in charge. And their news judgment was consistently suspect.

During my tenure, CBC News conducted a major project to evaluate its role in Canadian society. Part of it was a survey which boiled down to asking people on the street to define news. Obviously, if the people running CBC News had to ask "what is news" it was in big trouble. But the News Study, as it was titled, was lauded by the top banana at CBC News, Tony Burman, who called himself the editor in chief. (With apologies to Walter Cronkite, an old wire service hand who made himself managing editor at CBS News, I find it a joke that TV types take newspaper titles.)

Burman called it "the most extensive study of its kind in Canada" and a guide "to shape the CBC News strategy." What the hell is a news strategy? And why would any self-respecting journalist want to have one? But, as I've said, CBC was more consumed with managing the news than simply reporting it well.

Such efforts reached an inglorious climax in the spring of 2007, after a lunatic named Seung Hui Cho killed thirty-two people and himself at Virginia Tech University.

I wasn't working when the news broke. I was home, in front of the TV, transfixed. But once the story of the rampage was told, once the sad tales of the victims were recorded, I had only one question: *Who the hell was this guy?*

The shooter responded, having sent a package of twenty-seven videos, forty-three still photos and a twenty-three page statement – "manifesto" in the language of homicidal maniacs and the media – to NBC News.

I tuned to MSNBC to see the first pictures broadcast by the network, which promised that lead anchor Brian Williams would roll out more of the material on his nightly news show. Seeing and hearing the little turd with the gun made me want to slap him.

After I'd seen all NBC had to offer, I switched to the CBC, to see how it was handling the story. It broadcast a couple of the less crazy-looking stills of Cho. Otherwise, zip. Nada. Why?

I got the answer from Tony Burman, in a note to staff which was posted in his online column: *At the CBC, we debated the issue throughout the evening and made the decision that we would not broadcast any video or audio of this bizarre collection ... We would report the essence of what the killer was saying, but not do what he so clearly hoped all media would do. To decide otherwise – in our view – would be to risk copycat killings.*

The next weekend, my first at CBC after the Virginia Tech shooting, I told a colleague I found Burman's manifesto an embarrassment.

"It's about time someone said that," replied a website editor I had worked with at United Press Canada and

Canadian Press. "I couldn't believe all the people around here who were congratulating themselves."

"You're kidding," I said.

"No, everybody I heard seemed to agree with the decision."

Really? Or were they spineless civil servants just following the leader.

"Personally," I said, "I'm ashamed to work in a place where the first instinct on a touchy subject is: How do we *not* touch it."

She laughed. "And," I added, "I bet we would have gone wall-to-wall with the pictures if the shooter had been a red-blooded American instead of a pimply faced Korean kid."

The political correctness of CBC leaked into every decision and detail of the operation. Since appearance is often judged as important as content in TV news, CBC was undergoing a makeover. A couple of the best and most seasoned reporters, who happened to be white men, were squeezed out and snapped up by other networks. Meanwhile, many of the new reporters sent up through the ranks were young and non-white. Competence was not a prerequisite.

One of the most solid anchors at Newsworld came back from a leave of absence to be told, "There's no way we're putting a middle-aged white woman on the air." She was relegated to the desk, writing for anchors who had more trouble delivering the news than Ted Baxter.

I worked closely for years at Newsworld with Ken Ernhofer, a serious journalist who had been a national reporter and foreign correspondent in Moscow for rival

CTV. But at CBC he was stuck as a news writer and lineup editor, told there was no chance his pale complexion and gray hair would appear on camera at CBC.

None of the management machinations improved the product. If anything, it was worse. For me, it was frustrating. Pointless. Stupid.

I found myself in a familiar spot. Another news factory had worn me down. Loved the work. Was good at it too. But couldn't abide the bullshit. And this time, at this age, I couldn't imagine another dance in journalism.

I took some time off. My instinct had always been – when in doubt, hit the road.

In May 2008, I packed Lacey and her boyfriend Hugh in my Blazer to see the U.S.A. in my Chevrolet. We drove across the northern states. The highlight, for me, was my first look at the Little Big Horn. The interpretive signs helped me visualize how the Sioux and Cheyenne warriors baited, trapped and thrashed Custer's Seventh Cavalry. I never tired of walking the paths of history. I felt the same awe when I visited Gettysburg a few years earlier.

My journey with Lacey and Hugh ended in Vancouver. They flew home after a reunion with Jodie. I recharged for a couple of days before Jodie and I drove down to San Francisco. She'd been an affable road-trip partner since she was six. Now, at twenty-four, it was different and still the same. I showed her the San Francisco of my youth, the places I'd lived and first explored.

We drove back to her home in Vancouver and then across Canada to my home, where Jodie was a surprise guest at a family function.

The trip from the West Coast to southern Ontario reminded me that Canada remained a work in progress. If there is an excuse for only one highway crossing the country, there is no excuse for it being routed through cities and hick towns and being only two lanes in too many places.

I hung in at CBC for a couple more months. When I started counting down the days, I thought of the good times, the good people, the good stories. Being at the helm when big news broke never stopped being an adrenaline rush. But the juices also flowed on the offbeat stories, like the couple who thought they booked a honeymoon in Australia and found themselves in Sydney, Nova Scotia.

The second weekend in August 2008 was my last at CBC News. In advance, a longtime colleague, a veteran of nearly my vintage, Brian Currie, sent a note to all Toronto staff.

> *Anyone who's worked in this newsroom on the weekends knows the force of nature named Ken Becker. And every one of us has learned a lot from watching him work (on the news, and on us) in his unique, colorful (mostly blue) way ...*
> *Saturday is his last day working at Newsworld. And a lot of people feel a sense of loss about that. He's made a lot of friends and been a good friend to a lot of people.*
> *The point of this note is, he doesn't want a party, or a fuss, or a poignant goodbye. Doesn't fit with his brusk image, or maybe he's afraid he'll tear up and show he's really a softie.*

The note went on to suggest people flood me with messages so "he'll know how we feel about him leaving."

There were a lot of messages – and emails, and cards – from the grunts. Not a word from the bosses.

My young colleagues, including some former students, showered me with words like "mentor." A couple said I would remain in their heads, that they would ask themselves in a crunch, *What would Becker do?*

I sent a goodbye note to all CBC News staff in Canada and in foreign bureaus. My message to them was heartfelt. *Over the years, I've worked with some real pros, in Toronto, across the country, and around the world. I love those who also want to be on deck when IT hits the fan. I'll miss you …*

I now had only one job.

CHAPTER 34
LAST CALL

I've described myself as a "rugged individualist" a couple of times. I'm not subscribing to Herbert Hoover's use of the term as a Depression era Republican con to shelter the rich and tell the poor they're on their own. I'm saying I always believed I could stand up for myself, that my words and work and actions spoke for me, that I didn't need a union or a government to shield me from a cruel world. Pal Joey wrote a column in the *Star* about me a long time ago.

> *I want to tell you about my friend the Bronx Bomber. The Bronx Bomber, an American, from the Bronx, has, thanks to his Constitution and perhaps genetically imprinted, a clear sense of citizens' rights, particularly his own.*
> *He lives among us in a state of constant amazement at how we allow ourselves to be walked over by just about anybody at all – not just by our bosses, but our waiters,*

> *our police, our bus drivers, our movie ushers, our landlords, our doctors, our teachers, our petty bureaucrats and our tin-pot functionaries – even when we know we are in the right and even though, in most instances, it is their job to serve us.*

Being out of sync with my Canadian family and friends for all these years is often disorienting. Constantly fighting what I consider the good fight is fatiguing.

It didn't help that I spent ten years at what I called the People's Wire Service – a cooperative, like one of Mao's farms – and another ten at what I called the People's Network, a public broadcaster funded by the Canadian government. At Humber College, I was in the employ of the Ontario government.

To me, they were all civil service institutions – akin to the post office or the DMV – that attracted too many lazy lifers and ass kissers who meekly followed orders and kowtowed to the bosses. The height of rebelliousness by a colleague during my ten years at CP was exhibited by a copy editor who changed "backyard" to "backmetre" when CP style went metric.

One young ass kisser at CP weaseled his way into a semi-lofty position at the wire service and later at CBC and at Humber. He was a careerist, barely a journalist. I'd put him in his place a couple of times when he tried to exert authority over me, ridiculed his lack of editorial judgment. His one retort had been calling me a "fucking American" and storming off in a snit.

But, by 2010, he was one of the coordinators of the journalism program at Humber. Since I was a part-time teacher, a coordinator could get rid of me without cause by simply not giving me classes to teach. I should have known something was up when several of my students informed me this coordinator had told them about his younger days at Canadian Press, when Ken Becker told him to fuck off.

Early in 2011, he called to say he didn't have any classes for me. He called back to say I could teach one of my two classes. I survived another semester. Then, nothing. No call. No classes. Adios.

Another Humber teacher, a friend, suggested the weasel had engineered my departure because he had been carrying a grudge since CP and was finally getting his revenge. It was a spiteful child's game. For him, it may have been proportionate payback for a long-ago putdown. For me, it was a sudden crash, upsetting my life and livelihood.

In early December, I told my students in an email that "the frauds and flunkies" running the journalism program had cut me loose, that I was sorry I would not be able to see them through the school year. I learned that they had all signed a petition to have me back, that a few of them had pleaded their case with an associate dean, only to be rebuffed.

My email inbox was swamped with messages of outrage and thanks from them, and from other students I had taught during my eleven years at Humber.

Now, I had no job. No income. I was just past my sixty-fifth birthday. But I wasn't retired. Writers don't retire.

I had taken a whack at a memoir a few years earlier. Opened all the dusty file folders of my career. Organized the narrative. Put it all down. When I finished a second draft, I got in touch with an author I'd really hit it off with, Nelson DeMille.

I'd interviewed the novelist three times. Been a fan since I read *The Gold Coast*, the story of a lawyer, his wife, and the Mafia don who moves into the mansion next door on Long Island's north shore. DeMille really hooked me with a subsequent series of novels featuring the wiseass NYPD detective turned terrorist-hunter John Corey.

For one interview, DeMille came to my house in Lorne Park, met Linda and Jasper. He and I sat at the dining room table, talking and smoking.

When the publicist arrived to pick him up, to take him to an event at a bookstore down the highway in Burlington, he waved her off. "That's okay. Ken says he'll give me a lift."

We chatted some more in the car. DeMille was only a couple of years older than me, a New Yorker. We spoke the same language.

So, when I told him in an email that I'd written a memoir and wasn't sure what to do next, he offered to read it. He got back to me with praise, a list of literary agents in New York to contact – I never considered any small potatoes Canadian agency or publisher – and the okay to drop his name. I spent the next several weeks corresponding with agents.

The only positive reply came from a woman who said she loved the writing and the stories, but could not sell it in a market where it would compete with upcoming memoirs by Barbara Walters and Valerie Bertinelli, a former TV child star who was writing about her battle with fat. I pushed the memoir aside.

A short time later, a former Canadian Press colleague, Betsy Powell, contacted me about a book she was working on. Betsy was one of the kids on the Ontario Desk when I was news editor. We shared a love of mystery novels and Sanibel Island.

She had a contract with a small Canadian publisher to write a true crime book about black street gangs in Toronto, pegged to a murder trial she covered for the *Toronto Star.*

She asked for my help. We met. I read the few pages she had written. We talked. I scribbled an outline of how to organize the manuscript.

Over several months, Betsy wrote, I edited. The subject matter was compelling. I wrote and signed a foreword.

> *When my friend Betsy Powell told me she was writing a book about black street gangs in Toronto, I thought: It's about time. For too long, people in this city, in this country, have lived in blissful ignorance. Gangs were an American phenomenon. Black ghettos were an American problem. Not here. No way ...*
>
> *As long as the gangsters are killing each other in their own neighbourhoods, who cares? It's only when they bring their guns downtown that anybody – the politicians and media that fuel outbreaks of hysteria – notices.*
>
> *In Toronto, starting in the early 1990s, there were episodic eruptions: the race riot that the white power structure insisted was not a race riot; the shotgun blast fired by a black robber, killing a young white woman sitting in a trendy café; the 15-year-old white girl gunned down by black kids in a shootout on a busy downtown street. These*

were the stories that created the boldest headlines– each time young blacks broke the peace in Toronto the Good.
But this book takes a look at Toronto the Bad, the separate society that exists across an unmarked border, where poverty, drugs and guns create an explosive mix, where people live in fear in their neighborhoods, where a generation of Canadians has been lost to the lure of crime, where clueless cops sometimes crash the party, and oblivious politicians show up only during an election campaign.

That was me, the streetwise New Yorker, stickin' it to the man. Never mind that I never went to school with black kids, never had a black friend, or dated a black girl.

My one contribution to race relations was after one of Linda's nieces, who'd been born and raised in Michigan, married a black man and was basically disowned by her parents. Linda and I invited the couple *and* the parents to a party – surprise! – at our house in Clarkson. They all showed up and, as far as I know, lived happily ever after.

After I finished my work with Betsy, after I got the boot from Humber, I picked up the jumbled threads of that novel I started north of Superior. I finished it. Hatched the plot from that tale of rape told to me by the flight attendant in the No Name bar in Sausalito. Was happy with it. The few people who read said it was suspenseful – and funny. I sent it around to literary agents. No takers.

"The truth is, nobody's going to invest their time in a first novel by someone of your age," confided an old acquaintance from my time on the book beat, working for an international literary agency. She was right.

I wrote a screenplay. The reviews from writer friends were unanimous. It too was funny and suspenseful. A smash. I had no clue how to pitch it.

Just after my sixty-eighth birthday, in late November 2014, I gave up drinking. I hadn't planned on it. Hadn't taken the pledge. It just happened.

I was sick in bed for about a week. Not sure what was wrong. Linda checked my symptoms on the internet. I either had an intestinal flu, kidney failure, or cholera. Didn't go to a doctor. Didn't get a diagnosis.

When I came out of it, I felt okay. That evening, as was my habit, I poured a glass of red wine. Tasted awful. That was it. Not a drop since.

I'd been drinking for more than fifty years – scotch, beer, vodka, wine, anything and everything. For more years than I could count, I drank every day, starting in the evening, ending when I went to bed.

Booze never made me illiterate or inarticulate. All those manuscripts, all those words, had been written while I polished off a big bottle of Yellow Tail Shiraz. Then, from one week to the next, I couldn't stand the taste, the smell, of anything with alcohol.

In July 2015, I began writing a blog. I called it *thebeckerfiles* because kenbecker was taken.

I needed a break from projects that took months, or years, to complete. I fell back into an op-ed mindset, the eight-hundred-word column that slapped and tickled. Having people read my words, compliment my stuff, never lost its kick.

I set out to write media criticism. I had the credentials. And there was a lot to criticize.

In my first several columns, I used the word shit a lot. *If the foo shits, wear it,* as the punchline of the old joke goes. I heaped shit on newspapers and TV networks on both sides of the border.

Within about a month of Donald Trump declaring his candidacy for president, I was already nauseated by the coverage.

> *Every time Trump opens his yap, it's breaking news from Iowa to Uranus, with an endless echo on cable news, the internet, talk shows and comedy shows, the entertainment media and business media, newspapers, magazines, political forums and network news ...*
>
> *So, is it any wonder the most incorrigible head-case in the GOP psycho ward is leading in the polls?*
>
> *But does that validate giving Trump so much ink and airtime?*
>
> *Evidently.*
>
> *If Trump is the egg, the media are the chickens.*

I went gonzo on him a couple of times. After election night, all that was left was muted fear and loathing. It didn't help that Canadians were obnoxiously smug with young Justin Trudeau in his daddy's old office in Ottawa and the creature from the gold-plated lagoon in the White House.

Writing *thebeckerfiles* violated one of the lessons I taught my students – don't work for free. I crossed farther across the line when the Huffington Post contacted me and offered to reprint my columns – with no payment, of course. I succumbed to the scam, sent a couple of stories, before deciding *no mas.*

The internet, that free, endless space where all words are supposedly created equal, has managed to devalue the work of all writers. When I started freelancing in the late 1970s, I was regularly paid a buck a word. By the 2000s, the job title had become FREElancing.

In two years, writing more than a hundred columns, I turned only one into a check – $200 from the Washington Post for a piece on my 1972 Phillips Collection caper – to augment my paltry Social Security and Canadian government pension funds. No company pension for this rugged individualist. But I often wonder if I would have put in the required years at Canadian Press if I had been left alone to do what I did best – work with young reporters and direct coverage.

In November 2016, I turned seventy, exceeding my expectations and the prediction of the *Times* editor who said I wouldn't make it past twenty-five. I started a business, interviewing people and writing their life stories. I created a website and a Facebook page to promote it. The reception was unanimous. Great idea! Brilliant!

I sent out press releases. My local paper, the *Mississauga News*, did a story. So did the *Toronto Sun*. In the first several months, I gave as many interviews as I conducted with clients. "I think people love this stuff until they have to pay for it," a former colleague, a journalist turned entrepreneur, told me.

For Canada's sesquicentennial in 2017, I wrote a series of five columns on my forty-plus years in this country. The first part, headlined *The Expat Experience*, began:

> *When people ask me why I came to Canada and why I've stayed here this long, I usually say something like:*

> "I was working for UPI in New York and my first marriage was breaking up and I wanted to go somewhere, anywhere, because all my friends and family were in New York and I didn't want them to think, 'poor Ken,' and a pal at UPI was then the Canadian news editor and, when he asked if I wanted to take over the Vancouver bureau, I said, 'Where's Vancouver?'
> "Anyway, I went to Vancouver, and then transferred to UPI-Montreal and then to Toronto, where I met Linda, who, of course, is Canadian, and we got married and had a couple of kids who are, of course, Canadian – so I just stayed."

All my daughters are all grown up. Kate remains in Tucson, where she ended her marriage to Jorge, my favorite German. She runs a business, blending and bottling essential oils, and has a singing career.

Jodie came back from Vancouver in 2012 and lives down the road in Oakville. She abandoned the corporate world to start her own business, promoting fitness for mental health, and competes in triathlons. She's come a long way since she failed to finish the race in Thunder Bay.

Lacey and Hugh married – I survived the father-of-the-bride speech at their wedding – and have two Canadian granddaughters, named from A to Zed, Annie and Zoey. They all live a bit farther down the road in Burlington.

All daughters. All granddaughters. I often think of my only son, wonder what kind of man he would have turned out to be. The only evidence of Sean's life is a thick file stuffed with his birth certificate, hospital and post-mortem documents, correspondence with his doctors, notes and cards of condolence, a lock of his light brown hair, a footprint in faded purple ink, a photo, in black and white, of Linda holding our newborn, and a color photo of his grave.

Linda's mother, Edith, died in 2009 at the age of ninety-seven. I had written her life story, a gift for her family, which gave me something to work with when I wrote a eulogy. Great lady.

My mother, Dot, died at the age of ninety-four. Amazing she lived that long, with all the ailments and all the surgeries. She added to the inventory after moving north from Florida. A broken hip, followed by a broken fibula, finally persuaded her to use a walker. She was nearly blind by the spring of 2014, when she moved into my sister Janice's house in Tarrytown.

Two years later, Dot got pneumonia and faded fast. I talked with her on the phone. She was barely coherent. But she had been that way before, through other serious illnesses. How can you discern when someone is really at death's door?

Kate flew to New York to be with her grandma. I talked with her and Janice on the phone. Jodie wanted to go but was waiting for me. Finally, I said, "let's go tomorrow."

On May 10, 2016, Jodie and I drove to Tarrytown. We arrived in late afternoon, in time for the final hours. Dot couldn't speak. Her eyes were closed. Her breathing labored. She looked tiny in the bed. I took her hand. She seemed to respond.

"Ken's here," Jan said.

"She's been waiting for you," Kate said.

A couple of hours later, I was on the patio having a smoke with Jan when Kate and Jodie came out to say she was gone.

Linda, Lacey, Hugh, Annie and Zoey made it to the funeral, as did other close family. Rabbi Brian flew in from Portland, Oregon, to preside at the service. I eulogized Dot's toughness. Her casket was flown to Florida and lifted into her assigned place in the wall, beside dad.

Jan and I now try to talk regularly. We've gotten closer over the years, even closer now.

The drive to Tarrytown was the farthest I strayed from home in years. I rarely go into Toronto. Every time I do, the skyline has changed, the lakefront mushrooming with new, ugly highrise condos.

I can't help but compare it to New York, to streets lined with buildings older than I am, the scent of saltwater, big bridges over wide rivers. But I haven't been in The City in many years.

I'm still in the townhouse in Clarkson, in the condo complex called Walden Spinney, with a swimming pool called Walden Pond. It's not that I like it here. It's just where I happen to be. Linda is here. Going on forty years of marriage.

My closest companion is here too. I named him Brady – not for Tom Brady, though I've rooted for the Pats since 2001, but for Brady Coyne, a fictional Boston lawyer in William Tapply's fine series of mysteries.

Brady was a surprise Christmas gift from the kids in 2010. He's a standard poodle, we think. He's nothing like Yaz or Jasper. For one thing, he's white. For another, he's nuts.

I still have the pedigree papers for Yaz and Jasper. Know who their parents were. With Brady, I'm just guessing. Son of Rain Man and Sybil?

He arrived at about four months old – again, just guessing, no papers. He was scared of everything. Flinched when I raised my hand to pet him. Obviously abused. Probably the inbred spawn of an outlaw puppy mill or the House of Windsor.

A crack of thunder still leaves him shaking with fear. He also is spooked by bicycles, kids on skateboards, most men, and people with Eastern European accents.

While Linda goes to her real estate office or elsewhere, Brady follows me from room to room. Never out of sight. I talk to him constantly. He never argues or contradicts.

I start my day scanning the headlines in the *New York Times.* Not much worth reading, except Timothy Egan's op-ed column on Fridays. I miss Red Smith – long dead – Russell Baker – long retired – and Rick Bragg – long moved on.

I turn on CNN for the latest turd from the turd in the White House. He was born the same year I was. Also grew up in Queens. The accident of birth intrigues me. What if I had been born into a wealthy family? Or in Bangladesh? Or Amish?

There is plenty of time to think about such things as I spend my days in my home office. The framed red, white and blue poster of a smiling JFK – *Kennedy for President, Leadership for the 60's* – is on the wall behind me.

I am surrounded by books on American history, politics and media – Vietnam, Watergate, the Kennedys; *Fear and Loathing on the Campaign Trail '72, All the President's Men, The Kingdom and the Power.*

The TV is always tuned to an American program – sports, movies, serial dramas. I've watched all the episodes of *The West Wing, Homeland, Mad Men,* and *The Newsroom* too many times to count.

I'm unplugged from the country where I live. Would be hard pressed to name a Canadian TV show or movie, or any of the current crop of politicians beyond the prime minister and the premier of Ontario. I haven't watched a hockey game in decades.

I was at a bank recently, doing some cross-border business. I had no trouble reciting the U.S. Social Security number I got at fourteen but had to dig into my wallet to read off the number on my Canadian Social Insurance card. It was tucked into the same fold as my draft card.

Once, long ago, I arrived at Pearson airport in Toronto and the Canadian customs' guy expressed outrage that I had been in this country so long without taking citizenship. I shrugged. "No law says I have to," I said, and went on my way.

The fact is, I've always held the belief, my American optimism, that some great success would call me back across the border. Maybe it still will.

EPILOGUE

Some of the early chapters, the stories when I was young, were stirring in the retelling. The final chapters, getting old, the stories still raw, were tougher to write. In every case, I just opened a vein and bled.

Some words about the words
I used American spellings and imperial measurements throughout because words like cheque and labour will never look right to me and the metric system will forever be a bafflement.

Since I endeavored to write in the moment, I stuck with words – stewardess, Indian, Arab terrorists – that were commonplace and acceptable in their time in the narrative.

Some words about some people
My uncle **Jack Banning**, who helped me get started in the news business, died in 2005 at the age of seventy-three. The only reason I know this is because I came across his obit in the *San Diego Union-Tribune* while researching this

book. Jack went back to the theater, and was successful enough to rate an eight-hundred-word newspaper obit. The last time I saw him was my dad's funeral.

Lucien Carr, my imperfect journalism hero, also died in 2005, at the age of seventy-nine. He rated obits in the *New York Times*, the *Times of London* and many other newspapers, only because they all could call him a "muse" to Kerouac, Ginsberg and the rest of the Beat Generation writers. After I left New York, I never saw him again.

Barry Ginsberg, my little league catcher, died in October 2016 at the age of seventy. I hadn't seen him since we met in Sausalito in 1978, when he told me he'd been abducted by aliens. But we chatted a bit when he phoned after my mother died, and a couple times more to catch up. He sounded like my childhood pal. I thought we'd keep in touch. Then he was gone.

Rick Bosetti, who couldn't keep his pants zipped as a ballplayer, became a Republican politician and mayor of his hometown of Redding, California.

Les Pyette, the city editor who wanted me to kill a baby seal, became publisher of the *Sun* and was inducted into the Canadian News Hall of Fame.

ACKNOWLEDGMENTS

While I've mentioned my reporter's knack for recalling people and places and conversations – the Who, Where and What – I relied on others to help with the When on family matters. For this, I owe thanks to **Linda**, sister **Janice**, and cousin **Ylain**.

An old Long Island friend, recently found in Montana, **Steve Bloom**, also refreshed my memory of the years in my late teens, which are deservedly forgettable. He also read an early draft of the manuscript and encouraged me to get it published. Thanks, Steve.

I am most grateful to my personal unpaid editors – pal **Judy Charles** and, again, Linda. Judy is a crackerjack when it comes to spotting clunky sentences and passages that fail to make the grade. Linda is the best live-in proofreader on the planet.

And a special thanks to my nephew, **Mathew Lighty**, for designing the cover, and for all his hard work in helping me through the technical rigmarole of publishing this book.